CHILTON'S
REPAIR & TUNE-UP GUIDE

DATSUN 1200·210 NISSAN SENTRA 1973-82

1200 1973 • B210 1974-78
210 1979-82 • Sentra 1982

Managing Editor KERRY A. FREEMAN, S.A.E.
Senior Editor RICHARD J. RIVELE, S.A.E.
Editor A. LINDSAY BROOKE

President WILLIAM A. BARBOUR
Executive Vice President JAMES A. MIADES
Vice President and General Manager JOHN P. KUSHNERICK

CHILTON BOOK COMPANY
Radnor, Pennsylvania
19089

SAFETY NOTICE

Proper service and repair procedures are vital to the safe, reliable operation of all motor vehicles, as well as the personal safety of those performing repairs. This book outlines procedures for servicing and repairing vehicles using safe, effective methods. The procedures contain many NOTES, CAUTIONS and WARNINGS which should be followed along with standard safety procedures to eliminate the possibility of personal injury or improper service which could damage the vehicle or compromise its safety.

It is important to note that repair procedures and techniques, tools and parts for servicing motor vehicles, as well as the skill and experience of the individual performing the work vary widely. It is not possible to anticipate all of the conceivable ways or conditions under which vehicles may be serviced, or to provide cautions as to all of the possible hazards that may result. Standard and accepted safety precautions and equipment should be used when handling toxic or flammable fluids, and safety goggles or other protection should be used during cutting, grinding, chiseling, prying, or any other process that can cause material removal or projectiles.

Some procedures require the use of tools specially designed for a specific purpose. Before substituting another tool or procedure, you must be completely satisfied that neither your personal safety, nor the performance of the vehicle will be endangered.

Although information in this guide is based on industry sources and is as complete as possible at the time of publication, the possibility exists that the manufacturer made later changes which could not be included here. While striving for total accuracy, Chilton Book Company cannot assume responsibility for any errors, changes, or omissions that may occur in the compilation of this data.

PART NUMBERS

Part numbers listed in this reference are not recommendations by Chilton for any product by brand name. They are references that can be used with interchange manuals and aftermarket supplier catalogs to locate each brand supplier's discrete part number.

ACKNOWLEDGMENTS

The Chilton Book Company thanks the Nissan Motor Corporation in U.S.A., Gardena, California 90247, and Devon Datsun, Devon, Pennsylvania, for their assistance in the preparation of this book.

Copyright © 1982 by Chilton Book Company
All Rights Reserved
Published in Radnor, Pa. by Chilton Book Company
and simultaneously in Canada
by VNR Publishers, 1410 Birchmount Road,
Scarborough, Ontario M1P 2E7

Manufactured in the United States of America
234567890   1098765432

Chilton's Repair & Tune-Up Guide: Datsun 1200, 210 and Nissan Sentra 1973–82
ISBN 0-8019-7197-7 pbk.
Library of Congress Catalog Card No. 81-70237

CONTENTS

1 General Information and Maintenance

1 How to Use this Book
2 Tools and Equipment
6 Routine Maintenance and Lubrication

2 Tune-Up

27 Tune-Up Procedures
28 Tune-Up Specifications

3 Engine and Engine Rebuilding

44 Engine Electrical System
51 Engine Service and Specifications
70 Engine Rebuilding

4 Emission Controls and Fuel System

92 Emission Control System and Service
103 Fuel System Service

5 Chassis Electrical

117 Accessory Service
121 Instrument Panel Service
125 Lights, Fuses and Flashers

6 Clutch and Transmission

128 Manual Transmission
131 Clutch
135 Automatic Transmission

7 Drive Train

139 Driveshaft and U-Joints
142 Rear Axle

8 Suspension and Steering

145 Front Suspension
152 Rear Suspension
157 Steering

9 Brakes

164 Front Brakes
170 Brake Specifications
173 Rear Brakes

10 Body

179 Repairing Scratches and Small Dents
183 Repairing Rust
189 Body Care

11 Troubleshooting

194 Problem Diagnosis

226 Appendix
230 Index

108 Chiltons Fuel Economy and Tune-Up Tips

Quick Reference
Specifications For Your Vehicle

Fill in this chart with the most commonly used specifications for your vehicle. Specifications can be found in Chapters 1 through 3 or on the tune-up decal under the hood of the vehicle.

Tune-Up

Firing Order_____

Spark Plugs:

    Type_____

    Gap (in.)_____

Point Gap (in.)_____

Dwell Angle (°)_____

Ignition Timing (°)_____

    Vacuum (Connected/Disconnected)_____

Valve Clearance (in.)

    Intake_____   **Exhaust**_____

Capacities

Engine Oil (qts)

    With Filter Change_____

    Without Filter Change_____

Cooling System (qts)_____

Manual Transmission (pts)_____

    Type_____

Automatic Transmission (pts)_____

    Type_____

Front Differential (pts)_____

    Type_____

Rear Differential (pts)_____

    Type_____

Transfer Case (pts)_____

    Type_____

FREQUENTLY REPLACED PARTS

Use these spaces to record the part numbers of frequently replaced parts.

PCV VALVE   **OIL FILTER**   **AIR FILTER**

Manufacturer_____   **Manufacturer**_____   **Manufacturer**_____

Part No._____   **Part No.**_____   **Part No.**_____

General Information and Maintenance

HOW TO USE THIS BOOK

This book is divided into ten easy to follow chapters, avoiding "mechanic's jargon" and highlighting important procedures with illustrations wherever possible. As time goes by, you'll probably find that some chapters such as Chapter 2 (Tune Up) naturally accumulate more dirty fingerprints than others, but everything from engine rebuilding to waxing the car is covered here. Of course, even professional mechanics won't attempt a repair without the proper tools and a thorough knowledge of the work required. This is why operations like rebuilding your transmission or rear axle assembly are not covered here—they require a range of special tools which are too expensive, and a technical knowledge too extensive to be useful to you, the owner/mechanic.

Before loosening a single nut, read through the entire section you are dealing with and make sure you have the time, tools, and replacement parts necessary to do the job. This will save you much frustration, many hassles, and a walk to the bus stop Monday morning because you needed a part or were without a tool Saturday afternoon. Remember, too, that auto parts stores sometimes have to order certain parts, so it's wise to run through a procedure and make a couple phone calls to be sure a part will be available when you need it.

Each section begins with a brief description of the particular system and the basic theory behind it. When repairs involve a level of technical knowhow beyond most owner/mechanics, we tell you how to remove the part and replace it with a new or rebuilt unit. This way you can at least save the cost of labor, and the percentage that is often placed on top of the retail cost of new parts.

There are a few basic mechanic's rules that should be followed:

1. Left side of the car means the driver's side; right side is the passenger's side;

2. Most screws, bolts and nuts are "right handed"—they are tightened by turning them clockwise and removed by turning them counterclockwise;

3. *Never* crawl under a car supported only by a bumper jack—jack the car up, then support it with jackstands;

4. *Never* smoke or position an exposed flame near the battery or *any part* of the fuel system;

5. USE COMMON SENSE DURING ALL OPERATIONS.

TOOLS AND EQUIPMENT

The following list contains the basic tools needed to perform most of the maintenance and repair procedures covered in this book. All nuts, bolts and thread sizes in your Datsun are metric—you'll need a set of metric wrenches and sockets to work on the car. SAE (U.S. size) wrenches will be either too loose or too tight and will ruin nuts and boltheads if used.

1. Metric sockets, including a $^{13}/_{16}$ in.

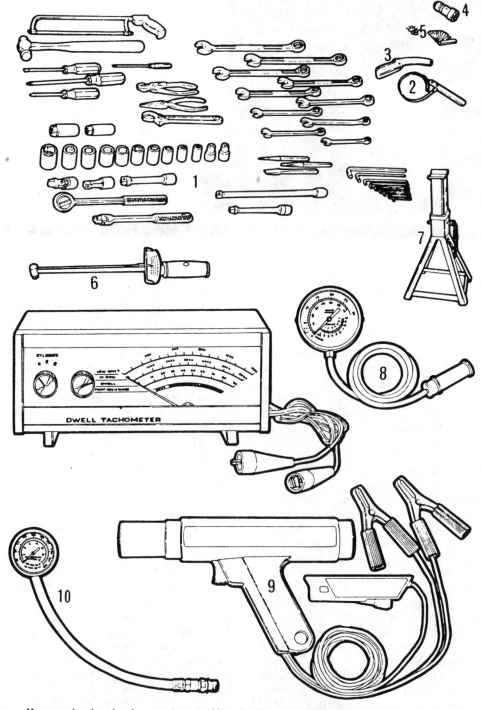

You need only a basic assortment of handtools for most maintenance and repair jobs

spark plug socket. Various length socket drive extensions are also very useful. One break in this area, from a monetary standpoint, is that metric sockets available in this country will all fit standard U.S. (SAE) ratchet handles and extensions (¼, ⅜, and ½ in. drive);

2. Set of metric "combination" (one end open and one end box) wrenches;

3. Wire-type spark plug feeler gauge;

4. Blade-type feeler gauge for ignition and valve settings;

5. Slot and Phillips head screwdrivers in various sizes;

6. Oil filter strap wrench. Necessary for removing oil filters (never used, though, for installing the filters);

7. Oil can filler spout, for pouring fresh oil from quart cans;

8. Pair of slip-lock pliers;

9. Two (at least) sturdy jackstands for working underneath the car—any other type of support (bricks, wood and especially cinderblocks) is just plain dangerous;

10. Pair of vise-type pliers;

11. Timing light, preferably a DC battery hook up type, and preferably an inductive type for use on cars with electronic ignition.

This is an adequate set of tools, and the more work you do yourself on your car, the larger you'll find the set growing—a pair of pliers here, a wrench or two there. It makes more sense to have a comprehensive set of basic tools as listed above, and then to acquire more along the lines as you need them, than to go out and plunk down big money for a professional size set you may never use. In addition to these basic tools, there are several other tools and gauges you may find useful. These include:

1. A hydraulic floor jack (1½ ton is fine for the Datsun). If you are serious about maintaining your own car, then a floor jack is as necessary as a spark plug socket. The greatly increased utility, strength, and *safety* of a hydraulic floor jack makes it pay for itself many times over through the years;

2. A compression gauge. The screw-in type is slower to use but it eliminates the possibility of a faulty reading due to escaping pressure;

3. A manifold vacuum gauge, very useful in troubleshooting ignition and emissions problems;

4. A drop light, to light up the work area (make sure yours is Underwriters' approved, and has a shielded bulb);

5. A volt/ohm meter, used for determining whether or not there is current in a wire. These are handy for use if a wire is broken somewhere; it is especially necessary for working on today's electronics-laden cars;

As a final note, a torque wrench is necessary for all but the most basic work—it should even be used when installing spark plugs. The more common beam-type models are perfectly adequate and are usually less expensive than the more precise "click" type (on which you pre-set the torque and the wrench "clicks" when that setting arrives on the fastener you are torquing).

NOTE: *Datsun special tools referred to in this guide are available through Kent-Moore Corporation, 29784 Little Mack, Roseville, Michigan 48066. For Canada, contact Kent-Moore of Canada, Ltd., 2395 Cawthra Mississauga, Ontario, Canada L5A 3Ps.*

SERVICING YOUR CAR SAFELY

It is virtually impossible to anticipate all of the hazards involved with automotive maintenance and service, but care and common sense will prevent most accidents.

The rules of safety for mechanics range from "don't smoke around gasoline," to "use the proper tool for the job." The trick to avoiding injuries is to develop safe work habits and take every possible precaution.

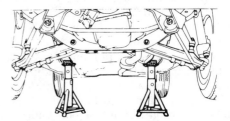

Always use support stands when working under your car

Dos

• Do keep a fire extinguisher and first aid kit within easy reach.

• Do wear safety glasses or goggles when cutting, drilling, grinding or prying, even if you have 20–20 vision. If you wear glasses for the sake of vision, they should be made of hardened glass that can serve also as safety glasses, or wear safety goggles over your regular glasses.

• Do shield your eyes whenever you work around the battery. Batteries contain sulphuric acid. In case of contact with the eyes or skin, flush the area with water or a mixture of water and baking soda and get medical attention immediately.

• Do use safety stands for any undercar service. Jacks are for raising vehicles; safety stands are for making sure the vehicle stays raised until you want it to come down. Whenever the car is raised, block the wheels remaining on the ground and set the parking brake.

• Do use adequate ventilation when working with any chemicals or hazardous materials. Like carbon monoxide, the asbestos dust resulting from brake lining wear can be poisonous in sufficient quantities.

• Do disconnect the negative battery cable when working on the electrical system. The secondary ignition system can contain up to 40,000 volts.

• Do follow manufacturer's directions whenever working with potentially hazardous materials. Both brake fluid and antifreeze are poisonous if taken internally.

• Do properly maintain your tools. Loose hammerheads, mushroomed punches and chisels, frayed or poorly grounded electrical cords, excessively worn screwdrivers, spread wrenches (open end), cracked sockets, slipping ratchets, or faulty droplight sockets can cause accidents.

• Keep your tools clean; a greasy wrench can slip off a bolthead, ruining the bolt and often ruining your knuckles in the process.

• Do use the proper size and type of tool for the job being done.

• Do when possible, pull on a wrench handle rather than push on it, and adjust your stance to prevent a fall.

• Do be sure that adjustable wrenches are tightly closed on the nut or bolt and pulled so that the face is on the side of the fixed jaw.

• Do select a wrench or socket that fits the nut or bolt. The wrench or socket should sit straight, not cocked.

• Do strike squarely with a hammer; avoid glancing blows.

• Do set the parking brake and block the drive wheels if the work requires the engine running.

Don'ts

• Don't run an engine in a garage or anywhere else without proper ventilation—EVER! Carbon monoxide is poisonous; it takes a long time to leave the human body

and you can build up a deadly supply of it in your system by simply breathing in a little every day. You may not realize you are slowly poisoning yourself. Always use power vents, windows, fans or open the garage doors.

• Don't work around moving parts while wearing necktie or other loose clothing. Short sleeves are much safer than long, loose sleeves; hard-toed shoes with neoprene soles protect your toes and give a better grip on slippery surfaces. Jewelry such as watches, fancy belt buckles, beads or body adornment of any kind is not safe working around a car. Long hair should be hidden under a hat or cap.

• Don't use pockets for toolboxes. A fall or bump can drive a screwdriver deep into your body. Even a wiping cloth hanging from the back pocket can wrap around a spinning shaft or fan.

• Don't smoke when working around gasoline, cleaning solvent or other flammable material.

• Don't smoke when working around the battery. When the battery is being charged, it gives off explosive hydrogen gas.

• Don't use gasoline to wash your hands; there are excellent soaps available. Gasoline may contain lead, and lead can enter the body through a cut, accumulating in the body until you are very ill. Gasoline also removes all the natural oils from the skin so that bone dry hands will suck up oil and grease.

• Don't service the air conditioning system unless you are equipped with the necessary tools and training. The refrigerant, R-12, is extremely cold when compressed, and when released into the air will instantly freeze any surface it contacts, including your eyes. Although the refrigerant is normally non-toxic, R-12 becomes a deadly poisonous gas in the presence of an open flame. One good whiff of the vapors from burning refrigerant can be fatal.

• Don't use screwdrivers for anything other than driving screws! A screwdriver used as a prying tool can snap when you least expect it, causing injuries.

• Don't use a bumper jack (that little scissors or pantograph jack supplied with the car) for anything other than changing a flat! These jacks were only intended for emergency use out on the road; they were NOT designed as a maintenance and repair tool. If you are serious about meintaining your car yourself, invest in a hydraulic floor jack (1½ ton for the Datsun).

HISTORY

The first Datsun automobile was built in 1914, a small 10 horsepower car with motorcycle fenders. The original name of the company, D.A.T., was derived from the last initials of the company's three main financial backers. A sports-type two seater was produced in 1918 and called the "son of D.A.T.", which later evolved into Datsun. Throughout the '20s and '30s the Datsun automobile looked like the English Austin after which it was closely patterned, while the company also began to branch out into the truck market. The year 1933 saw the formation of Nissan Motor Company, and was also the first year Datsuns were exported.

Following the end of World Wer II (in which Nissan produced military vehicles and aircraft engines), the company managed to resume truck and passenger car production. It wasn't until 1960 that the first Datsun was imported into the United States; since then, Datsun has moved up into second place in imported car sales. The company's introduction of the Sentra model (under the Nissan badge) in 1982 moved Nissan into the forefront of the fuel mileage competition for gasoline-engined cars.

This guide covers all Datsun 1200, B210, and 210 coupes, sedans, hatchbacks and station wagons from 1973 to 1982 (the "A-series" models). It also covers the Nissan Sentra.

SERIAL NUMBER IDENTIFICATION

Chassis

The chassis serial number is stamped into the firewall. The model designation, such as B210, precedes the serial number. The chassis number is also located on a dashboard plate which is visible through the windshield.

Vehicle Identification Plate

The vehicle identification plate is attached to the firewall. This plate gives the vehicle model, engine displacement in cubic centimeters (cc), SAE horsepower rating, wheelbase, engine number, and chassis number.

Engine

All 1200, B210, and 210 series engines are classified as "A-series" engines. Sentra en-

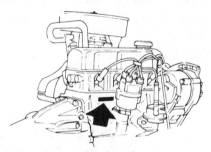

A-series engine number location

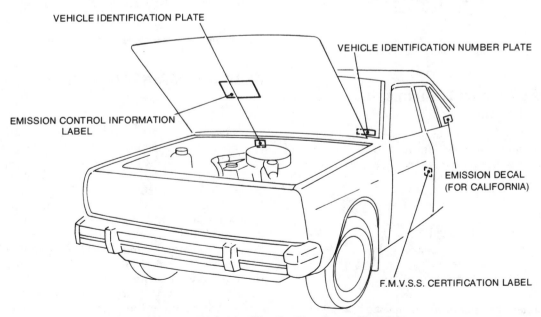

VEHICLE IDENTIFICATION PLATE

VEHICLE IDENTIFICATION NUMBER PLATE

EMISSION CONTROL INFORMATION LABEL

EMISSION DECAL (FOR CALIFORNIA)

F.M.V.S.S. CERTIFICATION LABEL

General vehicle identification locations, all models

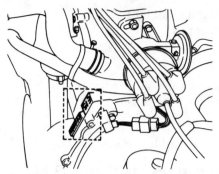

E-series (Sentra) engine number location

gines are "E-series." The engine number is stamped on the right side top edge of the cylinder block on all A-series models, and on the upper right front corner just below the distributor on the Sentra. This serial number is preceded by the engine model code.

Manual Transmission Number

The manual transmission serial number is stamped on the front upper face of the transmission bell housing (case).

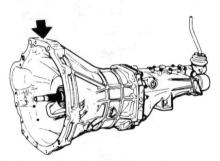

A-series manual transmission number location

Automatic Transmission Number

Automatic transmission serial numbers are found on a plate attached to the right-hand side of the transmission case.

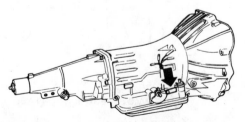

Automatic transmission number location, A-series

Manual Transaxle Number

The Sentra manual transaxle serial number is attached to the clutch withdrawal lever on the upper end of the transaxle.

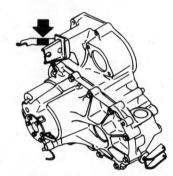

Sentra manual transaxle number location

Automatic Transaxle Number

The Sentra automatic transaxle serial number label is attached to the upper face of the transaxle case.

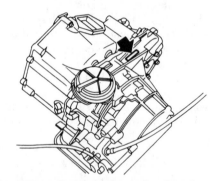

Sentra automatic transaxle number location

ROUTINE MAINTENANCE

Air Cleaner

All Datsuns covered in this guide are equipped with a disposable paper cartridge air cleaner element. At every tuneup, or sooner if the car is operated in a dusty or smoggy area, undo the wing nut, remove the housing top, and withdraw the element. Check the element. Replace the filter if it is extremely dirty. Loose dust can sometimes be removed by striking the filter against a hard surface several times or by blowing through it with compressed air. The filter should be replaced every 24,000 miles. Before installing either the original or a replacement filter, wipe out the inside of the air

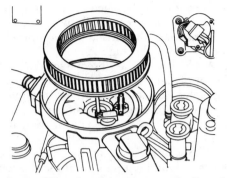

Air cleaner filter element replacement, all models

cleaner housing with a clean rag or paper towel. Install the paper air cleaner filter, seat the top cover on the bottom housing, and tighten the wing nut.

NOTE: *Some flat, cartridge, type air cleaner elements have the word "UP" printed on them. Be sure the side with "UP" on it faces up.*

Air Induction Valve Filter

This filter is located in the air cleaner of the later model 210 Datsuns and Sentra. Replace it when you replace your air filter element by removing the screws which attach the valve filter case, and remove the filter case. Install the new filter, paying attention to which direction the valve is facing so that exhaust gases will not flow backwards through the system.

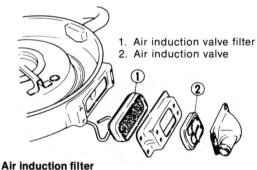

1. Air induction valve filter
2. Air induction valve

Air induction filter

Positive Crankcase Ventilation Valve

This valve feeds crankcase blow-by gases into the intake manifold to be burned with the normal air/fuel mixture. The PCV valve should also be replaced every 24,000 miles. The PCV filter, located inside the air cleaner canister, should be replaced every 24,000 miles or more frequently under dusty or

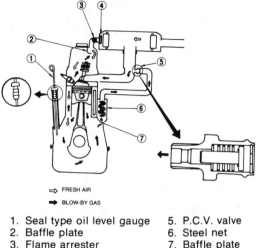

⇨ FRESH AIR
➡ BLOW-BY GAS

1. Seal type oil level gauge
2. Baffle plate
3. Flame arrester
4. Filter
5. P.C.V. valve
6. Steel net
7. Baffle plate

Typical PCV valve location

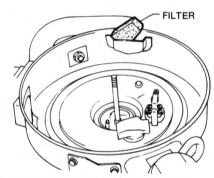

FILTER

PCV filter location in top of air cleaner

smoggy conditions. Make sure that all PCV connections are tight. Check that the connecting hoses are clear and not clogged. Replace any brittle or broken hoses.

To replace the valve, which is located in the intake manifold directly below the carburetor:

1. Squeeze the hose clamp with pliers and remove the hose.

2. Using a wrench, unscrew the PCV valve and remove the valve.

3. Disconnect the ventilation hoses and flush with solvent.

4. Install the new PCV valve and replace the hoses and clamp (check to make sure they are pliable and free of cracks first).

Fuel Evaporative Emissions System

Check the evaporation control system every 12,000 miles. Check the fuel and vapor lines for proper connections and correct routing as

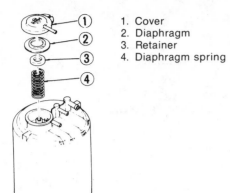

1. Cover
2. Diaphragm
3. Retainer
4. Diaphragm spring

1975 and later carbon canister fuel evaporative emissions system

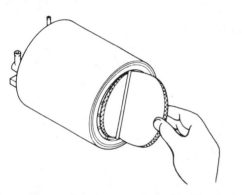

The carbon canister has a replaceable filter in the bottom

well as condition. Replace damaged or deteriorated parts as necessary. Remove and check the operation of the check value on pre-1975 models in the following manner.

1. With all the hoses disconnected from the valve, apply air pressure to the fuel tank side of the valve. The air should flow through the valve and exit the crankcase side of the valve. If the valve does not behave in the above manner, replace it.

2. Apply air pressure to the crankcase side valve. Air should not pass to either of the two outlets.

3. When air pressure is applied to the carburetor side of the valve, the air should pass through to exit out the fuel tank and/or the crankcase side of the valve.

On 1975 and later models, the flow guide valve is replaced with a carbon filled canister which stores fuel vapors until the engine is started and the vapors are drawn into the combustion chambers and burned.

To check the operation of the carbon canister purge control valve, disconnect the rubber hose between the canister control valve and the T-fitting, at the T-fitting. Apply vacuum to the hose leading to the control valve. The vacuum condition should be maintained indefinitely. If the control valve leaks, remove the top cover of the valve and check for a dislocated or cracked diaphragm. If the diaphragm is damaged, a repair kit containing a

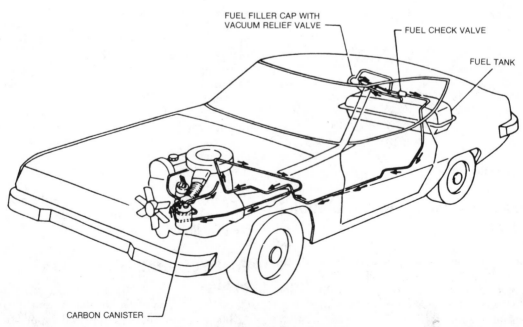

FUEL FILLER CAP WITH
VACUUM RELIEF VALVE

FUEL CHECK VALVE

FUEL TANK

CARBON CANISTER

Evaporative emissions schematic

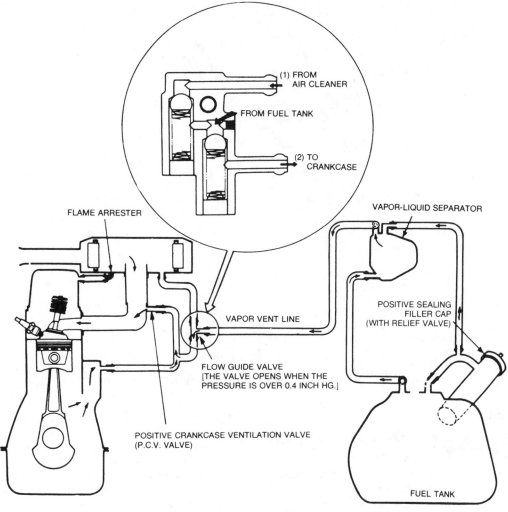

(1) FROM AIR CLEANER

FROM FUEL TANK

(2) TO CRANKCASE

FLAME ARRESTER

VAPOR-LIQUID SEPARATOR

VAPOR VENT LINE

POSITIVE SEALING FILLER CAP (WITH RELIEF VALVE)

FLOW GUIDE VALVE [THE VALVE OPENS WHEN THE PRESSURE IS OVER 0.4 INCH HG.]

POSITIVE CRANKCASE VENTILATION VALVE (P.C.V. VALVE)

FUEL TANK

1973–74 check valve fuel evaporative emissions system

new diaphragm, retainer, and spring is available and should be installed.

The carbon canister has an air filter in the bottom of the canister. The filter element should be checked once a year or every 12,000 miles; more frequently if the car is operated in dusty areas. Replace the filter by pulling it out of the bottom of the canister and installing a new one.

Heat Control Valve

The heat control valve, or Early Fuel Evaporative System, is a thermostically operated valve found in the exhaust manifold of 1200, B210 and early 210 models. It closes when the engine is warming up to direct hot exhaust gases to the intake manifold, in order to pre-heat the incoming fuel/air mixture. If it sticks shut, the result will be frequent stalling during warmup, especially in cold or damp weather. If it sticks open, the result will be a rough idle after the engine is warm.

The heat control valve should be checked for free operation every six months or 6,000 miles. Simply give the counterweight a twirl (engine cold) to make sure that no binding exists. If the valve sticks, apply a heat control solvent (usually available in spray cans) to the ends of the shaft. This type of solvent is available in most auto parts stores. Sometimes lightly rapping the end of the shaft with a hammer (engine hot) will break it loose. If this fails, the components will have to be removed from the car for repair.

NOTE: *The 1980 and later 210 engines do not use the heat control valve.*

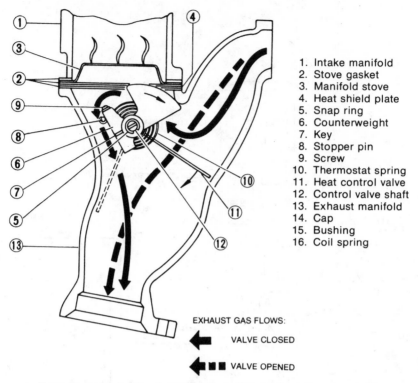

1. Intake manifold
2. Stove gasket
3. Manifold stove
4. Heat shield plate
5. Snap ring
6. Counterweight
7. Key
8. Stopper pin
9. Screw
10. Thermostat spring
11. Heat control valve
12. Control valve shaft
13. Exhaust manifold
14. Cap
15. Bushing
16. Coil spring

EXHAUST GAS FLOWS:

◀ VALVE CLOSED

◀■■ VALVE OPENED

Heat control valve (early fuel evaporative system) A-series engine

Belts

TENSION CHECKING, ADJUSTING, AND REPLACEMENT

Check the belts driving the fan, air pump, air conditioning compressor, and the alternator for cracks, fraying, wear, and tension every 6,000 miles. It is recommended that the belts be replaced every 24 months or 24,000 miles. Belt deflection at the midpoint of the longest span between pulleys should not be more than $7/16$ of an inch with 22 lbs of pressure applied to the belt.

To adjust the tension on all components *except* the air conditioning compressor, power steering pump, and some late model air pumps, loosen the pivot and mounting bolts of the component which the belt is driving, then, using a wooden lever, pry the component toward or away from the engine until the proper tension is achieved.

CAUTION: *Never tighten power steering*

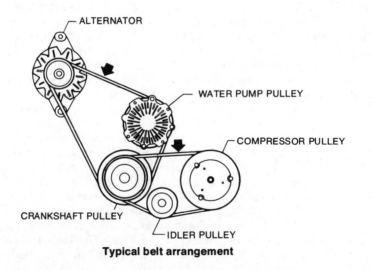

ALTERNATOR

WATER PUMP PULLEY

COMPRESSOR PULLEY

CRANKSHAFT PULLEY

IDLER PULLEY

Typical belt arrangement

HOW TO SPOT WORN V-BELTS

V-Belts are vital to efficient engine operation—they drive the fan, water pump and other accessories. They require little maintenance (occasional tightening) but they will not last forever. Slipping or failure of the V-belt will lead to overheating. If your V-belt looks like any of these, it should be replaced.

Cracking or weathering

This belt has deep cracks, which cause it to flex. Too much flexing leads to heat build-up and premature failure. These cracks can be caused by using the belt on a pulley that is too small. Notched belts are available for small diameter pulleys.

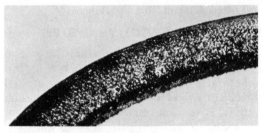

Softening (grease and oil)

Oil and grease on a belt can cause the belt's rubber compounds to soften and separate from the reinforcing cords that hold the belt together. The belt will first slip, then finally fail altogether.

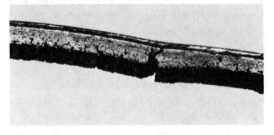

Glazing

Glazing is caused by a belt that is slipping. A slipping belt can cause a run-down battery, erratic power steering, overheating or poor accessory performance. The more the belt slips, the more glazing will be built up on the surface of the belt. The more the belt is glazed, the more it will slip. If the glazing is light, tighten the belt.

Worn cover

The cover of this belt is worn off and is peeling away. The reinforcing cords will begin to wear and the belt will shortly break. When the belt cover wears in spots or has a rough jagged appearance, check the pulley grooves for roughness.

Separation

This belt is on the verge of breaking and leaving you stranded. The layers of the belt are separating and the reinforcing cords are exposed. It's just a matter of time before it breaks completely.

pump, air conditioning compressor, and air pump belts by prying the pump or compressor away from the engine. Damage to the component will result. Also, do not overtighten belts—pulley bearings on the various components will wear out unusually fast.

Tighten the component mounting bolts securely. If a new belt is installed, recheck the tension after driving about 1,000 miles.

NOTE: *The replacement of the inner belt on multi-belted engines may require the removal of the outer belts.*

Belt tension adjustments for the factory installed air conditioning compressor and power steering pump are made at the idler pulley. The idler pulley is the smallest of the three pulleys. At the top of the slotted bracket holding the idler pulley there is a bolt which is used to either raise or lower the pulley. To free the bolt for adjustment, it is necessary to loosen the lock nut in the face of the idler pulley. After adjusting the belt tension, tighten the lock nut in the face of the idler pulley.

NOTE: *Some 1980 and later California Datsuns come equipped from the factory with special fan belts which, if loose, generate friction heat by slipping and shrink, taking up the slack. If your car is new or has low mileage on it, it may still have this type of belt(s) on it. The optical air conditioning drive belt is adjusted in a similar manner.*

NOTE: *Extra belts, especially alternator drive belts, should be part of your car's "emergency equipment," particularly if the brunt of your mileage is driven on the highway. Along with the new belts should be any tools (wrenches, wooden prybars, etc.) needed to install the belts while out on the road.*

Cooling System

Your Datsun's internal combustion gasoline engine generates power by the controlled explosion of a mixture of gasoline and air in the combustion chamber of each cylinder. The piston of each cylinder is at the top of its upward travel when this explosion occurs. The explosion (ignition) forces the piston downward, turning the crankshaft and creating mechanical energy. But not all of the force of the ignited fuel mixture is expended in forcing the piston downward; some heat is released, from the combustion, from the friction of the piston and piston rings moving up

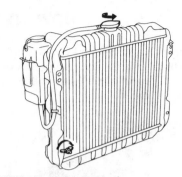

Radiator drain petcock location

and down against the inside of the cylinder bore, and from the movement of the engine's other internal parts. The job of the cooling system is to effectively remove that heat from the engine before it raises the cylinder head and block temperatures took greatly.

DRAINING THE COOLING SYSTEM

To drain the cooling system, allow the engine to cool down *before attempting to remove the radiator cap* Wrap a heavy rag or cloth around the cap to avoid burns, and turn it just enough until it hisses. This removes the pressure from the radiator; wait until the hissing stops before removing the cap. After removing the cap, drain the radiator by unscrewing the petcock or drain plug at the bottom of the radiator. See "Coolant" section under "Fluid Level Checks" in this chapter for refilling procedures.

COOLANT HOSE REPLACEMENT

Remove the radiator cap, unscrew the drain petcock or plug, and drain the radiator into a clean pan if you are going to use the old coolant. Disconnect the hose clamps and remove the hose by either cutting it off or twisting it to break its seal on the radiator and engine coolant inlets. Radiator hoses should always be pliable—any hose that feels brittle or hard should be replaced, as this condition indicates the hose could split anytime (usually when you are miles from any service facility). When installing the new hose, do not overtighten the hose clamps or you might slice the hose underneath. Refill the radiator, run the engine with the radiator cap on and recheck the coolant level.

NOTE: *As with your extra belts, you should carry extra radiator hoses if you plan to travel long distances, or if your normal mileage is on the highway. Don't forget whatever tools you may need to remove the hose clamps and hoses.*

HOW TO SPOT BAD HOSES

Both the upper and lower radiator hoses are called upon to perform difficult jobs in an inhospitable environment. They are subject to nearly 18 psi at under hood temperatures often over 280°F., and must circulate nearly 7500 gallons of coolant an hour—3 good reasons to have good hoses.

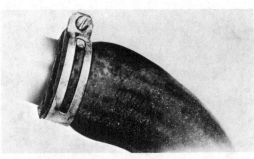

A good test for any hose is to feel it for soft or spongy spots. Frequently these will appear as swollen areas of the hose. The most likely cause is oil soaking. This hose could burst at any time, when hot or under pressure.

Swollen hose

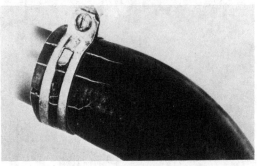

Cracked hoses can usually be seen but feel the hoses to be sure they have not hardened; a prime cause of cracking. This hose has cracked down to the reinforcing cords and could split at any of the cracks.

Cracked hose

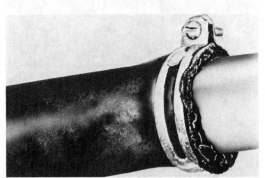

Weakened clamps frequently are the cause of hose and cooling system failure. The connection between the pipe and hose has deteriorated enough to allow coolant to escape when the engine is hot.

Frayed hose end (due to weak clamp)

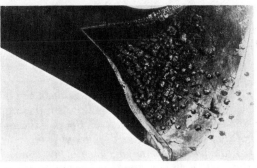

Debris, rust and scale in the cooling system can cause the inside of a hose to weaken. This can usually be felt on the outside of the hose as soft or thinner areas.

Debris in cooling system

Air Conditioning

This book contains no repair or maintenance procedures for the air conditioning system. It is recommended that any such repairs be left to the experts, whose personnel are well aware of the hazards and who have the proper equipment.

CAUTION: *The compressed refrigerant (R-12) used in the air conditioning system expands into the atmosphere at a temperature of −21.7°F or lower. This will freeze any surface, including your eyes, that it contacts. In addition, R-12 decomposes into a poisonous gas in the presence of flame. Do not open or disconnect any part of the air conditioning system.*

SIGHT GLASS CHECK

You can safely make a few simple checks to determine if your air conditioning system needs service. The tests work best if the temperature is warm (about 70°F).

NOTE: *If your vehicle is equipped with an after-market air conditioner, the following system check may not apply. You should contact the manufacturer of the unit for instructions on systems checks.*

1. Place the automatic transmission in Park or the manual transmission in Neutral. Set the parking brake.

2. Run the engine at a fast idle (about 1,500 rpm) either with the help of a friend, or by temporarily readjusting the idle speed screw.

3. Set the controls for maximum cold with the blower on high.

4. Locate the sight glass in one of the system lines. Uusually it is on the left alongside the top of the radiator.

5. If you see bubbles, the system must be recharged. Very likely there is a leak at some point.

6. If there are no bubbles, there is either no refrigerant at all or the system is fully charged. Feel the two hoses going to the belt-driven compressor. If they are both at the same temperature, the system is empty and must be recharged.

7. If one hose (high-pressure) is warm and the other (low-pressure) is cold, the system may be all right. However, you are probably making these tests because you think there is something wrong, so proceed to the next step.

8. Have an assistant in the car turn the fan control on and off to operate the compressor clutch. Watch the sight glass.

The sight glass is located in the head of the receiver-dryer (arrow)

9. If bubbles appear when the clutch is disengaged and disappear when it is engaged, the system is properly charged.

10. If the refrigerant takes more than 45 seconds to bubble when the clutch is disengaged, the system is overcharged. This usually causes poor cooling at low speeds.

CAUTION: *If it is determined that the system has a leak, it should be corrected as soon as possible. Leaks may allow moisture to enter and cause a very expensive rust problem.*

NOTE: *Operate the air conditioner for a few minutes, every two weeks or so, during the cold months. This avoids the possibility of the compressor seals drying out from lack of lubrication, a major cause of air conditioner system maintenance and repair.*

Fluid Level Checks

ENGINE OIL

The best time to check the engine oil is before operating the engine or after it has been sitting for at least 10 minutes in order to gain an accurate reading. This will allow the oil to drain back into the crankcase. To check the engine oil level, make sure that the vehicle is resting on a level surface, remove the oil dipstick, wipe it clean and reinsert the stick all the way down again until the cap seats itself in the tube. Pull the dipstick out again and "level" it for an accurate reading.

The oil dipstick has two marks on it to indicate high and low oil level. If the oil is at or below the "low level" mark on the dipstick, oil should be added as necessary. The oil level should be maintained in the safety margin, neither going above the "high level" mark or below the "low level" mark.

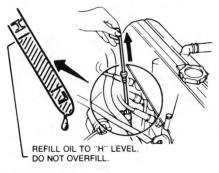

REFILL OIL TO "H" LEVEL.
DO NOT OVERFILL.

Oil dipstick markings

TRANSMISSION

Manual and Manual Transaxle (Sentra)

Check the level of the lubricant in the transmission every 3,000 miles. The lubricant level should be even with the bottom of the filler hole. Hold in on the filler plug when unscrewing it. When you are sure that all of the

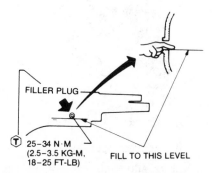

FILLER PLUG

ⓣ 25–34 N·M
(2.5–3.5 KG-M,
18–25 FT-LB)   FILL TO THIS LEVEL

Transmission oil should be level with the bottom of the filler plug on manual transmissions

threads of the plug are free of the transmission case, move the plug away from the case slightly. If lubricant begins to flow out of the transmission, then you know it is full. If not, add SAE90 gear oil as necessary. It is recommended that the transmission lubricant be changed every 24,000 miles.

Automatic

Check the level of the automatic transmission fluid every 2,000 miles. There is a dipstick at the right rear of the engine under the hood. It has a scale on each side, one for COLD and the other for HOT. The transmission is considered hot after 15 miles of highway driving.

Park the car on a level surface with the engine running. If the transmission is not hot, shift into Drive, Low, then Neutral or Park. Set the handbrake and block the wheels.

Remove the dipstick, wipe it clean, then reinsert it firmly. Remove the dipstick and check the fluid level on the appropriate scale. The level should be at the "Full" mark.

If the level is below the "Full" mark, add Type A or DEXRON® type automatic transmission fluid as necessary, with the engine running, through the dipstick tube. *Do not overfill*, as this may cause the transmission to malfunction and damage itself.

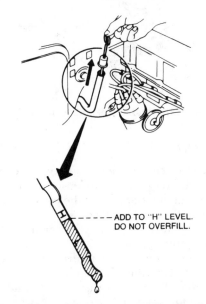

ADD TO "H" LEVEL.
DO NOT OVERFILL.

Remove the automatic transmission dipstick with engine warm and idling in Park

BRAKE AND CLUTCH MASTER CYLINDER

NOTE: *The clutch in your 1200, B210 or 210 model Datsun is operated hydraulic-*

ally, employing a system much the same as the hydraulic brake system in the car. Both systems use a DOT 3 type brake fluid. The Sentra does not have a hydraulic clutch.

Check the levels of brake fluid in the brake and clutch master cylinder reservoirs every 3,000 miles. The fluid level should be maintained to a level not below the bottom line on the reservoirs and not above the top line. Any sudden decrease in the level in either of the three reservoirs (two for the brakes and one for the clutch) indicates a probable leak in that particular system and the possibility of a leak should be checked out.

ADD TO "MAX" LEVEL - - - -

Brake master cylinder, all models similar

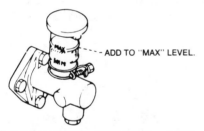

- ADD TO "MAX" LEVEL.

Clutch master cylinder, 1200, B210 and 210

COOLANT

Check the coolant level every time you change the oil. Check for loose connections and signs of deterioration of the coolant hoses. Maintain the coolant level 3 in. below the level of the filler neck when the engine is cold. Add a mixture of 70% to 50% water and 30% to 50% ethylene glycol antifreeze as necessary. See "Draining the Cooling System" in this chapter for radiator cap removal cautions and radiator draining.

Never add cold water to an overheated engine while the engine is not running; this can cause the engine block to crack. Run the engine until it reaches normal operating temperature after filling the radiator to make sure that the thermostat has opened and all air is bled from the system.

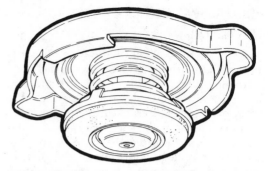

Check the rubber gasket on the cap when checking the coolant level

REAR AXLE

Check the rear axle lubricant on the 1200, B210 and 210 cars every 6,000 miles. Remove the filler plug in the axle housing. The lubricant should be up to the bottom of the filler hole with the vehicle resting on a level surface. Add SAE90 gear oil as necessary to bring the lubricant up to the proper level.

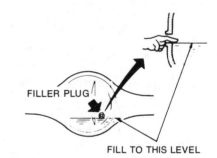

FILLER PLUG

FILL TO THIS LEVEL

Checking rear axle oil level, 1200, B210 and 210. Fill to the level of the filler plug hole

STEERING GEAR

Check the level of the lubricant in the steering gear box every 12,000 miles. If the level

⬤ : CHECK FLUID LEAKS.

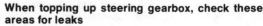 : ADD FLUID.

When topping up steering gearbox, check these areas for leaks

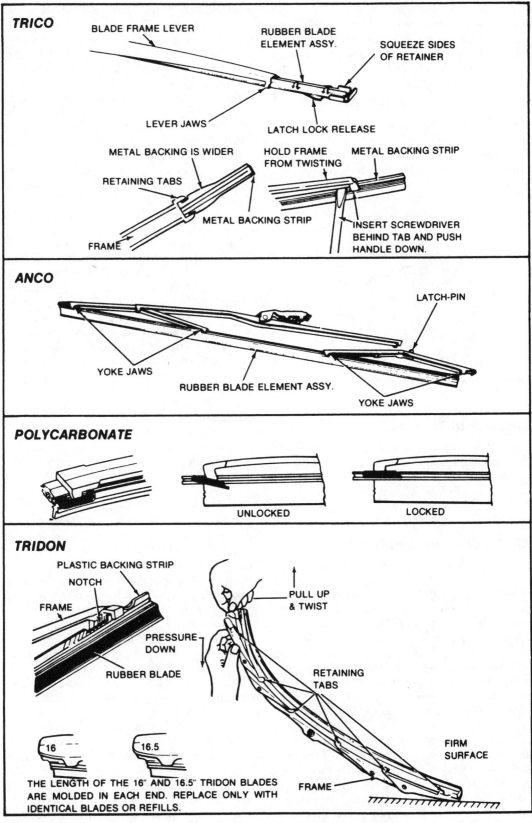

Popular styles of wiper refills

is low, check for leakage. An oily film is not considered a leak; solid grease must be present. Change the lubricant every 36,000 miles. Use steering gear lubricant. The lubricant is added and checked through the filler plug hole in the top of the steering gear.

POWER STEERING RESERVOIR

Check the fluid level in the reservoir by observing the dipstick when the fluid is cold. Add fluid as necessary to bring the level into the proper range on the dipstick. DO NOT OVERFILL.

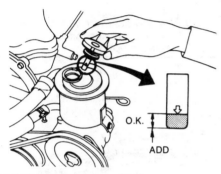

O.K.

ADD

Power steering reservoir check

Windshield Wipers

Intense heat from the sun, snow and ice, road oils and the chemicals used in windshield washer solvent combine to deteriorate the rubber wiper refills. The refills should be replaced about twice a year or whenever the blades begin to streak or chatter.

WIPER REFILL REPLACEMENT

Normally, if the wipers are not cleaning the windshield properly, only the refill has to be replaced. The blade and arm usually require replacement only in the event of damage. It is not necessary (except on new Tridon refills) to remove the arm or the blade to replace the refill (rubber part), though you may have to position the arm higher on the glass. You can do this by turning the ignition switch "on" and operating the wipers. When they are positioned where they are accessible, turn the ignition switch "off."

There are several types of refills and your car could have any kind, since aftermarket blades and arms may not use exactly the same type refill as the original equipment.

Most Trico styles use a release button that is pushed down to allow the refill to slide out of the yoke jaws. The new refill slides in and

locks in place. Some Trico refills are removed by locating where the metal backing strip or the refill is wider. Insert a small screwdriver blade between the frame and metal backing strip. Press down to release the refill from the retaining tab.

The Anco style is unlocked at one end by squeezing 2 metal tabs, and the refill is slid out of the framejaws. When the new refill is installed, the tabs will click into place, locking the refill.

The polycarbonate type is held in place by a locking lever that is pushed downward, out of the groove in the arm, to free the refill. When the new refill is installed, it will lock in place automatically.

The Tridon refill has a plastic backing strip with a notch about an inch from the end. Hold the blade (frame) on a hard surface so that the frame is tightly bowed. Grip the tip of the backing strip and pull up while twisting counterclockwise. The backing strip will snap out of the retaining tab. Do this for the remaining tabs until the refill is free of the arm. The length of these refills is molded into the end and they should be replaced with identical types.

No matter which type of refill you use, be sure that all of the frame claws engage the refill. Before operating the wipers, be sure that no part of the metal frame is contacting the windshield.

Battery

The battery in your Datsun is located in the engine compartment. Keep any eye on the battery electrolyte (fluid) level and its specific gravity. A few minutes occasionally spent monitoring battery condition is worth saving hours of frustration and hassle when your car won't start due to a dead battery. Use only distilled water (available in most supermarkets and hardware stores) to top up the battery, as tap water in many areas contains harmful chemicals and minerals.

Four tools that will make battery maintenance easier are a hydrometer, a squeeze bulb filler (syringe or common "turkey baster"), a battery terminal brush and a battery clamp puller. All of these tools are inexpensive and widely available at auto parts stores, hardware stores, etc. The specific gravity of the electrolyte should be between 1.27 and 1.20 (often shown by a color on the float of the hydrometer). Keep the top of the battery clean, as a film of dirt can sometimes com-

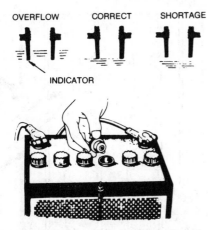

Make sure the electrolyte in the battery is level with the bottoms of the filler holes

Use the terminal brush to get the insides of the terminal clamps shiny

pletely discharge a battery. Clean this surface with a solution of baking soda and water, using an old toothbrush to remove the crystallized electrolyte (the whitish powder which sometimes builds up near the terminal posts). Flush the top of the battery with clear water.

Battery terminal posts and terminal clamps can be cleaned with the battery terminal brush. Unbolt the clamps from the terminals and remove them using the clamp puller (you can twist them up and off without the puller, but if they're stuck you may twist the terminal off with the clamp). Clean the insides of the clamps with the wire brush, until the insides are shiny. Clean the terminal posts with the female end of the brush unit, turning the brush around on the posts until the posts are shiny. The cleanliness of the posts and clamps is crucial to a good electrical connection.

Assemble the battery wire clamps to the

Capacities

Year	Model	Engine Crankcase (qts) With Filter	Engine Crankcase (qts) Without Filter	Transmission (pts) 4-Spd	Transmission (pts) 5-Spd	Automatic (total capacity)	Drive Axle (pts)	Gas Tank (gals)	Cooling System (qts)
1973	1200	3.6	2.6	2.5	—	11.8	1.8	10/10.5 (sedan)	5.2
1974	B-210	3.45	—	2.5	—	11.8	1.8	11.5	5.5
1975	B-210	4.2	3.7	2.7	—	11.4	1.89	11.5	6.25 ①
1976–78	B-210	3.8	3.4	2.75	3.6	11.8	1.8	11.5	6.25 ①
1979–82	210	3.5	3.0	②	2.5	11.8	1.8	13.25	5.25
1982–83	Sentra	4.1	3.6	4.8	5.75	13.1	—	13.25	5.0 ③

① Automatic transmission: 6 qts.
② A12A 2.5 pts.; A14, A15 2.75 pts.
③ Automatic transmission: 5.6 qts.

terminal posts and lightly coat the clamps with petroleum jelly to help retard corrosion.

CAUTION: *Battery electrolyte is an acid, and should be kept away from the skin, especially the eyes. If it is accidentally splashed, flush the area immediately with cold, clean water. Never smoke or place any open flame near a battery, as it is constantly giving off an explosive gas while charging.*

Tires

Check the air pressure in your tires every few weeks. Make sure that the tires are cool, as you will get a false reading when the tires are heated because air pressure increases with temperature. A decal (usually on a door jamb or inside the glove compartment) tells you the proper tire pressure for the standard equipment tires. Naturally, when you replace tires you will want to get the correct tire pressures for the new ones from the dealer or manufacturer. It pays to buy a tire pressure gauge to keep in the car, since those at service stations are usually inaccurate or broken.

While you are checking the tire pressure, take a look at the tread. The tread should be wearing evenly across the tire. Excessive wear in the center of the tread could indicate overinflation. Excessive wear on the outer edges could indicate underinflation. An irregular wear pattern is usually a sign of incorrect front wheel alignment or wheel balance. A front end that is out of alignment will usually pull the car to one side of a flat road when the

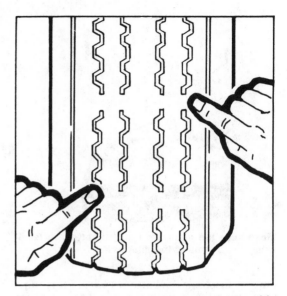

When bands appear as shown, your tire tread is below 1/16 inch. Tire should be replaced

steering wheel is released. Incorrect wheel balance will produce vibration in the steering wheel, while unbalanced rear wheels will result in floor or trunk vibration.

Rotating the tires every 6,000 miles or so will result in increased tread life. Use the correct pattern for your tire switching. Most automotive experts agree that radial tires are better all around performers, giving longer wear and better handling. An added benefit which you should consider when purchasing tires is that radials have less rolling resistance and, when properly inflated, can give up to a

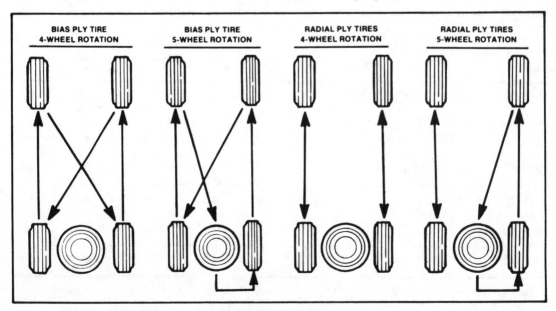

BIAS PLY TIRE 4-WHEEL ROTATION   BIAS PLY TIRE 5-WHEEL ROTATION   RADIAL PLY TIRES 4-WHEEL ROTATION   RADIAL PLY TIRES 5-WHEEL ROTATION

Tire rotation patterns

10% increase in fuel economy over a bias-ply tire.

Never mix bias tires and radials, or vice versa, as this can cause serious handling problems. Always replace tires in sets of four or five when switching tire types and never substitute a belted tire for a bias-ply, a radial for a belted tire, etc. An occasional pressure check and periodic rotation can make your tires last much longer than a neglected set, while maintaining the safety margin which was designed into them.

Fuel Filter

The fuel filter on all models is a disposable plastic unit. It's located on the right inner fender. The filter should be replaced at least every 24,000 miles. A dirty filter will starve the engine and cause poor running.

REPLACEMENT

1. Locate fuel filter on right-side of the engine compartment.
2. Disconnect the inlet and outlet hoses from the fuel filter. Make certain that the inlet hose (bottom) doesn't fall below the fuel tank level or the gasoline will drain out.
3. Pry the fuel filter from its clip and replace the assembly.
4. Replace the inlet and outlet lines; secure the hose clamps to prevent leaks.
5. Start the engine and check for leaks.

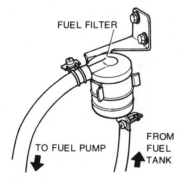

FUEL FILTER

TO FUEL PUMP

FROM FUEL TANK

Typical fuel filter, all models

LUBRICATION

Oil and Fuel Recommendations

Your Datsun is designed to operate on regular low lead or lead-free fuel. The octane ratings are listed on the inside of the fuel filler door, but these need only be checked when traveling outside of the United States. Should

you find the regular gasoline available, say in Mexico, to be of too low an octane, mix a 50/50 regular leaded-to-unleaded Premium ratio. This will give your car the lead it needs (if designed to run on leaded gas) and also the octane it needs. 1975 California cars and all 1976 and later models will run happily on the unleaded gasoline available in the United States.

Oil must be selected with regard to the anticipated temperatures during the period before the next oil change. Using the chart, select the oil viscosity for the lowest expected temperature and you will be assured of easy cold starting and sufficient engine protection. The oil you pour into your Datsun engine should have the designation "SE" marked on the top of its container. Under the classification system adopted by the American Petroleum Institute (API) in May, 1970, "SE" is the highest designation for passenger car use. The "S" stands for passenger car and the second letter denotes a more specific application. "SA" oil, for instance, contains no additives and is suitable only for very light-duty usage. Oil designated "MS" (motor severe) may also be used, since this was the highest classification under the old API rating system.

SYNTHETIC OIL

There are many excellent synthetic and fuel-efficient oils currently available that can provide better gas mileage, longer service life, and in some cases better engine protection. These benefits do not come without a few hitches, however—the main one being the price of synthetic oils, which is three or four times the price per quart of conventional oil.

Synthetic oil is not for every car and every type of driving, so you should consider your engine's condition and your type of driving. Also, check your car's warranty conditions regarding the use of synthetic oils.

Both brand new engines and older, high mileage engines are the wrong candidates for synthetic oil. The synthetic oils are so slippery that they can prevent the proper break-in of new engines; most manufacturers recommend that you wait until the engine is properly broken in (5,000 miles) until using synthetic oil. Older engines with wear have a different problem with synthetics: they "use" (consume during operation) more oil as they age. Slippery synthetic oils get past these worn parts easily—if your engine is "using" conventional oil, it will use synthetics much faster. Also, if your car is leaking oil past old seals you'll have a much greater leak problem with synthetics.

Consider your type of driving. If most of your accumulated mileage is high speed, highway type driving, the more expensive synthetic oils may be of benefit. Extended highway driving gives the engine a chance to warm up, accumulating less acids in the oil and putting less stress on the engine over the long run. Under these conditions, the oil change interval can be extended (as long as your oil filter can last the extended life of the oil) up to the advertised mileage claims of the synthetics. Cars with synthetic oils may show increased fuel economy in highway driving, due to less internal friction. However, many automotive experts agree that 50,000 miles is too long to keep any oil in your engine.

Cars used under harder circumstances, such as stop-and-go, city type driving, short trips, or extended idling, should be serviced more frequently. For the engines in these cars, the much greater cost of synthetic or fuel-efficient oils may not be worth the investment. Internal wear increases much quicker on these cars, causing greater oil consumption and leakage.

NOTE: *The mixing of conventional and synthetic oils is not recommended. If you are using synthetic oil, it might be wise to carry two or three quarts with you no matter where you drive, as not all service stations carry this type of lubricant.*

Oil Changes

The mileage figures given in your owner's manual are the Datsun recommended intervals for oil and filter changes assuming average driving. If your Datsun is being used under dusty, polluted, or off-road conditions, change the oil and filter sooner than specified. The same thing goes for cars driven in stop-and-go traffic or only for short distances.

Always drain the oil after the engine has been running long enough to bring it to operating temperature. Hot oil will flow easier and more contaminants will be removed along with the oil than if it were drained cold. You will need a large capacity drain pan, which you can purchase at any store which sells automotive parts. Another necessity is containers for the used oil. You will find that plastic bottles, such as those used for bleach or fabric softener, make excellent storage jugs. One ecologically desirable solution to the used oil

Oil Viscosity Selection Chart

	Anticipated Temperature Range	SAE Viscosity
Multi-grade	Above 32° F	10W—40 10W—50 20W—40 20W—50 10W—30
	May be used as low as −10° F	10W—30 10W—40
	Consistently below 10° F	5W—20 5W—30
Single-grade	Above 32° F	30
	Temperature between +32° F and −10° F	10W

disposal problem is to find a cooperative gas station owner who will allow you to dump your used oil into his tank or take the oil to a reclamation center (often at garages and gas stations).

Datsun recommends changing both the oil and filter during the first oil change and the filter every other oil change thereafter. For the small price of an oil filter, it's cheap insurance to replace the filter at *every oil change*. One of the larger filter manufacturers points out in its advertisements that not changing the filter leaves one quart of dirty oil in the engine. This claim is true and should be kept in mind when changing your oil.

CHANGING YOUR ENGINE OIL

1. Run the engine until it reaches normal operating temperature.

2. Jack up the front of the car and sup-

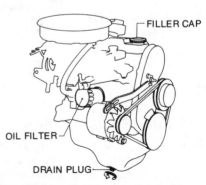

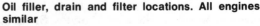

Oil filler, drain and filter locations. All engines similar

A strap wrench will make oil filter removal easier. Do not install a filter with a strap wrench

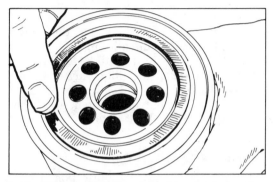

Apply a light coat of oil to the rubber gasket on the oil filter before installing it

port it on safety stands if necessary to gain access to the filter.

3. Slide a drain pan of at least 6 quarts capacity under the oil pan.

4. Loosen the drain plug. Turn the plug out by hand. By keeping an inward pressure on the plug as you unscrew it, oil won't escape past the threads and you can remove it without being burned by hot oil. Use a rag to unscrew the plug.

5. Allow the oil to drain completely and then install the drain plug. *Don't overtighten* the plug, or you'll be buying a new pan or a "trick" replacement plug for buggered threads.

6. Using the oil filter strap wrench, remove the oil filter. As the filter unscrews the final turn, "level" it as you pull it off the engine block. Keep in mind the filter is still filled with about a quart of *dirty, hot oil.*

7. Empty the old filter into the drain pan and dispose of the filter.

8. Using a clean rag, wipe off the filter adapter on the engine block. Be sure that the rag doesn't leave any lint which could clog an oil passage.

9. Coat the rubber gasket on the new filter with a wipe of fresh oil. Spin it onto the engine by hand; when the filter begins to snug

up against the mounting surface give it another ½–¾ turn. *Do not turn it any more* or you'll ruin the gasket and the filter will leak.

10. Refill the engine with the correct amount of fresh oil. See the "Capacities" chart.

11. Crank the engine over several times and then start it. If the oil pressure "idiot light" doesn't go out or the pressure gauge shows zero, shut the engine down and find out what's wrong.

12. If the oil pressure is OK and there are no leaks, shut the engine off and lower the car.

Transmission

MANUAL AND MANUAL TRANSAXLE

Change the transmission lubricant in your manual transmission every 36,000 miles as follows:

1. Park the car on a level surface and apply the parking brake. Jack up the car and support it on stands.

2. Remove the oil filler plug (the upper one). The Sentra filler plug is on the side of the transaxle.

3. Place a drain pan under the drain plug in the transmission bottom pan. Drain plug for the Sentra transaxle is on the side of the transaxle case, below the filler plug.

4. Slowly remove the drain plug keeping an upward pressure on it until you can quickly pull it out.

5. Allow all of the old gear oil to drain and then replace the plug. Don't overtighten it.

6. Fill the transmission with SAE 90 gear oil. Refill with the quantity shown in the "Capacities" chart. An oil suction gun or squeeze bulb filler (turkey baster") are handy for this chore and can be used for the rear axle, too (except on Sentra, which is front wheel drive).

7. Replace the filler plug and lower the car.

AUTOMATIC AND AUTOMATIC TRANSAXLE

The transmission fluid in an automatic transmission should be changed every 24,000 miles of normal driving or every 12,000 miles of driving under abnormal or severe conditions (such as frequent trailer-pulling). The fluid should be drained immediately after the vehicle has been driven, but before it has had the chance to cool. Follow the procedure given below:

1. Drain the automatic transmission fluid from the transmission into a large drain pan,

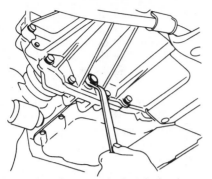

Sentra automatic transmission drain plug

by removing the transmission bottom pan screws, pan, and gasket on the 1200, B210 and 210. On the Sentra transaxle, remove the hexagon drain plug first. When all fluid has drained, remove the pan guard, pan, and gasket.

2. Thoroughly clean the bottom pan and position a new gasket on the pan mating surface. Use petroleum jelly on the gasket to seal it. Install the bottom pan and secure it with the attaching screws, tightening them to 3–5 ft. lbs.

3. Pour the correct amount of Type A DEXRON® automatic transmission fluid, as specified in the "Capacities" chart, in through the filler pipe. Make sure that the funnel, container, hose, or any other item used to assist in filling the transmission is clean.

4. Start the engine. Do NOT race it. Allow the engine to idle for a few minutes.

5. Place the selector lever in Park and ap-

ply the parking brake. With the transmission fluid at operating temperatures, check the fluid level; add fluid to bring the level to the "FULL" mark on the dip-stick.

Rear Axle

Change the gear oil in the rear axle every 36,000 miles as follows:

1. With the car on a level surface, jack up the rear and support it with stands.

2. Slide a drain pan under the drain plug, remove the plug, and allow the oil to drain out.

3. Install the drain plug, but don't overtighten it. Remove the filler plug.

4. Refill the rear axle with SAE 90 gear oil up to the level of the filler plug (a kitchen "turkey baster" is useful here in adding the oil. Also, some oil brands come in plastic bottles with useful built-in spouts).

Chassis Greasing

Datsun doesn't install lubrication fittings ("grease nipples") in lube points on the steering linkage or suspension. You can buy metric threaded fittings to grease these points or use a pointed, rubber end tip on your grease gun. Lubricate all joints equipped with a plug every 24,000 miles. When greasing, keep the grease gun as square with the fitting as possible, or grease will just squeeze out around the fitting instead of inside the fitting. Replace the plugs after lubrication.

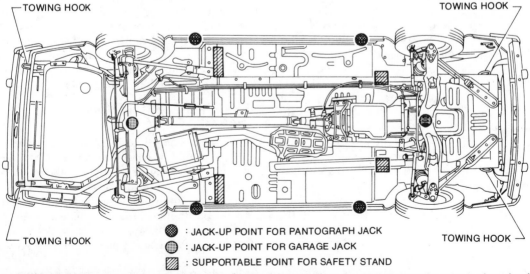

: JACK-UP POINT FOR PANTOGRAPH JACK
: JACK-UP POINT FOR GARAGE JACK
: SUPPORTABLE POINT FOR SAFETY STAND

Jacking and towing locations, 210. 1200 and B210 models similar except they use the rear spring shackles as tow hooks. Sentra has single central tow hook on each end.

JUMP STARTING A DEAD BATTERY

The chemical reaction in a battery produces explosive hydrogen gas. This is the safe way to jump start a dead battery, reducing the chances of an accidental spark that could cause an explosion.

Jump Starting Precautions

1. Be sure both batteries are of the same voltage.
2. Be sure both batteries are of the same polarity (have the same grounded terminal).
3. Be sure the vehicles are not touching.
4. Be sure the vent cap holes are not obstructed.
5. Do not smoke or allow sparks around the battery.
6. In cold weather, check for frozen electrolyte in the battery.
7. Do not allow electrolyte on your skin or clothing.
8. Be sure the electrolyte is not frozen.

Jump Starting Procedure

1. Determine voltages of the two batteries; they must be the same.
2. Bring the starting vehicle close (they must not touch) so that the batteries can be reached easily.
3. Turn off all accessories and both engines. Put both cars in Neutral or Park and set the handbrake.
4. Cover the cell caps with a rag—do not cover terminals.
5. If the terminals on the run-down battery are heavily corroded, clean them.
6. Identify the positive and negative posts on both batteries and connect the cables in the order shown.
7. Start the engine of the starting vehicle and run it at fast idle. Try to start the car with the dead battery. Crank it for no more than 10 seconds at a time and let it cool off for 20 seconds in between tries.
8. If it doesn't start in 3 tries, there is something else wrong.
9. Disconnect the cables in the reverse order.
10. Replace the cell covers and dispose of the rags.

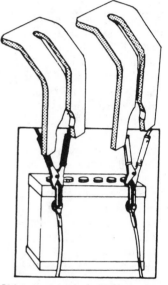

Side terminal batteries occasionally pose a problem when connecting jumper cables. There frequently isn't enough room to clamp the cables without touching sheet metal. Side terminal adaptors are available to alleviate this problem and should be removed after use.

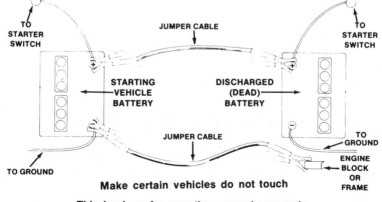

TO STARTER SWITCH   JUMPER CABLE   TO STARTER SWITCH

STARTING VEHICLE BATTERY   DISCHARGED (DEAD) BATTERY

JUMPER CABLE

TO GROUND

TO GROUND   ENGINE BLOCK OR FRAME

Make certain vehicles do not touch

This hook-up for negative ground cars only

PUSHING TOWING AND JUMP STARTING

All Datsun 1200, B210, 210 and Sentra models with manual transmissions can be push started, except 1976 and later California cars, as push starting may damage the catalytic converters. *All models* equipped with automatic transmissions, including Sentra, may NOT be push started.

Before starting, check to make sure that the bumpers of both vehicles are aligned as much as possible. An old tire placed between the bumpers of both vehicles makes a good cushion against damage to either car. Make sure that all electrical components are turned off (headlights, heater, etc.). Turn the ignition switch "on," push in the clutch pedal and place the shift lever in third gear. Give the driver of the push vehicle the signal to "go"; at about 15 mph, signal the driver to fall back, depress the accelerator pedal and release the clutch pedal slowly (check again to be certain the ignition switch is "on"). The engine should start.

You can perform the same procedure as above, but without a push car, if you are within access to a long hill (devoid of traffic, of course). In either situation, it is not advisable to tow-start your Datsun for fear of ramming the towing vehicle when the engine starts.

Both manual and automatic 1200, B210, and 210 Datsuns may be towed for short distances and at speeds no more than 20 mph. *Never* tow a Sentra model with automatic transmission with the front (drive) wheels touching the ground. If the car must be towed a long distance, it should be done with either the drive wheels off the ground or the driveshaft disconnected. Sentra manual transaxle models should be towed with their drive (front) wheels off the ground to avoid transaxle damage. If this is not possible, place the transaxle in neutral and make sure the ignition switch is NOT in the "LOCK" position. Try to restrict towing an automatic transmission car to a distance of less than 20 miles. Any towing of a manual transmission car over 50 miles should be done with the driveshaft disconnected.

Jump starting a dead battery is a procedure that should be known to every car owner (see illustration). Make sure the cars are not touching, the cables are not crossed, and the clamps connected positive-to-positive and negative-to-negative. You should carry a set of good quality jumper cables in your car at all times.

JACKING

NEVER use the bumper jack—the jack supplied with the car—for anything other than changing tires. If you are serious about performing your own maintenance, invest in a 1½ ton hydraulic floor jack and (at least) two sturdy jackstands. A hydraulic jack will pay for itself very quickly in safety, time saved, and overall utility.

ALWAYS chock the wheels when changing a tire or working beneath the car. This cannot be overemphasized: CLIMBING UNDER A CAR SUPPORTED BY ONLY A JACK IS EXTREMELY DANGEROUS.

Tune-Up

TUNE-UP PROCEDURES

The tune-up is a routine maintenance operation which is essential for the efficient and economical operation, as well as the long life, of your car's engine. The interval between tune-ups is a variable factor which depends upon the way you drive your car, the conditions under which you drive it (weather, road type, etc.) and the type of engine installed in your car. Manufacturer's recommended tune-up intervals should be followed if possible, but it is generally correct to say that no car should be driven more than 12,000 miles between tune-ups, especially in this age of emission controls and fuel shortages. Cars driven extremely hard or under severe weather conditions should be tuned at closer intervals.

The replacement parts involved in a tune-up include spark plugs, air filter, distributor cap, ignition points (if equipped), rotor, and spark plug wires. In addition to these parts and the adjustments involved in properly adapting them to your engine, there are several adjustments of other parts involved in completing the job. Included in these adjustments are carburetor idle speed and air/fuel mixture, ignition timing, and valve clearance adjustments.

This chapter gives specific procedures on how to tune-up your 1200, B210 or 210 model Datsun, and Nissan Sentra. It is intended to be as complete as possible. Chapter 11, "Troubleshooting," is intended to go hand-in-hand with this chapter; it includes troubleshooting diagnosis for the more experienced owner/mechanic.

Tune up time is also a good time to look around the engine compartment for potential problems, such as fuel and oil leaks, cracking or hard radiator or heater hoses, loose or frayed belts, loose wire connections, etc.

CAUTION: *When working around a running engine, always be certain there is plenty of ventilation. Make sure the transmission is in Neutral (unless otherwise specified) and the parking brake is fully applied. Always keep hands, hair, and clothing away from the fan, hot manifolds and radiator. Remove any jewelry or neckties. When the engine is running, do not grasp the ignition wires, distributor cap or coil wire, as a shock in excess of 20,000 volts may result. Whenever working around the distributor, even if the engine is not running, make sure that the ignition is switched off. Removing or disturbing the distributor cap on an electronic ignition system with the ignition switch "on" can often cause the system to fire.*

For 1973–79 models, Datsun recommends

Tune-Up Specifications

When analyzing compression test results, look for uniformity among cylinders, rather than specific pressures.

| Year | Model | Spark Plug | | Distributor | | Ignition Timing (deg) | | Fuel Pump Pressure (psi) | Idle Speed (rpm) * | | Valve Clearance | | Percentage of CO at Idle |
		Type	Gap (in.)	Point Dwell (deg)	Point Gap (in.)	MT	AT		MT	AT	In	Ex	
1973	1200	BP5-ES	.034	49–55	.020	5B @ 700	5B @ 600	2.6	800	650	0.010 cold 0.014 hot	0.010 cold 0.014 hot	1.5
1974	B-210	BP5-ES	.033	49–55	.020	5B @ 800	5B @ 650	3.4	800	650	0.014 hot	0.014 hot	1.5
1975	B210 (Federal)	BP5-ES	.033	49–55	.020	10B	10B	3.8	700	650	0.014 hot	0.014 hot	2.0
	B210 (California)	BP6-ES	.033	Electronic	①	10B	10B	3.8	750	650	0.014 hot	0.014 hot	2.0
1976	B210 (Federal)	BP5-ES	.033	44–55	.020	10B	10B	3.8	700	650	0.014 hot	0.014 hot	2.0
	B210 (California)	BP5-ES	.033	Electronic	①	10B	10B	3.8	700	650	0.014 hot	0.014 hot	2.0
1977	B210 (Federal)	BP5-ES	.041	49–55	.020	10B	8B	3.8	700	650	0.014 hot	0.014 hot	2.0
	B210 (California)	BP5-ES	.041	Electronic	①	10B	10B	3.8	700	650	0.014 hot	0.014 hot	2.0

Year	Model	Spark Plug Type	Gap (in.)	Ignition	①	Timing	Timing	Fuel Pump Pressure	Idle Speed	Idle Speed	Valve Clearance	CO
1978	B210 (except FU)	BP5-ES	.041	Electronic	①	10B	8B②	3.9	700	650	0.014 hot	2.0
	B210 (FU model)	BP5-EQ	.047	Electronic	①	5B	—	3.9	700	—	0.014 hot	1.0
1979	210	BP5-ES⑥	.041⑦	Electronic	①	10B③⑤	8B③	3.8	700	650	0.014 hot	2.0
1980	210	BP5-ES	.041	Electronic	①	10B②	8B	3.8	700	650	0.014 hot	2.0
1981–82	210	BP5-ES11, BPR5-ES11	.041	Electronic	①	5B⑧	5B	3.8	700	650	0.014 hot	2.0
1982–83	Sentra	BPR5ES-11	.041	Electronic	①	4A	6A	3.8	750	650	0.011 hot	2.0

NOTE: Emission control requires a very precise approach to tune-up. Timing and idle speed are peculiar to the engine and its application, rather than to the engine alone. Data for the particular application is on a sticker in the engine compartment on all late models. If the sticker disagrees with this chart, use the sticker figure. The results of any adjustments or modifications should be checked with a CO meter. On many 1980 cars, CO levels are not adjustable.

EFI: electronic fuel injection

NOTE: FU models are Hatchbacks with 5-speed transmissions sold in the U.S.A. except for California

① Electronic ignition—reluctor (air) gap: 0.008–0.016 in. (1975–78); 0.012–0.020 in. (1979–82)
② A14, A15 engine: 8B
③ California models: 5B
④ California: 10B
⑤ FU model: 5B
⑥ FU model: BP-5EQ
⑦ FU model: 0.043–0.051 in.
⑧ A12A with M/T, 10B; Canada 10B

a tune-up, including distributor points (unless equipped with electronic ignition), and spark plugs every 12,000 miles. In 1980 and on later models, Datsun and Nissan have been using a new, more durable spark plug in all models sold in the United States. Datsun recommends that the new plugs be replaced every 30,000 miles or 24 months, whichever comes first. (Of course, the Datsun plugs can be replaced with quality spark plugs from any major manufacturer). Certain Canadian 1980 and later Datsuns still use the conventional 12 month, 12,000 mile plugs. Even though the manufacturer suggests such a long lifespan for the spark plugs on these models, it would be wise to remove, clean, inspect, and re-gap them every 12,000 miles.

Spark Plugs

A typical spark plug consists of a metal shell surrounding a ceramic insulator. A metal electrode extends downward through the center of the insulator and protrudes a small distance. Located at the end of the plug and attached to the side of the outer metal shell is the side electrode. The side electrode bends in at a 90 degree angle so that its tip is even with, and parallel to, the tip of the center electrode. The distance between these two electrodes (measured in thousandths of an inch) is called the spark plug gap. The spark plug in no way produces a spark but merely provides a gap across which the current can arc. The coil produces anywhere from 20,000 to 40,000 volts, which travels to the distributor where it is distributed through the spark plug wires to the spark plugs. The current passes along the center electrode and jumps the gap to the side electrode, and, in so doing, ignites the air/fuel mixture in the combustion chamber.

Spark plug life and efficiency depend upon the condition of the engine and the temperatures to which the plug is exposed. Combustion chamber temperatures are affected by many factors such as compression ratio of the engine, air/fuel mixtures, exhaust emission equipment, and the type of driving you do. Spark plugs are designed and classified by number according to the heat range at which they will operate most efficiently.

SPARK PLUG HEAT RANGE

Spark plug heat range is actually quite simple: the amount of heat the plug absorbs is determined by the length of the lower insu-

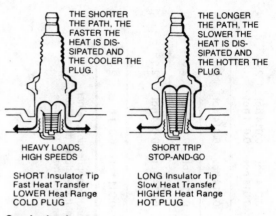

THE SHORTER THE PATH, THE FASTER THE HEAT IS DISSIPATED AND THE COOLER THE PLUG.

THE LONGER THE PATH, THE SLOWER THE HEAT IS DISSIPATED AND THE HOTTER THE PLUG.

HEAVY LOADS, HIGH SPEEDS

SHORT TRIP STOP-AND-GO

SHORT Insulator Tip
Fast Heat Transfer
LOWER Heat Range
COLD PLUG

LONG Insulator Tip
Slow Heat Transfer
HIGHER Heat Range
HOT PLUG

Spark plug heat range

lator. The longer the insulator (or the farther it extends into the engine), the hotter the plug will operate; the shorter the insulator the cooler it will operate. A plug that absorbs little heat and remains too cool will quickly accumulate deposits of oil and carbon since it is not hot enough to burn them off. This leads to plug fouling and consequently to misfiring. A plug that absorbs too much heat will have no deposits, but, due to the excessive heat, the electrodes will burn away quickly and in some instances, preignition may result. Preignition takes place when plug tips get so hot that they glow sufficiently to ignite the fuel/air mixture before the actual spark occurs. This early ignition will usually cause a pinging during low speeds and heavy loads. In severe cases, the heat may become high enough to start the fuel/air mixture burning throughout the combustion chamber rather than just to the front of the plug as in normal operation. At this time, the piston is rising in the cylinder making its compression stroke. The burning mass is compressed and an explosion results, forcing the piston back down in the cylinder while it is still trying to go up. Obviously, something must go, and it does—pistons are often damaged.

The general rule of thumb for choosing the correct heat range when picking a spark plug is: if most of your driving is long distance, high speed travel, use a colder plug; if most of your driving is stop and go, use a hotter plug. Factory-installed plugs are, of course, compromise plugs, since the factory has no way of knowing what sort of driving you do. It should be noted that most people never have occasion to change their plugs from the factory-recommended heat range, but if you spend most of your driving on the highway, or around town, you may want to try a set of cooler or hotter-than-normal spark plugs and run them until the next tune up. Then check the condition of the plugs, comparing them to the color photos in the center of this book.

REMOVAL AND INSTALLATION

1. Grasp the spark plug boot and pull it straight out. *Don't* pull on the wire. If the boot(s) are cracked, replace them.

2. Place the spark plug socket firmly on the plug. Turn the spark plug out of the cylinder head in a counterclockwise direction.

NOTE: *The Datsun cylinder head is aluminum, which is easily stripped. Remove plugs only when the engine is cold.*

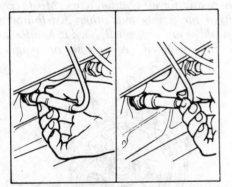

Correct method of removing spark plug wires on left. Pulling the wire instead of the boot on the right is incorrect

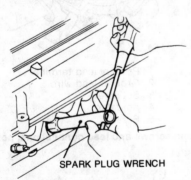

SPARK PLUG WRENCH

Keep the plug socket square on the spark plug

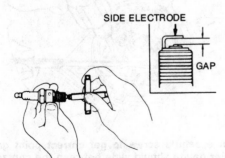

SIDE ELECTRODE

GAP

Check the spark plug gap with a wire gauge

Removal should not be difficult, but if it is loosen the plug only slightly and drip penetrating oil onto the threads. Allow the oil time enough to work and then unscrew the plug. Proceeding in this manner will prevent damaging the threads in the cylinder head. Be sure to keep the socket straight to avoid breaking the ceramic insulator.

3. Continue and remove the remaining spark plugs.

4. Inspect the plugs using the "color center" section illustrations and then clean or discard them according to condition.

New spark plugs come pre-gapped, but always double check the setting. The recommended spark plug gap is listed in the "Tune-Up Specifications" chart. Use a spark plug wire gauge for checking the gap. The wire should pass through the electrode with just a slight drag. Avoid adjusting the plug gap with a flat-bladed feeler gauge; a false reading could result. Using the electrode bending tool on the end of the gauge, bend the side electrode to adjust the gap. Never attempt to adjust the center electrode. Lightly oil the threads of the replacement plug and install it hand-tight. It is a good practice to use a torque wrench to tighten the spark plugs on any car and especially on the Datsun, since the head is aluminum. Torque the spark plugs to 14–22 ft. lbs. Install the ignition wire boots firmly on the spark plugs.

CHECKING AND REPLACING SPARK PLUG CABLES

Visually inspect the spark plug cables for burns, cuts, or any breaks in the insulation. Check the spark plug boots and the rubber nipples on the distributor and coil for the same. Any damaged wiring must be replaced.

If there is no obvious physical damage to the wires, check them for excessive resistance with an ohmmeter:

1. Remove the distributor cap and leave the wires connected to the cap.

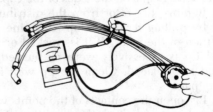

Connect an ohmmeter between the spark plug terminal (in boot) and the electrode inside the cap to check spark plug cable resistance

2. Connect one lead of the ohmmeter to the corresponding electrode inside the cap and the other lead to the spark plug terminal (remove it from the spark plug for the test).

3. Replace any wire that shows over 50,000 ohms (resistance should not run over 35,000 ohms and 50,000 ohms should be considered the outer limits of acceptability).

Test the coil wire by connecting the ohmmeter between the center contact in the cap and either of the primary terminals at the coil. If the total resistance of the coil and cable is more than 25,000 ohms, remove the cable from the coil and check the resistance of the cable alone. If the resistance is higher than 15,000 ohms, replace the cable.

It should be remembered that wire resistance is a function of length—the longer the cable the greater the resistance. Thus, if your cables are longer than factory originals, their resistance could be greater.

When installing a new set of spark plug cables, replace the cables one at a time so there will be no mixup. Start by replacing the longest cable first. Install the boot firmly over the spark plug. Route the wire exactly the same as the original. Insert the nipple firmly into the tower on the distributor cap. Repeat the process for each cable.

Breaker Points and Condenser

NOTE: *Datsun California B210 models manufactured in 1975–77, and all 1978 and later B210, 210 and Sentra models are equipped with electronic, breakerless ignition systems. The 1200 series and the non-California B210 models prior to 1978 have the points-type ignition systems. The following section covers maintenance procedures for these points systems.*

INSPECTION OF THE POINTS

1. Disconnect the high-tension wire from the top of the distributor and the coil.

2. Remove the distributor cap by prying off the spring clips on the sides of the cap.

3. Remove the rotor from the distributor shaft by pulling it straight up. Examine the condition of the rotor. If it is cracked or the metal tip is excessively worn or burned, it should be replaced. Clean the tip with fine emery paper.

4. Pry open the contacts of the points with a screwdriver and check the condition of the contacts. If they are excessively worn, burned or pitted, they should be replaced.

5. If the points are in good condition, adjust them and replace the rotor and the distributor cap. If the points need to be replaced, follow the replacement procedure given below.

REPLACEMENT OF THE BREAKER POINTS AND CONDENSER

1. Remove the coil high-tension wire from the top of the distributor cap. Remove the distributor cap and place it out of the way. Remove the rotor from the distributor shaft by pulling up.

NOTE: *A magnetic screwdriver or one with a holding (locking) mechanism is very handy here and for all ignition work. Most screws used for points and other distributor assemblies are very small, hard to handle, and easily dropped. A locking or magnetic*

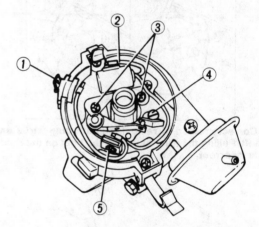

1. Primary lead terminal
2. Ground lead wire
3. Set screw
4. Adjuster
5. Screw

Adjusting screws and lead connections, points type distributor

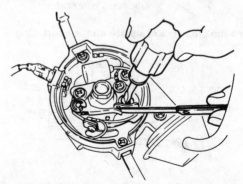

Turn eccentric screw to get correct point gap. Feeler gauge should slide between the contacts with a slight drag

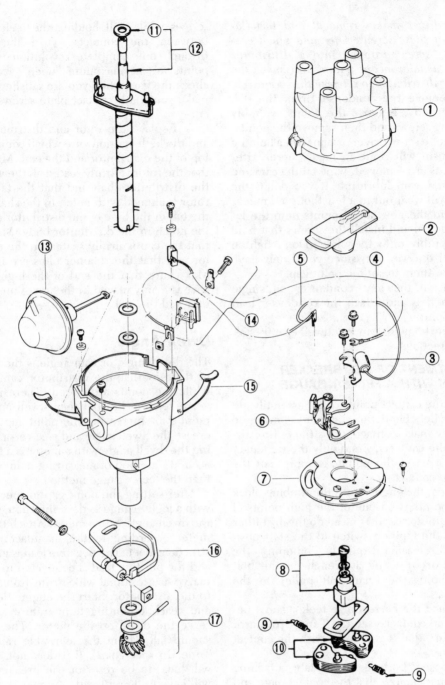

1. Cap
2. Rotor
3. Condenser
4. Ground wire
5. Lead wire
6. Breaker points
7. Breaker plate
8. Cam assembly
9. Governor spring
10. Governor weight
11. Thrust washer
12. Shaft assembly
13. Vacuum control assembly
14. Terminal assembly
15. Clamp
16. Retaining plate
17. Gear set

Exploded view of points type distributor

screwdriver makes removal and installation of these screws safer and much easier—a screw dropped into a distributor body usually means having to remove the entire distributor to retrieve the screw.

2. Remove the condenser from the distributor body. Remove the points assembly attaching screws and then remove the points. A magnetic screwdriver or one with a holding mechanism will come in handy here. After the points are removed, wipe off the cam and apply new cam lubricant. If you don't, the points will wear out in a few thousand miles.

3. Slip the new set of points onto the locating dowel and install the screws that hold the assembly onto the plate. Don't tighten them all the way yet, since you'll only have to loosen them to set the point gap.

4. Install the new condenser on single point models and attach the condenser lead to the points.

5. Set the point gap and dwell (see the following sections).

ADJUSTMENT OF THE BREAKER POINTS WITH A FEELER GAUGE

1. If the contact points of the assembly are not parallel, bend the stationary contact so that they make contact across the entire surface of the contacts. Bend only the stationary bracket part of the point assembly; not the movable contact.

2. Turn the engine until the rubbing block of the points is on one of the high points of the distributor cam. You can do this by either turning the ignition switch to the start position and releasing it quickly ("bumping" the engine) or by using a wrench on the bolt which holds the crankshaft pulley to the crankshaft.

3. Place the correct size feeler gauge between the contacts (see the Tune-Up Chart). Make sure that it is parallel with the contact surfaces.

4. Loosen both contact plate attaching screws *just enough* that the contact plate and points gap can be adjusted with the adjusting screw.

5. While holding the feeler gauge in one hand between the points contacts, insert a screwdriver into the eccentric adjusting screw with the other hand. Turn the adjusting screw to either increase or decrease the gap to the proper setting. When the correct gap is found, there should be a moderate drag on the feeler gauge as you pass it through both contacts.

6. Tighten both contact plate attaching

screws while still holding the feeler gauge between the contacts. Turn the engine through one complete revolution until the points are at maximum "open" again. Recheck the gap; when you are satisfied with it, make sure both contact plate screws are secure.

7. Replace the rotor and distributor cap, and the high-tension wire which connects the top of the distributor and the coil. Make sure that the rotor is firmly seated all the way onto the distributor shaft and that the tab of the rotor is aligned with notch in the shaft. Align the tab in the base of the distributor cap with the notch in the distributor body. Make sure that the cap is firmly seated on the distributor and that the retainer clips are in place. Make sure that the end of the high-tension wire is firmly placed in the top of the distributor and the coil.

Dwell Angle

The dwell angle or cam angle is the number of degrees that the distributor cam rotates while the points are closed. There is an inverse relationship between dwell angle and point gap. Increasing the point gap will decrease the dwell angle and vice versa. Checking the dwell angle with a meter is a far more accurate method of measuring point opening than the feeler gauge method.

After setting the point gap to specification with a feeler gauge as described above, check the dwell angle with a meter. Attach the dwell meter according to the manufacturer's instruction sheet. The negative lead is grounded and the positive lead is connected to the primary wire terminal which runs from the coil to the distributor. Start the engine, let it idle and reach operating temperature, and observe the dwell on the meter. The reading should fall within the allowable range (see Tune Up spec chart). If it does not, the gap will have to be reset or the breaker points will have to be replaced.

ADJUSTMENT OF THE BREAKER POINTS WITH A DWELL METER

1. Adjust the points with a feeler gauge as previously described.

2. Connect the dwell meter to the ignition circuit as according to the manufacturer's instructions. One lead of the meter is connected to a ground and the other lead is connected to the distributor post on the coil. An adapter is usually provided for this purpose.

3. If the dwell meter has a set line on it, adjust the meter to zero the indicator.

4. Start the engine.

NOTE: *Be careful when working on any vehicle while the engine is running. Make sure that the transmission is in Neutral and that the parking brake is applied. Keep hands, clothing, tools and the wires of the test instruments clear of the rotating fan blades.*

5. Observe the reading on the dwell meter. If the reading is within the specified range, turn off the engine and remove the dwell meter.

NOTE: *If the meter does not have a scale for 4 cylinder engines, multiply the 8 cylinder reading by two.*

6. If the reading is above the specified range, the breaker point gap is too small. If the reading is below the specified range, the gap is too large. In either case, the engine must be stopped and the gap adjusted in the manner previously covered.

After making the adjustment, start the engine and check the reading on the dwell meter. When the correct reading is obtained, disconnect the dwell meter.

7. Check the adjustment of the ignition timing.

Datsun Electronic Ignition

In 1975, in order to comply with California's tougher emissions laws, Datsun introduced electronic ignition systems for all models sold in that state. Since that time, the Datsun and Nissan electronic ignition system has undergone a metamorphosis from a standard transistorized circuit (1975–78) to an Integrated Circuit system (IC), 1979 and later. Some

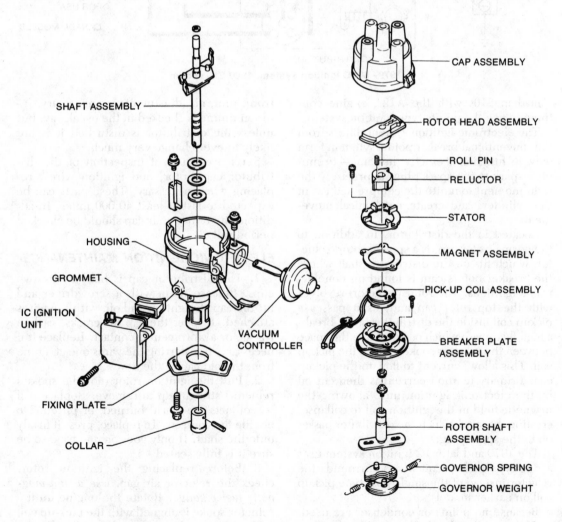

IC (electronic) ignition distributor, 1979 and later A-series. Sentra unit similar

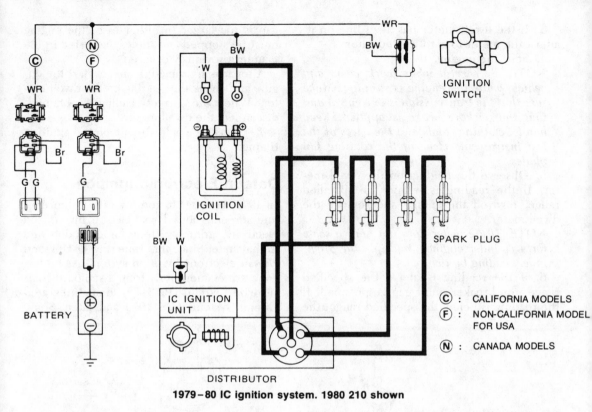

1979–80 IC ignition system. 1980 210 shown

Canadian 210s with the A12A engine continue to use the points type ignition system.

The electronic ignition system differs from the conventional breaker points sytem in form only; its function is exactly the same—to supply a spark to the spark plugs at precisely the right moment to ignite the compressed gas in the cylinders and create mechanical movement.

Located in the distributor, in addition to the normal rotor cap, is a spoked rotor (reluctor) which fits on the distributor shaft where the breaker points cam is found on nonelectronic ignitions. The rotor (reluctor) revolves with the top rotor cap and, as it passes a pickup coil inside the distributor body, breaks a high flux phase which occurs while the space between the reluctor spokes passes the pickup coil. This allows current to flow to the pickup coil. Primary ignition current is then cut off by the electronic ignition unit, allowing the magnetic field in the ignition coil to collapse, creating the spark which the distributor passes on to the spark plug.

The 1979 and later IC ignition system uses a ring-type pickup coil which surrounds the reluctor instead of the single post type pickup coil on earlier models.

Because no points or condenser are used, and because dwell is determined by the electronic unit, no adjustments are necessary. Ignition timing is checked in the usual way, but unless the distributor is disturbed it is not likely to ever change very much.

Service consists of inspection of the distributor cap, rotor, and ignition wires, replacing when necessary. These parts can be expected to last at least 40,000 miles. In addition, the reluctor air gap should be checked periodically.

ELECTRONIC IGNITION MAINTENANCE

1. The distributor cap is held on by two clips. Release them with a screwdriver and lift the cap straight up and off, with the wires attached. Inspect the cap for cracks, carbon tracks, or a worn center contact. Replace it if necessary, transferring the wires one at a time from the old cap to the new.

2. Pull the ignition rotor (not the spoked reluctor) straight up to remove. Replace it if its contacts are worn, burned, or pitted. Do not file the contacts. To replace, press it firmly onto the shaft. It only goes on one way, so be sure it is fully seated.

3. Before replacing the ignition rotor, check the reluctor air gap. *Use a non-magnetic feeler gauge.* Rotate the engine until a reluctor spoke is aligned with the pick-up coil (either bump the engine around with the

starter, or turn it with a wrench on the crankshaft pulley bolt). The gap should measure 0.008–0.016 in. through 1978, or 0.012–0.020 in. for 1979 and later. Adjustment, if necessary, is made by loosening the pickup coil mounting screws and shifting the coil either closer to or farther from the reluctor. On 1979 and later models, center the pickup coil (ring) around the reluctor. Tighten the screws and recheck the gap.

4. Inspect the wires for cracks or brittleness. Replace them one at a time to prevent crosswiring, carefully pressing the replacement wires into place. The cores of electronic wires are more susceptible to breakage than those of standard wires, so treat them gently.

TROUBLESHOOTING

1975–78

The main differences between the 1975–77 and 1978 systems are: (1) the 1975–77 system uses an external ballast resistor located next to the ignition coil, and (2) the earlier system uses a wiring harness with individual eyelet connectors to the electronic unit, while the later system uses a multiple plug connector. You will need an accurate voltmeter and ohmmeter for these tests, which must be performed in the order given.

1. Check all connections for corrosion, looseness, breaks, etc., and correct if necessary. Clean and gap the spark plugs.

2a. Disconnect the harness (connector or plug) from the electronic unit. Turn the ignition switch On. Set the voltmeter to the DC 50v range. Connect the positive (+) voltmeter lead to the black/white wire terminal, and the negative (−) lead to the black wire terminal. Battery voltage should be obtained. If not, check the black/white and black wires for continuity; check the battery terminals for corrosion; check the battery state of charge.

2b. Next, connect the voltmeter + lead to the blue wire and the − lead to the black wire. Battery voltage should be obtained. If not, check the blue wire for continuity; check the ignition coil terminals for corrosion or looseness; check the coil for continuity. On 1975–77 models, also check the external ballast resistor.

3. Disconnect the distributor harness wires from the ignition coil ballast resistor on 1975–77 models, leaving the ballast resistor-to-coil wires attached. On 1978 models, disconnect the ignition coil wires. Connect the leads of an ohmmeter to the ballast resistor outside

terminals (at each end) for 1975–77, and to the two coil terminals for 1978. With the ohmmeter set in the X1 range, the 1975–78 B210 should show a reading of approximately 0 ohms. The maximum allowable limit for the 0 ohm models is 1.8 ohms. If a reading higher than the limit is received, replace the ignition coil assembly.

4. Discount the harness from the electronic control unit. Connect an ohmmeter to the red and the green wire terminals. Resistance should be 720 ohms. If far more or far less, replace the distributor pick-up coil.

5. Disconnect the anti-dieseling solenoid connector (see Chapter 4). Connect a voltmeter to the red and green terminals of the electronic control harness. When the starter is cranked, the needle should deflect slightly. If not, replace the distributor pick-up coil.

6. Reconnect the ignition coil and the electronic control unit. Leave the anti-dieseling solenoid wire disconnected. Unplug the high tension lead (coil to distributor) from the distributor and hold it ⅛–½ in. from the cylinder head with a pair of insulated pliers and a heavy glove. When the engine is cranked, a spark should be observed. If not, check the lead, and replace if necessary. If still no spark, replace the electronic control unit.

7. Reconnect all wires.

1976–77: connect the voltmeter + lead to the blue electronic control harness connector and the −− lead to the black wire. The harness should be attached to the control unit.

1978: connect the voltmeter + lead to the − terminal of the ignition coil and the − lead to ground.

As soon as the ignition switch is turned On, the meter should indicate battery voltage. If not, replace the electronic control unit.

1979 and Later

1. Make a check of the power supply circuit. Turn the ignition OFF. Disconnect the connector from the top of the IC unit. Turn the ignition ON. Measure the voltage at each terminal of the connector in turn by touching the probe of the positive lead of the voltmeter to one of the terminals, and touching the probe of the negative lead of the voltmeter to a ground, such as the engine. In each case, battery voltage should be indicated. If not, check all wiring, the ignition switch, and all connectors for breaks, corrosion, discontinuity, etc., and repair as necessary.

2. Check the primary windings of the ignition coil. Turn the ignition OFF. Discon-

nect the harness connector from the negative coil terminal. Use an ohmmeter to measure the resistance between the positive and negative coil terminals. If resistance is 0.84–1.02 ohms (1.04–1.27 ohms on the Sentra the coil is OK. Replace if far from this range.

If the power supply, circuits, wiring, and coil are in good shape, check the IC unit and pick-up coil, as follows:

3. Turn the ignition OFF. Remove the distributor cap and ignition rotor. Use an ohmmeter to measure the resistance between the two terminals of the pick-up coil, where they attach to the IC unit. Measure the resistance by reversing the polarity of the probes. If approximately 400 ohms are indicated, the pick-up coil is OK, but the IC unit is bad and must be replaced. If other than 400 ohms are measured, go to the next Step.

4. Be certain the two pin connector to the IC unit is secure. Turn the ignition ON. Measure the voltage at the ignition coil negative terminal. Turn the ignition OFF.

CAUTION: *Remove the tester probe from the coil negative terminal before switching the ignition OFF, to prevent burning out the tester.*

If zero voltage is indicated, the IC unit is bad and must be replaced. If battery voltage is indicated, proceed.

5. Remove the IC unit from the distributor:

   a. Disconnect the battery ground (negative) cable.

   b. Remove the distributor cap and ignition rotor.

   c. Disconnect the harness connector at the top of the IC unit.

   d. Remove the two screws securing the IC unit to the distributor.

   e. Disconnect the two pick-up coil wires from the IC unit.

CAUTION: *Pull the connectors free with a pair of needlenosed pliers. Do not pull on the wires to detach the connectors.*

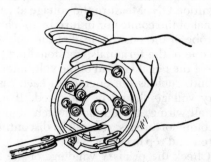

Checking air gap, electronic ignition distributors

f. Remove the IC unit.

6. Measure the resistance between the terminals of the pick-up coil. It should be approximately 400 ohms. If so, the pick-up coil is OK, and the IC unit is bad. If not approximately 400 ohms, the pick-up coil is bad and must be replaced.

7. With a new pick-up coil installed, install the IC unit. Check for a spark at one of the spark plugs (see Chapter 11). If a good spark is obtained, the IC unit is OK. If not, replace the IC unit.

Ignition Timing

Ignition timing is an important part of the tune-up. It is always adjusted after the points are gapped (dwell angle changed), since altering the dwell affects the timing. Three basic types of timing lights are available, the neon, the DC, and the AC powered. Of the three, the inductive DC light is the most frequently used by professional tuners. The bright flash put out by the DC light makes the timing marks stand out on even the brightest of days. Another advantage of the DC light is that you don't need to be near an electrical outlet. Neon lights are available for a few dollars, but their weak flash makes it necessary to use them in a fairly dark work area. One neon light lead is attached to the spark plug and the other to the plug wire. The DC light attaches to the spark plug and the wire with an adapter and two clips attach to the battery posts for power. The AC unit is similar, except that the power cable is plugged into a house outlet.

CAUTION: *When performing this or any other operation with the engine running, be very careful of the alternator belt and pulleys. Make sure that your timing light wires don't interfere with the belt.*

Ignition timing is the measurement, in degrees of crankshaft rotation, of the point at which the spark plugs fire in each of the cylinders. It is measured in degrees before or after Top Dead Center (TDC) of the compression stroke. Ignition timing is by turning the distributor body in the engine.

Ideally, the air/fuel mixture in the cylinder will be ignited by the spark plug just as the piston passes TDC of the compression stroke. If this happens, the piston will be beginning its downward motion of the power stroke just as the compressed and ignited air/fuel mixture starts to expand. The expansion of the air/fuel mixture then forces the piston down

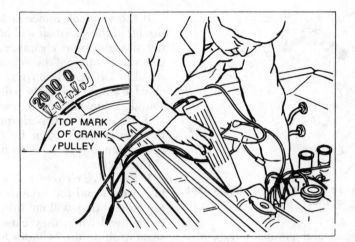

TOP MARK
OF CRANK
PULLEY

Checking ignition timing with timing light. Timing marks shown at left

on the power stroke and turns the crankshaft.

Because it takes a fraction of a second for the spark plug to ignite the mixture in the cylinder, the spark plug must fire a little before the piston reaches TDC. Otherwise, the mixture will not be completely ignited as the piston passes TDC and the full power of the explosion will not be used by the engine.

The timing measurement is given in degrees of crankshaft rotation before the piston reaches TDC (BTDC). If the setting for the ignition timing is 5° BTDC (5B), the spark plug must fire 5° before each piston reaches TDC. This only holds true, however, when the engine is at idle speed.

As the engine speed increases, the pistons go faster. The spark plugs have to ignite the fuel even sooner if it is to be completely ignited when the piston reaches TDC. To do this, the distributor has a means to advance the timing of the spark as the engine speed increases. This is accomplished by centrifugal weights within the distributor and a vacuum diaphragm, mounted on the side of the distributor. It is necessary to disconnect the vacuum line from the diaphragm when the ignition timing is being set.

If the ignition is set too far advanced (BTDC), the ignition and expansion of the fuel in the cylinder will occur too soon and tend to force the piston down while it is still traveling up. This causes engine ping. If the ignition spark is set too far retarded, after TDC (ATDC), the piston will have already passed TDC and started on its way down when the fuel is ignited. This will cause the piston to be forced down for only a portion of its travel, resulting in poor engine performance and lack of power.

The timing is best checked with a timing light. This device is connected in series with the No. 1 spark plug. The current which fires the spark plug also causes the timing light to flash.

The timing marks are located at the front crankshaft pulley and consist of a notch on the crankshaft pulley and a scale of degrees of crankshaft rotation attached to the front cover.

When the engine is running, the timing light is aimed at the marks on the flywheel pulley and the pointer.

IGNITION TIMING ADJUSTMENT

NOTE: *Datsun does not give ignition timing adjustments for 1980 and later California Datsuns and Nissans. The procedure has been discontinued.*

1. Set the dwell to the proper specification.

2. Locate the timing marks on the crankshaft pulley and the front of the engine.

3. Clean off the timing marks so that you can see them (the numbers correspond to degrees before and after Top Dead Center).

4. Use chalk or white paint to color the mark on the crankshaft pulley and the mark on the scale which will indicate the correct timing when aligned with the notch on the crankshaft pulley.

5. Attach a tachometer to the engine (some dwell meters have a tachometer built in).

6. Attach a timing light to the engine, according to the manufacturer's instructions.

7. Leave the vacuum line connected to the distributor vacuum diaphragm on all models except 1979 210 wagons equipped

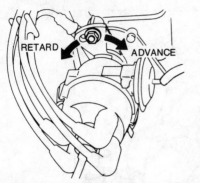

Sentra (E-series) distributor timing adjustment showing adjusting locknut

with the A15 engine and automatic transmission, and all 1980 and later 210s and Sentra. Plug disconnected vacuum hoses with golf tees. On Canadian 210 models and Sentra, disconnect the air induction hose from the air cleaner, cap or plug the air pipe.

8. Check to make sure that all of the wires clear the fan and then start the engine. Allow the engine to reach normal operating temperature.

9. Adjust the idle to the correct rpm setting.

10. Aim the timing light at the timing marks. If the marks that you put on the pulley and the engine are aligned when the light flashes, the timing is correct. Turn off the engine and remove the tachometer and the timing light. If the marks are not in alignment, proceed with the following steps.

11. Turn off the engine.

12. Loosen the distributor lockbolt just enough so that the distributor can be turned with a little effort.

13. Start the engine. Keep the wires of the timing light clear of the fan.

14. With the timing light aimed at the pulley and the marks on the engine, turn the distributor in the direction of rotor rotation (see "Firing Order" illustration in Chapter 3 for rotor rotation if you do not know it) to retard the spark, and in the opposite direction of rotor rotation to advance the spark.

15. Align the marks on the pulley and the engine with the flashes of the timing light.

16. Tighten the distributor hold-down bolt when proper timing is found.

Valve Lash

Valve adjustment determines how far the valves enter the cylinder and how long they stay open and closed.

If the valve clearance is too large, part of the lift of the camshaft will be used in removing the excessive clearance. Consequently, the valve will not be opening as far as it should. This condition has two effects: the valve train components will emit a tapping sound as they take up the excessive clearance and the engine will perform poorly because the valves don't open fully and allow the proper amount of gases to flow into and out of the engine.

If the valve clearance is too small, the intake valves and the exhaust valves will open too far and they will not fully seat on the cylinder head when they close. When a valve seats itself on the cylinder head, it does two things: it seals the combustion chamber so that none of the gases in the cylinder escape and it cools itself by transferring some of the heat it absorbs from the combustion in the cylinder to the cylinder head and to the engine's cooling system. If the valve clearance is too small, the engine will run poorly because of the gases escaping from the combustion chamber. The valves will also become overheated and will warp, since they cannot transfer heat unless they are touching the valve seat in the cylinder head.

NOTE: *While all valve adjustments must be made as accurately as possible, it is better to have the valve adjustment slightly loose than slightly tight, as a burned valve may result from overly tight adjustments.* This holds true for valve adjustments on most engines.

VALVE ADJUSTMENT—200, B210, AND 210

1. Run the engine until it reaches normal operating temperature. Oil temperature, not water temperature, is critical to valve adjustment. With this in mind, make sure the engine is fully warmed up since this is the only

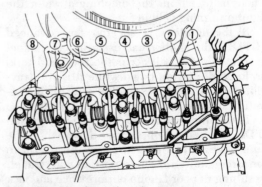

Adjusting A-series valve clearances

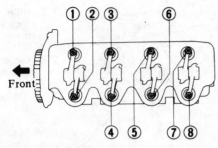

Sentra valve arrangement

way to make sure the parts have reached their full expansion. Generally speaking, this takes around fifteen minutes. After the engine has reached normal operating temperature, shut it off.

2. Purchase a new valve cover gasket before removing the valve cover. The new silicone gasket sealers, available in tubes, are just as good or better if you can't find a gasket. Remove valve cover.

3. Note the location of any hoses or wires which may interfere with valve cover removal, disconnect them and move them aside. Then, remove the bolts which hold the valve cover in place.

4. After the valve cover has been removed, the next step is to get the number one piston at TDC on the compression stroke. There are at least two ways to do it; you can bump the engine over with the starter or turn it over by using a wrench on the front pulley attaching bolt. The easiest way to find TDC is to turn the engine over slowly with a wrench (after first removing no. 1 plug) until the piston is at the top of its stroke and the TDC timing mark on the crankshaft pulley is in alignment with the timing mark pointer. Make sure transmission is in Neutral and battery ground cable is disconnected. At this point, the valves for No. 1 cylinder should be checked.

NOTE: *Make sure both valves are closed with the valve springs up as high as they will go. An easy way to find the compression stroke is to remove the distributor cap and see toward which spark plug lead the rotor is pointing. If the rotor points to number one spark plug lead, number one cylinder is on its compression stroke. When the rotor points to number two spark plug lead, number two cylinder is on its compression stroke, etc.*

5. With no. 1 piston at TDC of the compression stroke, check the clearance on valves Nos. 1, 2, 3, and 5 (counting from the front to the rear).

6. To adjust the clearance, loosen the locknut with a wrench and turn the adjuster with a screwdriver while holding the locknut. The correct size feeler gauge should pass with a slight drag between the rocker arm and the valve stem.

7. Turn the crankshaft one full revolution to position the no. 4 piston at TDC of the compression stroke. Adjust valves nos. 4, 6, 7, and 8 in the same manner as the first four.

8. Replace the valve cover.

VALVE ADJUSTMENT—SENTRA

1. Start engine and run it until normal operating temperature has been reached (usually after about fifteen minutes). Turn off engine.

2. Remove air cleaner securing bolts, disconnect air cleaner hoses and remove air cleaner.

3. Remove valve rocker cover.

4. Rotate the crankshaft pulley until TDC of the compression stroke of No. 1 cylinder is found (see valve adjustment procedure for the 1200/B210 series for more details on finding TDC).

5. With the No. 1 piston at Top Dead Center on its compression stroke, adjust valve clearance of valves 1, 2, 3 and 6 (see valve arrangement diagram). Adjust the valve by loosening the rocker adjusting screw locknut, inserting the proper feeler gauge between the rocker and the end of the valve stem, and turning the adjusting screw until the specified clearance (0.011 in.) is obtained. After adjustment, tighten the locknut and recheck the clearance (the feeler gauge should drag slightly but should not be tight).

6. Set the No. 4 cylinder at TDC of its compression stroke and adjust valve clearance of valves 4, 5, 7 and 8.

7. Replace the rocker cover, using a new gasket. Replace the air cleaner assembly.

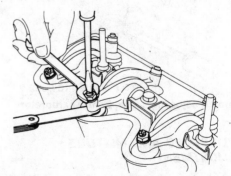

Adjusting the Sentra valves. There should be a slight drag on the feeler gauge

Carburetor

This section contains only tune-up adjustment procedures for carburetors. Descriptions, adjustments, and overhaul procedures for carburetors can be found in Chapter 4.

When the engine in your Datsun or Nissan is running, the air-fuel mixture from the carburetor is being drawn into the engine by a partial vacuum which is created by the movement of the pistons downward on the intake stroke. The amount of air-fuel mixture that enters into the engine is controlled by the throttle plate(s) in the bottom of the carburetor. When the engine is not running the throttle plate(s) is closed, completely blocking off the bottom of the carburetor from the inside of the engine. The throttle plates are connected by the throttle linkage to the accelerator pedal in the passenger compartment of the Datsun. When you depress the pedal, you open the throttle plates in the carburetor to admit more air-fuel mixture to the engine.

When the engine is not running, the throttle plates are closed. When the engine is idling, it is necessary to have the throttle plates open slightly. To prevent having to hold your foot on the pedal when the engine is idling, an idle speed adjusting screw was added to the carburetor linkage.

The idle adjusting screw contacts a lever (throttle lever) on the outside of the carburetor. When the screw is turned, it either opens or closes the throttle plates of the carburetor, raising or lowering the idle speed of the engine. This screw is called the curb idle adjusting screw.

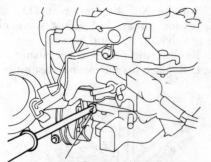

THROTTLE ADJUSTING SCREW

Throttle adjusting screw, Sentra carburetor

IDLE SPEED AND MIXTURE ADJUSTMENT

NOTE: *1980 and later model Datsuns require a CO Meter to adjust their mixture*

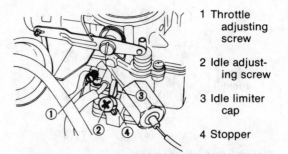

1 Throttle adjusting screw

2 Idle adjusting screw

3 Idle limiter cap

4 Stopper

Carburetor adjusting screws, A-series engines

A-series mixture screw. Note limiter tab

ratios, therefore no procedures concerning this adjustment are given. Also, many model Datsuns have a plug over their mixture control screw. It is suggested that on these models mixture adjustment be left to a qualified technician.

1. Start the engine and allow it to run until it reaches normal operating temperature.

2. Allow the engine idle speed to stabilize by running the engine at idle for at least two minutes.

3. If you have not done so already, check and adjust the ignition timing to the proper setting.

4. Shut off the engine and connect a tachometer.

5. Disconnect and plug the air hose between the three way connector and the check valve, if equipped. On 1980 and later models, disconnect the air induction hose to the air cleaner and plug the pipe. With the transmission in Neutral, check the idle speed on

the tachometer. If the reading is correct, continue on to Step 6 for 1973–79 Datsuns. For 1980 and later, and certain California models, proceed to step 10 below if the idle is correct. If the idle is not correct, for all 1200, B210 and 210 models, turn the idle speed adjusting screw clockwise with a screwdriver to increase idle speed or counterclockwise to decrease it, until the proper idle speed is achieved. On Sentra, turn the throttle adjusting screw.

6. With the automatic transmission in Drive (wheels blocked and parking brake on) or the manual transmission in Neutral, turn the mixture screw out until the engine rpm starts to drop due to an overly rich mixture (transmission placed in Drive in order to put a load on the engine for this procedure).

CAUTION: *While making the idle adjustments on automatic transmission cars (transmission in "Drive"), DO NOT race the engine, or even raise the rpm above those engine speeds recommended. The parking brake and wheel chocks cannot be expected to hold the car in this situation, and injury and/or damage will most certainly occur. Before racing the engine, place the trans-*

mission in Neutral, make sure the parking brake is firmly applied and the wheels chocked.

7. Turn the adjusting screw until just before the rpm starts to drop due to an overly lean mixture. Turn the mixture screw in until the idle speed drops 60–70 rpm with manual transmission, or 15—25 rpm with automatic transmission (in Drive) for 1975–76 B210; 35–45 rpm with manual transmission or 10–20 rpm with automatic for 1977–78 B210, 1979 210. If the mixture limiter cap will not allow this adjustment, remove it, make the adjustment, and re-install it. Go on to step 10 for all 1975–79 models.

8. On 1973–74 models, turn the mixture screw back out to the point midway between the two extreme positions where the engine began losing rpm to achieve the fastest and smoothest idle.

9. Adjust the curb idle speed to the proper specification, on 1973–74 models, with the idle speed adjusting screw.

10. Install the air hose. If the engine speed increases, reduce it with the idle speed screw until a smooth idle as listed in the Tune-Up specifications chart is achieved.

Engine and Engine Rebuilding

ENGINE ELECTRICAL

Distributor

REMOVAL

All Models

1. Unfasten the retaining clips and lift the distributor cap straight up. It will be easier to install the distributor if the wiring is not disconnected from the cap. If the wires must be removed from the cap, mark their positions to aid in installation.

2. Disconnect the distributor wiring harness.

3. Disconnect the vacuum lines.

4. Note the position of the rotor in relation

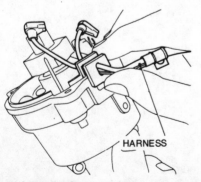

Disconnecting distributor wiring harness, all models

to the base. Scribe or paint a mark on the base of the distributor and on the engine block (on the end of the head on Sentra) so the marks can be lined up for reinstallation. Align the marks with the direction the metal tip of the rotor is pointing.

5. Remove the bolt(s) which holds the distributor to the engine.

6. Lift the distributor assembly from the engine on the A-series engines. On Sentra, pull the distributor straight out from the end of the head.

INSTALLATION

1. Lightly oil the distributor shaft and insert the shaft and assembly into the engine. Line up the mark on the distributor and the one on the engine with the metal tip of the rotor. Make sure that the vacuum advance diaphragm is pointed in the same direction as it was pointed originally. This will be done automatically if the marks on the engine and the distributor are lined up with the rotor.

2. Install the distributor hold-down bolt and clamp. Leave the screw loose enough so that you can move the distributor with heavy hand pressure.

3. Connect the primary wire to the coil. Install the distributor cap on the distributor housing. Secure the distributor cap with the spring clips.

4. Install the spark plug wires if removed. Make sure that the wires are pressed all the way into the top of the distributor cap and firmly onto the spark plug.

5. Adjust the point dwell and set the ignition timing(see Chapter 2 "Tune-Up").

NOTE: *If the crankshaft has been turned or the engine disturbed in any manner (i.e., disassembled and rebuilt) while the distributor was removed, or if the marks were not drawn, it will be necessary to initially time the engine. Follow the procedure given below.*

INSTALLATION—ENGINE DISTURBED

1. It is necessary to place the No. 1 cylinder in the firing position to correctly install the distributor. To locate this position, the ignition timing marks on the crankshaft front pulley are used.

2. Remove the No. 1 cylinder spark plug. Turn the crankshaft until the piston in the no. 1 cylinder is moving up on the compression stroke. This can be determined by placing your thumb over the spark plug hole and feeling the air being forced out of the cylinder. Stop turning the crankshaft when the timing marks that are used to time the engine on the front pulley are aligned.

3. Oil the distributor housing lightly where the distributor bears on its mounting flange. Oil the distributor drive gear on A-series engines.

4. Install the distributor so that the rotor, which is mounted on the shaft, points toward the No. 1 spark plug terminal tower position when the cap is installed. Of course, you won't be able to see the direction in which the rotor is pointing if the cap is on the distributor, so lay the cap on the top of the distributor. Make a mark on the side of the distributor housing just below the No. 1 spark plug terminal. Make sure that the rotor points toward that mark when you install the distributor.

5. When the distributor shaft has reached the bottom of the hole, move the rotor back and forth slightly until the driving gear on the end of the shaft enters the slots cut in the end of the oil pump shaft and the distributor assembly slides down into place.

6. When the distributor is correctly installed, the breaker points (if equipped) should be in such a position that they are just ready to break contact with each other. On electronic ignition distributors, the reluctor tooth will be very close to approaching the stator pole. This is accomplished by rotating

the distributor body after it has been installed in the engine. Once again, line up the marks that you made before the distributor was removed from the engine.

7. Install the distributor hold-down bolt.

8. Install the spark plug into the No. 1 spark plug hole and continue from Step 3 of the preceding distributor installation procedure.

Firing Order

To avoid confusion, replace the spark plug wires one at a time.

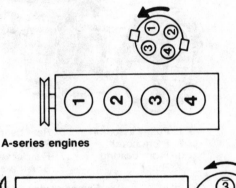

A-series engines

E-series (Sentra) engines

Alternator

ALTERNATOR PRECAUTIONS

To prevent damage to the alternator and regulator, the following precautionary measures must be taken when working with the electrical system.

1. Never reverse battery connections; make sure positive is attached to positive, and negative to negative.

2. Booster batteries for starting must be connected properly. Make sure that the positive cable of the booster battery is connected to the positive terminal of the battery that is getting the boost. This applies to both negative and ground cables.

3. Disconnect the battery cables before using a fast charger; the charger has a tendency to force current through the diodes in the opposite direction for which they are designed. This burns out the diodes.

4. *Never* use a fast charger as a booster for starting the vehicle.

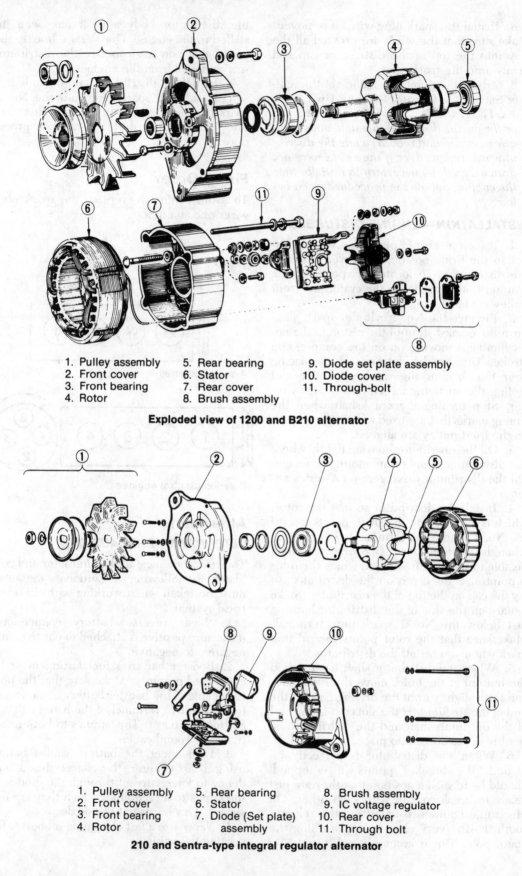

1. Pulley assembly
2. Front cover
3. Front bearing
4. Rotor
5. Rear bearing
6. Stator
7. Rear cover
8. Brush assembly
9. Diode set plate assembly
10. Diode cover
11. Through-bolt

Exploded view of 1200 and B210 alternator

1. Pulley assembly
2. Front cover
3. Front bearing
4. Rotor
5. Rear bearing
6. Stator
7. Diode (Set plate) assembly
8. Brush assembly
9. IC voltage regulator
10. Rear cover
11. Through bolt

210 and Sentra-type integral regulator alternator

Alternator and Regulator Specifications

Model	Year	Alternator Identification Number	Rated Output @ 5000 RPM	Output @ 2500 RPM (not less than)	Brush Length	Brush Spring Tension (oz.)	Regulated Voltage
1200	1973	LT135-138	35	14	0.571	8.80–12.32	14.3–15.3
B210	1973–74	LT135-13B LT150-05 ③	35 50	14 28	0.571 0.571	8.99–12.17 8.99–12.17	14.3–15.3 14.3–15.3
B210	1975–76	LT150-19	50	37.5	0.295	9.0–12.2	14.3–15.3
B210	1977	LT150-26	50	37.5	0.295	9.0–12.2	14.3–15.3
B210	1978	LT150-36 ①	50	40	0.295	9.0–12.2	14.3–15.3
210	1979–80	LR150-36 ①	50	40	0.295	8.99–12.17	14.4–15.0
210	1981–82	LR150-99 ② ①	50	40	0.28	8.99–12.17	14.4–15.0
Sentra	1982–83	LR150-125B ①	50	42	0.28	8.99–12.17	14.4–15.0

① Uses integral voltage regulator
② LR150-99B in 1982
③ Optional

5. Never disconnect the voltage regulator while the engine is running.

6. Do not ground the alternator output terminal.

7. Do not operate the alternator on an open circuit with the field energized.

8. Do not attempt to polarize an alternator.

REMOVAL AND INSTALLATION

1. Disconnect the negative battery terminal.

2. Disconnect the two lead wires and connector from the alternator.

3. Loosen the drive belt adjusting bolt and remove the belt.

4. Unscrew the alternator attaching bolts and remove the alternator from the vehicle.

5. Install the alternator in the reverse order of removal.

Regulator

REMOVAL AND INSTALLATION

NOTE: *1978–83 models are equipped with integral regulator alternators. Since the regulator is part of the alternator, no adjustments are possible or necessary on these models.*

1. Disconnect the negative battery terminal.

2. Disconnect the electrical lead connector of the regulator.

3. Remove the two mounting screws and remove the regulator from the vehicle.

4. Install the regulator in the reverse order of removal.

ADJUSTMENT

1. Adjust the voltage regulator core gap by loosening the screw which is used to secure the contact set on the yoke, and move the contact up or down as necessary. Retighten the screw. The gap should be 0.024–0.039 in.

2. Adjust the point gap of the voltage regulator coil by loosening the screw used to secure the upper contact and move the upper

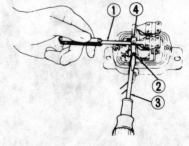

1. Feeler gauge   3. Phillips screwdriver
2. Screw   4. Upper contact

Adjusting voltage regulator point gap

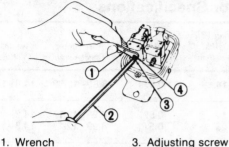

1. Wrench
2. Phillips screwdriver
3. Adjusting screw
4. Locknut

Adjusting the regulated voltage, voltage regulator models

contact up or down. The gap for 1973–76 1200 and B210 models is 0.012–0.016 in. The point gap for all other models with separate regulators is 0.014–0.018 in.

3. The core gap and point gap on the charge relay coil are adjusted in the same manner as previously outlined for the voltage regulator coil. The core gap is to be set at 0.032–0.039 in. and the point gap adjusted to 0.016–0.024 in.

4. The regulated voltage is adjusted by loosening the locknut and turning the adjusting screw clockwise to increase, or counterclockwise to decrease the regulated voltage. The voltage should be between 14.3–15.3 volts at 68°F.

Starter

Datsun began using a gear reduction starter in 1978 and later Canadian models. The differences between the gear reduction and conventional starters are: the gear reduction starter has a set of ratio reduction gears while the conventional starter does not; the brushes on the gear reduction starter are located on a plate behind the starter drive housing, while the conventional starter's brushes are located in its rear cover. The extra gears on the gear reduction starter make the starter pinion gear turn at about half the speed of the starter, giving the starter twice the turning power of a conventional starter. There is no difference in removal and installation procedures between the two.

REMOVAL AND INSTALLATION

1. Disconnect the negative battery cable from the battery.
2. Disconnect the starter wiring at the starter, taking note of the positions for correct reinstallation.
3. Remove the bolts attaching the starter to the engine and remove the starter from the vehicle.
4. Install the starter in the reverse order of removal.

BRUSH REPLACEMENT

Non-Reduction Gear Type

1. With the starter out of the vehicle, remove the bolts holding the solenoid to the top of the starter and remove the solenoid.
2. To remove the brushes, remove the two thru-bolts, and the two rear cover attaching screws and remove the rear cover.
3. Disconnect the electrical leads, lift up the brush spring with a wire hook and remove the brushes.
4. Install the brushes in the reverse order of removal.

Note the wire locations before removing the starter

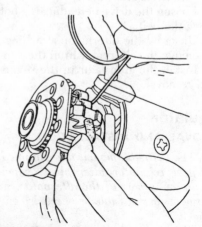

Lift brush spring with a wire hook and remove brush on non-reduction starters

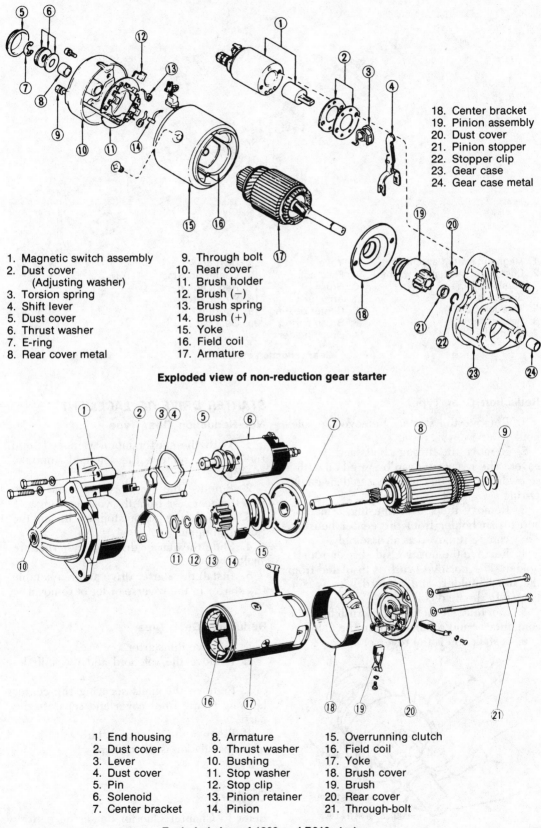

18. Center bracket
19. Pinion assembly
20. Dust cover
21. Pinion stopper
22. Stopper clip
23. Gear case
24. Gear case metal

1. Magnetic switch assembly
2. Dust cover
   (Adjusting washer)
3. Torsion spring
4. Shift lever
5. Dust cover
6. Thrust washer
7. E-ring
8. Rear cover metal

9. Through bolt
10. Rear cover
11. Brush holder
12. Brush (−)
13. Brush spring
14. Brush (+)
15. Yoke
16. Field coil
17. Armature

Exploded view of non-reduction gear starter

1. End housing
2. Dust cover
3. Lever
4. Dust cover
5. Pin
6. Solenoid
7. Center bracket

8. Armature
9. Thrust washer
10. Bushing
11. Stop washer
12. Stop clip
13. Pinion retainer
14. Pinion

15. Overrunning clutch
16. Field coil
17. Yoke
18. Brush cover
19. Brush
20. Rear cover
21. Through-bolt

Exploded view of 1200 and B210 starter

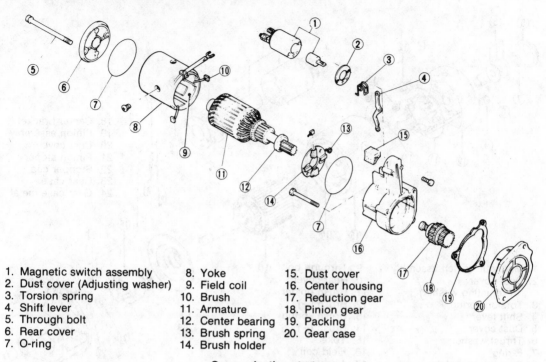

1. Magnetic switch assembly
2. Dust cover (Adjusting washer)
3. Torsion spring
4. Shift lever
5. Through bolt
6. Rear cover
7. O-ring

8. Yoke
9. Field coil
10. Brush
11. Armature
12. Center bearing
13. Brush spring
14. Brush holder

15. Dust cover
16. Center housing
17. Reduction gear
18. Pinion gear
19. Packing
20. Gear case

Gear reduction starter

Reduction Gear Type

1. Remove the starter. Remove the solenoid.

2. Remove the through bolts and the rear cover. The rear cover can be pried off with a screwdriver, but be careful not to damage the O-ring.

3. Remove the starter housing, armature, and brush holder from the center housing. They can be removed as an assembly.

4. Remove the positive side brush from its holder. The positive brush is insulated from the brush holder, and its lead wire is connected to the field coil.

5. Carefully lift the negative brush from the commutator and remove it from the holder.

6. Installation is the reverse.

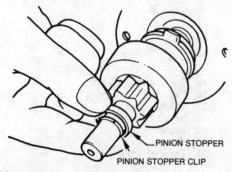

PINION STOPPER
PINION STOPPER CLIP

Pinion stopper removal

STARTER DRIVE REPLACEMENT

Non-Reduction Gear Type

1. With the starter motor removed from the vehicle, remove the solenoid from the starter.

2. Remove the two thru-bolts and separate the gear case from the yoke housing.

3. Remove the pinion stopper clip and the pinion stopper.

4. Slide the starter drive off the armature shaft.

5. Install the starter drive and reassemble the starter in the reverse order of removal.

Reduction Gear Type

1. Remove the starter.

2. Remove the solenoid and the shift lever.

3. Remove the bolts securing the center housing to the front cover and separate the parts.

4. Remove the gears and starter drive.

5. Installation is the reverse.

Battery

Refer to Chapter One for details on battery maintenance.

Battery and Starter Specifications

All cars use 12 volt, negative ground electrical systems

		Battery Amp Hour Capacity	Lock Test		Torque (ft. lbs)	Starter No Load Test			Brush Spring Tension (oz)	Min Brush Length (in)
Year	Model		Amps	Volts		Amps	Volts	RPM		
1973	1200	45	420	6.3	6.5 MT	60	12	7,000	56	0.26
					7.2 AT	60	12	6,000	29	0.37
1974–78	B210	60	420	6.3	6.5	60	12	7,000	49–64	0.47
			—	—	—	60	12	6,000①	29	0.37
			—	—	—	100 RG	12	4,300 RG	56–70	0.43
1979–82	210	60	—	—	—	60	11.5	7,000	50–64	0.47
						100 RG	11	3,900	56–70	0.43
1982–83	Sentra	60②	—	—	—	60	11.5	7,000	50–64	0.43

MT: Manual Transmission
AT: Automatic Transmission
RG: Reduction gear type starter (Canada)

① 1974 Automatic Transmission models only
—: Not recommended
② 30A U.S.A. MPG model; 65A Canada

REMOVAL AND INSTALLATION

1. Disconnect the negative (ground) cable from the terminal, and then the positive cable. Special pullers are available to remove the cable clamps, if they seem stuck.

NOTE: *To avoid sparks, always disconnect the ground cable first, and connect it last.*

2. Remove the battery hold-down clamp.

3. Remove the battery, being careful not to spill the acid.

NOTE: *Spilled acid can be neutralized with a baking soda/water solution. If you somehow get acid into your eyes, flush it out with lots of water and get to a doctor.*

4. Clean the battery posts thoroughly before reinstalling, or when installing a new battery.

5. Clean the cable clamps, using a wire brush, both inside and out.

6. Install the battery and the hold-down clamp or strap. Connect the positive, and the negative cable (see "Note" above). Do not hammer the cables onto the terminal posts. The complete terminals should be coated lightly (externally) with petroleum jelly or grease to help prevent corrosion. There are also felt washers impregnated with an anti corrosion substance which are slipped over the battery posts before installing the cables; these are available in most auto parts stores.

CAUTION: *Make absolutely sure that the battery is connected properly (positive to positive, negative to negative) before you turn the ignition key. Reversed polarity can burn out your alternator and regulator in a matter of seconds.*

ENGINE MECHANICAL

Design

The "A series" engines used in the 1200, B210 and 210 models covered in this book are all members of the same "family." The A12, A12A, A13, A14 and A15 series of engines are all water-cooled, inline, overhead valve, four cylinder powerplants. All of these engines utilize a cast iron block and an aluminum cylinder head. Camshafts in these engines are placed high in the block, allowing for short pushrods, which in turn means low valve train reciprocating weight and higher engine speeds. The A12 through A15s also have in common a five main bearing crankshaft. The engines differ mainly in displacement, which becomes greater as the number after the "A" prefix becomes greater (A12s are 1200 cubic centimeters, A13s 1300, and so on).

The "E series" engines used in the Nissan Sentra retain the displacement of the A15 (1500 cc) Datsun engines, while departing significantly in engine design. The Sentra E15 utilizes a single overhead camshaft and "hemi" combustion chambers. The cylinder block is much smaller and lighter than the A15. Distributor drive on the E15 also departs from its Datsun cousins, and follows proven European practice of driving the distributor directly off of the overhead cam.

Engines are referred to by model designation codes throughout this book. Use the "General Engine Specifications" table in this chapter for the identification of engines by model and displacement.

Engine Removal and Installation

All A-series Models

The engine and transmission are removed together and then separated when out of the car.

1. Mark the location of the hinges on the bottom of the hood with a scribe or grease pencil for later installation. Unbolt and remove the hood.

2. Disconnect the battery cables.

3. Drain the coolant from the radiator, and drain the automatic transmission fluid.

4. Remove the radiator and radiator shroud after disconnecting the automatic transmission coolant tubes (if equipped).

5. Remove the air cleaner.

6. Remove the fan and pulley.

7. Disconnect:

  a. water temperature gauge wire;
  b. oil pressure sending unit wire;
  c. ignition distributor primary wire;

Engine I.D. Table

Vehicle	Number of Cylinders	Displacement cu. in. (cc)	Type	Engine Model Code
1200	4	71.5 (1171)	OHV	A12
B210	4	78.59 (1288)	OHV	A13
	4	85.24 (1397)	OHV	A14
210	4	75.5 (1237)	OHV	A12A
	4	85.3 (1397)	OHV	A14
	4	90.8 (1488)	OHV	A15
Sentra	4	90.8 (1488)	OHC	E15

NOTE: OHV is Overhead Valve
       OHC is Overhead Cam

  d. starter motor connections;
  e. fuel hose;
  f. alternator leads;
  g. heater hoses;
  h. throttle and choke connections;
  i. engine ground cable;
  j. thermal transmitter wire;
  k. wire to fuel cut-off solenoid;
  l. vacuum cut solenoid wire.

NOTE: *A good rule of thumb when disconnecting the rather complex engine wiring of today's cars is to put a piece of masking tape on the wire and on the connection you removed the wire from, then mark both*

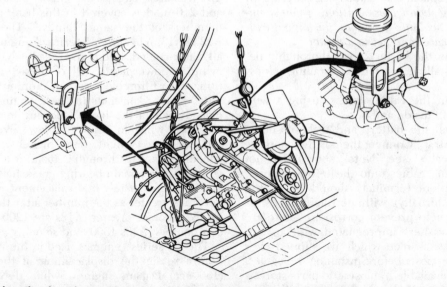

Removing the A-series engine. All engines removed in a similar manner, except Sentra which is removed sideways

Gearshift lever removal: 1200, B210. 210 similar

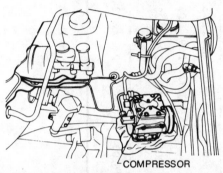

COMPRESSOR

Secure A/C compressor to the inside of the fender or frame when removing engine on all models

pieces of tape 1,2,3, etc. When replacing wiring, simply match the pieces of tape.
CAUTION: *On models with air conditioning, it is necessary to remove the compressor and the condenser from their mounts. DO NOT ATTEMPT TO UNFASTEN ANY OF THE AIR CONDITIONER HOSES. See chapter one for additional warnings.*

8. Disconnect the power brake booster hose from the engine.

9. Remove the clutch operating cylinder and return spring.

10. Disconnect the speedometer cable from the transmission. Disconnect the backup light switch and any other wiring or attachments to the transmission.

11. Disconnect the column shift linkage. Remove the floorshift lever. On 1200 and B210 models, remove the boot, withdraw the lock pin, and remove the lever from inside the car.

12. Detach the exhaust pipe from the exhaust manifold. Remove the front section of the exhaust manifold.

13. Mark the relationship of the driveshaft flanges with a centerpunch or scribe and remove the driveshaft. The marks are matched up later during installation; the driveshaft must be installed in the same relationship as it was removed.

14. Place a jack under the transmission. Remove the rear crossmember, keeping the jack underneath just enough for support. On 1200 and B210 models, remove the rear engine mounting nuts. Remove the front engine mount bolts from all models.

15. Attach a strong (heavy chain or heavy rope in good condition) lifting sling to the lifting eyelets on the engine. Run the sling through both eyelets, and then through a suitable pulley or other lifting device.

NOTE: *Make sure that whatever will be supporting the engine as you pull it out of the car will be able to support the weight of both engine and transmission. Many children's swing sets are not sturdy enough for this and are not recommended. Engine lifting tripods are available at many equipment rental shops, and are designed for this work.*

16. Drape a heavy cloth across the grille of the car. This will protect and cushion the grille, crossmember and engine from any damage. Slowly lift the engine up and out of the car. It is helpful to have at least two people working on this job, especially to help the transmission clear its tunnel and engine compartment. When the engine is out of the car, do not rest the weight of the entire unit on the oil pan.

17. Installation is the reverse of removal. If the buffer rod length has not been altered, it should still be correct.

E SERIES ENGINES

NOTE: *The engine and transaxle must be removed as a unit. Since the Sentra is a front wheel drive car, this is a fairly involved procedure. It is very important to label and mark all cables, hoses and vacuum lines during this procedure. Masking tape works well here. Marking both the disconnected hose, etc., and where it was attached will help to avoid the "where did that go?" later.*

CAUTION: *Be sure the car is on a flat, solid surface with the wheels chocked before beginning. Do not remove the engine until the exhaust system has cooled off completely; you will avoid burns and fuel line fires this way. Also, when unbolting the air conditioner compressor and idler pulley mount, DO NOT disconnect any A/C fittings or hoses.*

1. Scribe or draw a line around the hood mounting brackets on the underside of the

General Engine Specifications

Year	Model	Type (model)	Engine Displacement Cu In. (cc)	Carburetor Type	Horsepower (SAE) @ rpm	Horsepower (SAE) @ rpm	Torque @ rpm (ft. lbs.)	Bore x Stroke (in.)	Compression Ratio	Normal Oil Pressure (psi)
1973	1200 Sedan 1200 Coupe	OHV 4 (A12)	71.5 (1171)	Two barrel downdraft	69 @ 6000	69 @ 6000	70 @ 4000	2.87 x 2.76	8.5:1	54–60
1974	B210 Sedan, Coupe	OHV 4 (A13)	78.6 (1288)	Two barrel downdraft	75 @ 6000	75 @ 6000	77 @ 3600	2.87 x 3.03	8.5:1	43–50
1975	B210 Sedan, Coupe	OHV 4 (A14)	85.24 (1397)	Two barrel downdraft	78 @ 6000	78 @ 6000	75 @ 4000	3.09 x 3.03	8.5:1	43–50
1976–78	B210	OHV 4 (A14)	85.2 (1397)	Two barrel downdraft	80 @ 6000	80 @ 6000	83 @ 3600	2.99 x 3.03	8.5:1	43–50
1979–82	210	OHV 4 (A12A)	75.5 (1237)	Two barrel downdraft	58 @ 5600	58 @ 5600	67 @ 3600	2.95 x 2.75	8.5:1	43–50
	210 MPG	OHV 4 (A14)	85.3 (1397)	Two barrel downdraft	65 @ 5600	65 @ 5600	75 @ 3600	2.99 x 3.03	8.5:1 ①	43–50
		OHV 4 (A15)	90.8 (1488)	Two barrel downdraft	67 @ 5200	67 @ 5200	80 @ 3200	2.99 x 3.23	8.9:1	43–50
1982–83	Sentra	OHC 4 (E15)	90.8 (1488)	Two barrel downdraft	67 @ 5200	67 @ 5200	85 @ 3200	2.99 x 3.23	9.0:1	43–50

NOTE: Specifications given are for United States except California
① 8.9:1 on 1981–2

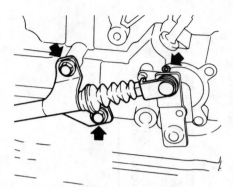

Sentra transaxle linkage attaching points

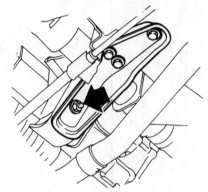

Sentra rear engine mount

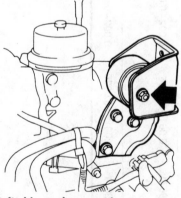

Sentra left side engine mount

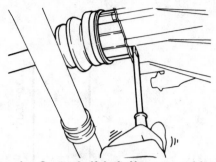

Removing Sentra halfshaft. Use care not to damage the grease seal

and idler pulley bracket from the cylinder block, observing the "Caution" above. Remove the compressor drive belt and hold the compressor unit upright, attached to the car with a wire or rope.

7. Disconnect the exhaust header pipe from the exhaust manifold.

8. Disconnect the manual transaxle control rod link support rod from the transaxle.

9. Disconnect the automatic transaxle control linkage from the transaxle.

10. Remove the lower ball joint. Do not reuse the nuts once they have been removed—replace them with new nuts.

11. Drain the transaxle gear oil or fluid.

12. Disconnect the right and left halfshafts from the transaxle.

NOTE: *When drawing out the halfshafts, it is necessary to loosen the strut head bolts. Be careful not to damage the grease seal on the transaxle side.*

13. Disconnect the clutch cable.

14. Remove the speedometer cable with the pinion from the transaxle. Plug the hole from which the pinion gear was removed with a clean rag to keep out dirt.

15. Disconnect the accelerator cable.

16. Disconnect any vacuum and air hoses between the engine and vehicle body. Disconnect all cables, wires and harness connectors.

17. Disconnect the fuel hoses from the fuel pump.

18. Attach a suitable sling to the lifting eyelets on the engine.

19. Unbolt the engine mounts, and lift the engine up and away from the car. Transaxle can now be separated from the engine.

INSTALLATION

1. Install engine with transaxle attached, in the reverse order of removal, and following these checks:

hood, to facilitate installation later. Remove the hood.

2. Remove battery and battery support bracket.

3. Remove air cleaner and related hoses. Plug the air horn of the carburetor with a clean rag to keep dirt out.

4. Drain engine coolant and remove radiator with the radiator cooling fan.

5. Remove the power steering pump, if equipped.

6. Unbolt the air conditioner compressor

Crankshaft and Connecting Rod Specifications

Engine Model	Crankshaft					Connecting Rod Bearings		
	Main Brg Journal Dia	Main Brg Oil Clearance	Shaft End-Play	Thrust on No.	Journal Dia	Oil Clearance	Side Clearance
A12 (1200)	1.9671–1.9668	0.001–0.002	0.002–0.006	3	1.7701–1.7706	0.001–0.002	0.007–0.012
A13	1.966–1.967	0.0008–0.002	0.002–0.006	3	1.7701–1.7706	0.0008–0.002	0.008–0.012
A14 (1975–78)	1.966–1.967	0.0008–0.002	0.002–0.006	3	1.7701–1.7706	0.0008–0.002	0.008–0.012
A12A, A14, A15 (1979–1982)	1.9663–1.9671	0.001–0.0035	0.002–0.0059	3	1.7701–1.7706	0.0012–0.0031	0.004–0.008
E15	1.9663–1.9671	0.0012–0.0030	0.002–0.0071	3	1.5730–1.5738	0.0012–0.0024	0.004–0.014

Piston and Ring Specifications

All measurements in inches

| Engine Model | Piston-to-Bore Clearance | Ring Gap | | | Ring Side Clearance | | |
		Top Compression	Bottom Compression	Oil Control	Top Clearance	Bottom Compression	Oil Control
A12 1973	0.001–0.002	0.008–0.014	0.008–0.014	0.012–0.035	0.002–0.003	0.002–0.003	0.002–0.003
A13	0.001–0.002	0.008–0.014	0.008–0.014	0.012–0.035	0.002–0.003	0.002–0.003	—
A14 1975–78	0.0009–0.002	0.008–0.014	0.008–0.014	0.012–0.035	0.002–0.003	0.001–0.002	Combined ring
A12A, A14, A15 1979–82	0.0010–0.0018	0.008–0.014	0.008–0.014	0.012–0.035	0.002–0.003	0.001–0.002	Combined ring
E15	0.0009–0.0017	0.0079–0.0138	0.0059–0.0118	0.0118–0.0354	0.0016–0.0029	0.0012–0.0025	0.0020–0.0057

Valve Specifications

Model	Seat Angle (deg)	Spring Test Pressure lbs @ in.	Free Length (in.)	Stem-to-Guide Clearance (in.)		Stem Diameter (in.)	
				Intake	Exhaust	Intake	Exhaust
A12, A13, A14 (1973–78)	45°	52.7 @ 1.52	1.83	0.0006– 0.0018	0.0016– 0.0028	0.3138– 0.3144	0.3128– 0.3134
A12A, A14 A15 (1979–82)	45°30'	52.7 @ 1.19	1.83	0.0006– 0.0018	0.0016– 0.0028	0.3138– 0.3144	0.3128– 0.3134
E15	45°15– 45°45'	127.8 @ 1.18	1.83	0.0008– 0.0020	0.0018– 0.0030	0.2744– 0.2750	0.2734– 0.2740

Torque Specifications
All readings in ft. lbs.

Engine Model	Cylinder Head Bolts	Main Bearing Bolts	Rod Bearing Bolts	Crankshaft Pulley Bolt	Flywheel to Crankshaft Bolts	Manifolds	
						Intake	Exhaust
A12	40–43	36–43	23–28	108–116	47–54	7–10	7–10
A13	51–54	36–43	23–27	108–145	54–61	7–10	7–10
A12A, A14, A15	51–54	36–43	23–27	108–145	58–65 ①	11–14	11–14
E15	51–54 ②	36–43	23–27	83–108	58–65	12–15	12–15

① 1975–77 A14: 54–61 ft. lbs.
② Second (final) torquing. First torque to 29–33 ft. lbs.

a. When installing, make sure that the brake lines, brake master cylinder, etc., do not interfere with the engine and trans-axle.

b. Make sure that the A/C compressor and power steering pump (if equipped) are securely out of the way when lowering the engine.

2. Tighten the engine mount bolts, making sure there is some clearance in the rubber insulator.

Cylinder Head
REMOVAL AND INSTALLATION
A Series Overhead Valve Engines
NOTE: *To prevent distortion or warping of the cylinder head, allow the engine to cool completely before removing the head bolts. Also, do not pry the head off of the block.*

If the head seems stuck, tap lightly around the lower perimeter of the head with a rubber mallet to loosen head from the block.
To remove the cylinder head on all "A" series OHV engines:

1. Drain the coolant.
2. Disconnect the battery ground cable.
3. Remove the upper radiator hose. Remove the water outlet elbow and the thermostat.
4. Remove the air cleaner, carburetor, rocker arm cover, and both manifolds.
5. Remove the spark plugs.
6. Disconnect the temperature gauge connection.
7. Remove the head bolts and remove the head and rocker arm assembly together. Rap the head with a mallet to loosen it from the block. Remove the head and discard the gasket.
8. Remove the pushrods one by one,

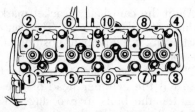

A-series cylinder head bolt loosening sequence

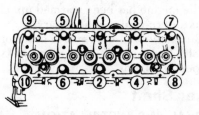

A-series cylinder head torque tightening sequence

marking them with tape to keep them in order.

To replace the cylinder head on OHV engines:

1. Make sure that head and block surfaces are clean. Check the cylinder head surface with a straightedge and a feeler gauge for flatness. If the head is warped more than 0.004 in., it must be trued. If this is not done, there will probably be a leak. The block surface should also be checked in the same way. If the block is warped more than 0.004 in., it must be trued (machined flat).

2. Install a new head gasket. Most gaskets have a TOP marking. Make sure that the proper head gasket is used on the A12 so that no water passages are blocked off.

3. Install the head. Install the pushrods in their original locations. Install the rocker arm assembly. Loosen the rocker arm adjusting screws to prevent bending the pushrods when tightening the head bolts. Tighten the head bolts finger tight. One of the head bolts is smaller in diameter than the others. This bolt should be inserted in hole number one, center in the illustration.

CAUTION: *The above mentioned bolt is thinner than the others because it acts as the oil passageway for the rocker components. It must be inserted in the correct hole or the valve train will seize up after a few hundred miles.*

4. Refer to the Torque Specifications" chart for the correct head bolt torque. Tighten the bolts to one third of the specified torque in the order shown in the head bolt tightening sequence illustration. Torque the rocker arm mounting bolts to 15–18 ft. lbs.

5. Tighten the bolts to two thirds of the specified torque in sequence.

6. Tighten the bolts to the fill specified torque in sequence.

7. Adjust the valves to the cold setting.

8. Reassemble the engine. Intake and exhaust manifold bolt torque for 1200 A12 engine is 7–10 ft. lbs., for all others 11–14 ft. lbs. Fill the cooling system. Start the engine and run it until normal temperature is reached. Remove the rocker arm cover. Torque the bolts in sequence once more. Check the valve clearances.

9. Retorque the head bolts after 600 miles of driving. Check the valve clearances after torquing, as this may disturb the settings.

E series Overhead Cam Engines

NOTE: *Make sure engine is cold before removing head: An aluminum head is prone to warpage if removed while warm.*

1. Crank the engine until the No. 1 piston is at Top Dead Center on its compression stroke and disconnect the negative battery cable. Drain the cooling system and remove the air cleaner assembly.

2. Remove the alternator.

3. Number all spark plug wires as to their respective cylinders and remove the distributor, with all wires attached.

4. Remove the EAI pipes bracket and EGR tube at the right (EGR valve) side. Disconnect the same pipes on the front (exhaust manifold) side from the manifold.

5. Remove the exhaust manifold cover and the exhaust manifold, taking note that the center manifold nut has a different diameter than the other nuts.

6. Remove the A/C compressor bracket

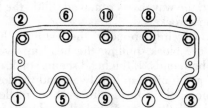

Head loosening sequence, Sentra

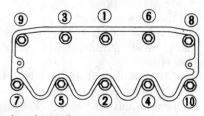

Sentra head torquing sequence

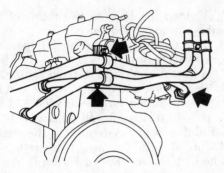

Disconnect EGR (upper) and EAI tubes on Sentra

and the power steering pump bracket (if equipped).

7. Label and disconnect the carburetor throttle linkage, fuel line, and all vacuum and electrical connections.

8. Remove the intake manifold with carburetor.

9. Remove water pump drive belt and pulley. Remove crankshaft pulley.

10. Remove the rocker (valve) cover.

11. Remove upper and lower dust cover on the camshaft timing belt shroud.

12. With the shroud removed, the cam sprocket, crankshaft sprocket, jackshaft sprocket, tensioner pulley, and toothed rubber timing belt are in front of you.

13. Mark the relationship of the camshaft sprocket to the timing belt and the crankshaft sprocket to the timing belt with paint or a grease pencil. This will make setting everything up during reassembly much easier if the engine is disturbed during disassembly.

14. Remove the belt tensioner pulley.

15. Mark an arrow on the timing belt showing direction of engine rotation, as the belt wears a certain way and should be replaced the way it was removed. Slide the belt off the sprockets.

16. Carefully remove the cylinder head from the block, pulling the head up evenly from both ends. If the head seems stuck, DO NOT pry it off. Tap lightly around the lower perimeter of the head with a rubber mallet to help break the joint. Label all head bolts with tape or magic marker, as they must go back in their original positions.

To install the cylinder head:

1. Thoroughly clean both the cylinder block and head mating surfaces. Avoid scratching either.

2. Turn the crankshaft and set No. 1 cylinder at TDC on its compression stroke. This causes the crankshaft timing sprocket mark to be aligned with the cylinder block cover mark.

3. Align the camshaft sprocket mark with the cylinder head cover mark. This causes the valves for No. 1 cylinder to position at TDC on the compression stroke.

4. Place a new gasket on the cylinder block.

5. Install the cylinder head on the block and tighten the bolts in two stages: first to 29–33 ft. lbs. on all bolts, then go around again and torque them all up to 51–54 ft. lbs. After the engine has been warmed up, check all bolts and re-torque if necessary.

6. Reassemble in the reverse order of disassembly, making sure all timing marks are in proper alignment.

Rocker Shaft

REMOVAL AND INSTALLATION

A12, A12A, A13, A14, A15 Engines

1. Remove rocker cover.

2. Loosen rocker adjusting bolts and push adjusting screws away from pushrods.

3. Unbolt and remove the rocker shaft assembly.

4. To install, reverse the above. Tighten the rocker shaft bolts to 14–18 ft. lbs. in a circular sequence. Adjust the valves.

NOTE: *Both the intake and the exhaust valve springs are the uneven pitch type. That is, the springs have narrow coils at the bottom and wide coils at the top. The narrow coils (painted white) must be the side making contact on the cylinder head surface.*

E Series Engines

1. Remove rocker cover.

2. Loosen each rocker adjusting locknut and screw slightly.

3. Unbolt the rocker shaft assembly and remove from head.

4. Reverse the procedure for installation, torquing the rocker shaft bolts to 12–15 ft. lbs. Adjust the valves.

NOTE: *Make sure that the oil holes in the ends of the rocker shaft face downward*

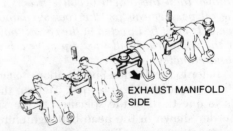

EXHAUST MANIFOLD SIDE

Make sure cutout on Sentra rocker shaft faces exhaust manifold

when the rocker shaft is installed. Also, be sure that the cutout in the center retainer of the rocker shaft faces toward the exhaust manifold side when installed.

Intake Manifold
REMOVAL AND INSTALLATION

1. Remove the air cleaner assembly together with all of the attending hoses.

2. Disconnect the throttle linkage and fuel and vacuum lines from the carburetor.

3. The carburetor can be removed from the manifold at this point or can be removed as an assembly with the intake manifold.

4. Disconnect the intake and exhaust manifold on the A series engines unless you are removing both. Loosen the intake manifold attaching nuts, working from the two ends toward the center, and then remove them.

5. Remove the intake manifold from the engine.

6. Install the intake manifold in the reverse order of removal.

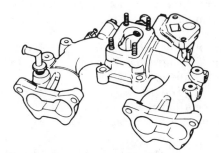

A-series engine intake manifold

Removing the A-series intake and exhaust manifolds as a unit

Exhaust Manifold
REMOVAL AND INSTALLATION

1. Remove the air cleaner assembly, if necessary for access. Remove the heat shield, if present.

2. Disconnect the exhaust pipe from the exhaust manifold. Disconnect the intake manifold from the exhaust manifold (A-series

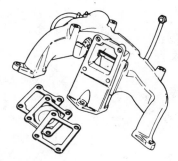

A-series engine exhaust manifold

engines only) unless you are removing both.

3. Remove all temperature sensors, air induction pipes and other attachments from the manifold. Disconnect the EAI and EGR tubes from their fittings on the E series manifolds.

4. Loosen and remove the exhaust manifold attaching nuts and remove the manifold from the engine.

5. Install the exhaust manifold in the reverse order of removal.

Timing Chain Cover
REMOVAL AND INSTALLATION
A12, A12A, A13, A14, A15 Overhead Valve Engines

1. Remove the radiator. Loosen the alternator adjustment and remove the belt. Loosen the air pump adjustment and remove the belt on engines with the air pump system.

2. Remove the fan and water pump.

3. Bend back the locktab from the crankshaft pulley nut. Remove the nut by affixing a heavy wrench and rapping the wrench with a hammer. The nut must be unscrewed in the opposite direction of normal engine rotation. Pull off the pulley.

4. It is recommended that the oil pan be removed or loosened before the front cover is removed.

5. Unbolt and remove the timing chain cover.

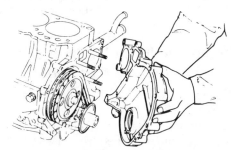

Removing the A-series engine timing cover

When removing the A-series engine timing cover it is necessary to loosen or remove the oil pan

A-series engine camshaft locating plate correctly installed

6. Replace the crankshaft oil seal in the cover. Most models use a felt seal.

7. Reverse the procedure to install, using new gaskets. Apply sealant to both sides of the timing cover gasket. Front cover bolt torque is 4 ft. lbs., water pump bolt torque is 7–10 ft. lbs., and oil pan bolt torque is 4 ft. lbs.

Timing Belt Cover
REMOVAL AND INSTALLATION
E series Overhead Cam Engines

1. Loosen the air conditioner belt and remove.

2. Loosen the alternator adjusting bolt, and remove the alternator belt. Unbolt the alternator mounting bracket and remove the alternator.

3. Remove the power steering belt (if equipped) by loosening the steering pump adjusting bolt.

4. Remove the water pump pulley.

5. Remove crankshaft pulley.

6. Loosen and remove the eight bolts securing the timing cover and remove the cover.

7. Installation is the reverse of removal. wadjust all accessory drive belts and tighten the mounting bolts. Torque the crank pulley bolt to 83–108 ft. lbs.; the water pump pulley bolt to 2.7–3.7 ft. lbs.; and the belt cover bolts to 2.7–3.7 ft. lbs.

Timing Chain and Camshaft
REMOVAL AND INSTALLATION
A12, A12A, A13, A14, A15 Overhead Valve Engines

It is recommended that this operation be done with the engine removed from the vehicle.

1. Remove the timing chain cover.

2. Unbolt and remove the chain tensioner.

3. Remove the camshaft sprocket retaining bolt.

4. Pull off the camshaft sprocket, easing off the crankshaft sprocket at the same time. Remove both sprockets and chain as an assembly. Be careful not to lose the shim and oil slinger from behind the crankshaft sprocket.

5. Remove the distributor, distributor drive spindle, pushrods, and valve lifters. Number all parts with tape.

NOTE: *The lifters cannot be removed until the camshaft has been removed.*

Remove the oil pump and pump driveshaft.

6. Unbolt and remove the camshaft locating plate.

7. Remove the camshaft carefully. This will be easier if the block is inverted to prevent the lifters from falling down.

8. The camshaft bearings can be pressed out and replaced. They are available in undersizes, should it be necessary to regrind the camshaft journals.

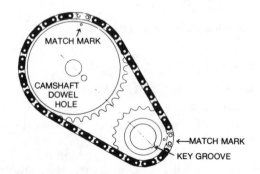

A-series engine timing mark alignment

9. Reinstall the camshaft. If the locating plate has an oil hole, it should be to the right of the engine. The locating plate is marked with the word LOWER and an arrow. Locating plate bolt torque is 3–4 ft. lbs. Be careful to engage the drive pin in the rear end of the camshaft with the slot in the oil pump driveshaft.

10. Camshaft end-play can be measured after temporarily replacing the camshaft sprocket and securing bolt.

The standard end-play specifications for the A12 engine are 0.001–0.003 in. with a service limit (largest allowable end-play limit) of 0.004 in. The A12A, A13, A14 and A15 engines have standard end-play specifications of 0.004–0.002 in. with a service limit of 0.004 in. If the end-play is excessive, replace the locating plate. New plates are available in several sizes.

11. If the crankshaft or camshaft has been replaced, install the sprockets temporarily and make sure that they are parallel. Adjust by shimming under the crankshaft sprocket.

12. Assemble the sprockets and chain, aligning them.

13. Turn the crankshaft until the keyway and the No. 1 piston is at top dead center. Install the sprockets and chain. The oil slinger behind the crankshaft sprocket must be replaced with the concave surface to the front. If the chain and sprocket installation is correct, the sprocket marks must be aligned between the shaft centers when the No. 1 piston is at top dead center. Engine camshaft sprocket retaining bolt torque is 33–36 ft. lbs.

14. The rest of the reassembly procedure is the reverse of disassembly. Engine chain tensioner bolt torque is 4–6 ft. lbs.

Camshaft

REMOVAL AND INSTALLATION

E series Overhead Cam Engines

1. Removal of the cylinder head from the engine is optional. Crank the engine until the No. 1 piston is at Top Dead Center on its compression stroke.

2. Follow the "Timing Belt Cover" removal procedure and remove the cover. Mark the relationship of the camshaft sprocket to the timing belt and the crankshaft sprocket to the timing belt with paint or a grease pencil. This will make setting everything up during reassembly much easier, if the engine is disturbed during disassembly.

3. Remove the distributor.

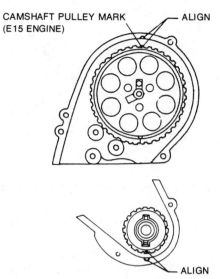

CAMSHAFT PULLEY MARK (E15 ENGINE) — ALIGN
— ALIGN

Camshaft and crankshaft sprocket alignment marks, E-series engine

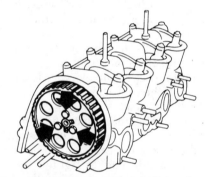

Remove three cam sprocket bolts and pull off sprocket, E-series

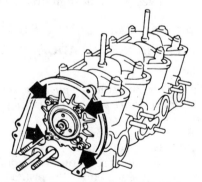

E-series front camshaft retainer screws

4. Remove the thermostat housing.

5. Remove the timing belt from the sprockets, after loosening the belt tensioner pulley.

6. Remove the rocker cover and remove the rocker shaft.

7. Loosen and remove the cam drive sprocket.

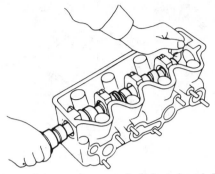

Use care in removing camshaft from head, E-series

8. Remove the camshaft front retainer plate.

NOTE: *Be careful not to damage the oil seal lip between the front retainer plate and the end of the camshaft.*

9. Squirt a small amount of clean oil around the camshaft bearings. Carefully slide the camshaft out of the carrier in the cylinder head.

10. To install, lightly oil the camshaft bearings with clean motor oil and slowly slide the cam into place in the cylinder head.

11. Install the camshaft front retainer plate on the cylinder head.

12. Reassemble the remainder of the head assembly in the reverse order of removal. Check the valve timing after all sprockets and timing belt are installed. Tighten the camshaft drive sprocket to 4.3–5.8 ft. lbs. Install a new gasket behind the thermostat housing. Adjust the valves, and adjust all drive belts.

Pistons and Connecting Rods
REMOVAL AND INSTALLATION
All Engines

NOTE: *This procedure may be easier on the Sentra (E series engines) if the engine is removed from the car.*

1. Remove the cylinder head.

2. Remove the oil pan.

3. Remove any carbon buildup from the cylinder wall at the top end of the piston travel with a ridge reamer tool.

4. Position the piston to be removed at the bottom of its stroke so that the connecting rod bearing cap can be reached easily from under the engine.

5. Unscrew the connecting rod bearing cap nuts and remove the cap and lower half of the bearing.

6. Push the piston and connecting rod up and out of the cylinder block with a length of wood or a wooden hammer handle. Use care not to scratch the cylinder wall with the connecting rod or the wooden tool.

7. Keep all of the components from each cylinder together and install them in the cylinder from which they were removed.

8. Coat the bearing face of the connecting rod and the outer face of the pistons with engine oil.

9. See the illustrations for the correct placement of the piston rings for your model and year Datsun.

10. Turn the crankshaft until the rod journal of the particular cylinder you are working on is brought to the TDC position.

11. With the piston and rings clamped in a ring compressor, the notched mark on the head of the piston toward the front of the engine, and the oil hole side of the connecting rod toward the fuel pump side of the engine, push the piston and connecting rod assembly into the cylinder bore until the big bearing end of the connecting rod contacts and is seated on the rod journal of the crankshaft. *Use care not to scratch the cylinder wall with the connecting rod.*

NOTE: *It is good practice to cut two lengths of rubber tubing to fit over the connecting rod bolts. The tubing should be long enough to reach through the cylinder bore and through the bottom of the crankcase. When the tubing is installed over the bolts, it reduces, if not eliminates, the chance of scratching the cylinder bore with the bolts as you install the piston assembly.*

12. Push down farther on the piston and turn the crankshaft while the connecting rod rides around on the crankshaft rod journal. Turn the crankshaft until the crankshaft rod journal is at BDC (bottom dead center).

13. Align the mark on the connecting rod bearing cap with that on the connecting rod and tighten the bearing cap bolts to the specified torque.

14. Install all of the piston/connecting rod assemblies in the manner outlined above and assemble the oil pan and cylinder head to the engine in the reverse order of removal.

IDENTIFICATION AND POSITIONING

The pistons are marked with a number or "F" in the piston head. When installed in the engine the number or "F" markings are to be facing toward the front of the engine.

The connecting rods are installed in the

engine with the oil hole facing toward the fuel pump side (right) of the engine.

NOTE: *It is advisable to number the pistons, connecting rods, and bearing caps in some manner so that they can be reinstalled in the same cylinder, facing in the same direction from which they are removed.*

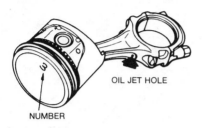

OIL JET HOLE

NUMBER

Piston and rod positioning—A-series engines

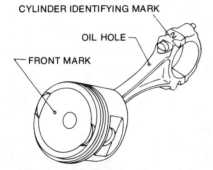

CYLINDER IDENTIFYING MARK

OIL HOLE

FRONT MARK

Piston and rod positioning, E-series

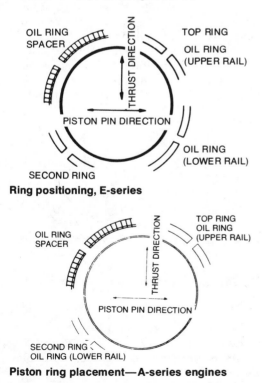

OIL RING SPACER

TOP RING

OIL RING (UPPER RAIL)

THRUST DIRECTION

PISTON PIN DIRECTION

OIL RING (LOWER RAIL)

SECOND RING

Ring positioning, E-series

OIL RING SPACER

TOP RING
OIL RING (UPPER RAIL)

THRUST DIRECTION

PISTON PIN DIRECTION

SECOND RING
OIL RING (LOWER RAIL)

Piston ring placement—A-series engines

ENGINE LUBRICATION

Oil Pan
REMOVAL AND INSTALLATION
All Engines

To remove the oil pan it will be necessary to unbolt the motor mounts and jack the engine to gain clearance. Drain the oil, remove the attaching screws, and remove the oil pan and gasket. Install the oil pan in the reverse order with a new gasket, tightening the screws to 4–7 ft. lbs. (3–4 ft. lbs. E series).

Rear Main Oil Seal
REPLACEMENT
A Series Engines

In order to replace the rear main oil seal, the rear main bearing cap must be removed. Removal of the rear main bearing cap requires the use of a special rear main bearing cap puller. Also, the oil seal is installed with a special crankshaft rear oil seal drift. Unless these or similar tools are available to you, it is recommended that the oil seal be replaced by a Datsun service center.

1. Remove the engine and transmission assembly from the vehicle.

2. Remove the transmission from the engine. Remove the oil pan.

Installing A-series rear oil seal using drift

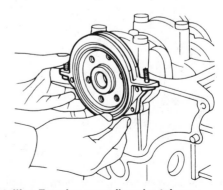

Installing E-series rear oil seal retainer

3. Remove the clutch from the flywheel.

4. Remove the flywheel from the crankshaft.

5. Remove the rear main bearing cap together with the bearing cap side seals.

6. Remove the rear main oil seal from around the crankshaft.

7. Apply lithium grease around the sealing lip of the oil seal and install the seal around the crankshaft using a suitable tool.

8. Apply sealer to the rear main bearing cap as indicated, install the rear main bearing cap, and tighten the cap bolts to 33–40 ft. lbs.

9. Apply sealant to the rear main bearing cap side seals and install the side seals, driving the seals into place with a suitable drift.

10. Assemble the engine and install it in the vehicle in the reverse order of removal.

E Series Engines

In order to replace the rear main oil seal in the E series engines, the transaxle must be removed, or the engine and transaxle assembly must be removed.

1. Remove transaxle from the car.

2. Remove the clutch from the flywheel.

3. Unbolt and remove the flywheel from the end of the crankshaft.

4. Unbolt the two bolts attaching the oil seal retainer to the oil pan.

5. Remove the three Phillips head screws that attach the oil seal retainer to the engine block, and remove the oil seal.

6. During installation of the new oil seal, apply a coating of clean oil to the outside edge of the seal. Install the new seal in the direction that the dust seal lip faces (to the outside of the crankcase). Coat the mating shaft with clean oil also, when installing the oil seal retainer, to prevent scratches and a folded lip.

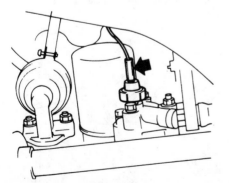

Removing oil pressure gauge harness from oil pump, E-series

Oil Pump

The oil pump is mounted externally on the engine, this eliminates the need to remove the oil pan in order to remove the oil pump. The oil pump is actually part of the oil filter mounting bracket.

Removing A-series engine oil pump

REMOVAL AND INSTALLATION
1973–82 All A Series Models

1. Drain the engine oil and remove oil filter.

2. Remove the front stabilizer bar if it is in the way of removing the oil pump (if equipped).

3. Remove the splash shield.

4. Remove the oil pump body with the drive spindle assembly.

5. Install the oil pump in the reverse order of removal, after removing any traces of the old gasket and installing a new gasket.

6. Make sure the pump mounting bolts are tight. Install the oil filter to the oil pump. Check the oil level mark on the dipstick and add oil if necessary. Start the engine and check for leaks.

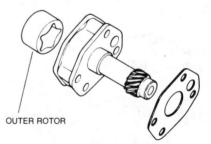

OUTER ROTOR

Exploded view of A-series engine oil pump

E Series Engines

1. Loosen alternator lower bolts.

2. Remove alternator belt and adjusting bar bolt. Move alternator aside so there is ample room to work.

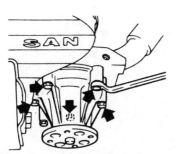

Water pump removal, E-series

3. Disconnect oil pressure gauge harness.

4. If necessary, remove oil filter from the engine to give proper access to oil pump bolts.

5. Unbolt the oil pump from the engine block and remove.

6. If the oil pump gasket is worn, replace it. Install the oil pump, making sure all bolts are tight. You may have to turn the pump body slightly when inserting the pump drive gear into the block, in order to properly engage the drive gear with its drive gear on the engine jackshaft.

ENGINE COOLING

Radiator

REMOVAL AND INSTALLATION

NOTE: *On some models it may be necessary to remove the front grille.*

1. Drain the engine coolant into a clean container.

2. Disconnect the upper and lower radiator hoses and the expansion tank hose.

3. Disconnect the automatic transmission oil cooler lines after draining the transmission. Cap the lines to keep dirt out of them.

4. If the fan has a shroud, unbolt the shroud and move it back, hanging it over the fan.

5. Remove the radiator mounting bolts and the radiator.

6. Installation is the reverse of removal. Fill the automatic transmission to the proper level. Fill the cooling system.

Water Pump

REMOVAL AND INSTALLATION

All Engines

1. Drain the engine coolant into a clean container.

2. On the A series, loosen the four bolts retaining the fan shroud to the radiator and remove the shroud.

3. Loosen the belt, then remove the fan and pulley from the water pump hub.

4. Remove the bolts retaining the pump and remove the pump together with the gasket from the front cover.

5. Remove all traces of gasket material and install the water pump in the reverse order

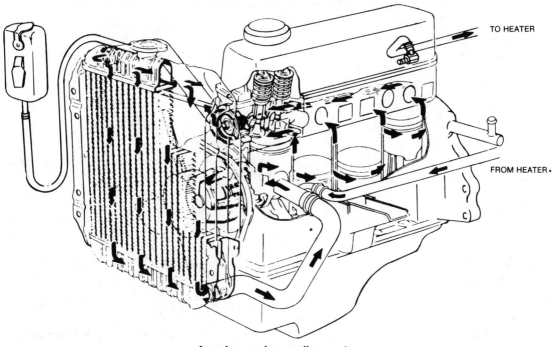

A-series engine cooling system

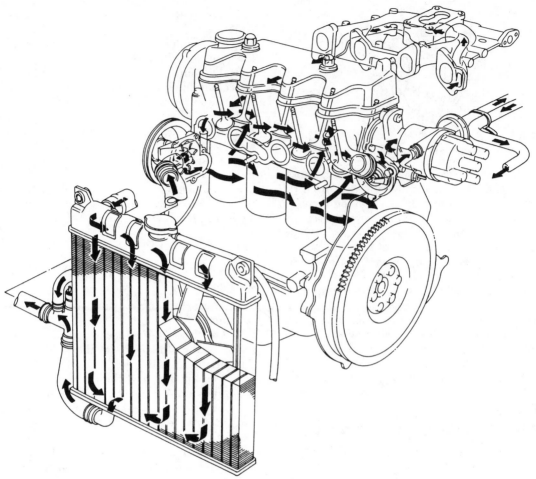

Sentra (E series) cooling system

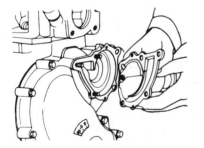

A-series engine water pump removal

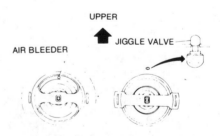

1980 A-series thermostat: place jiggle valve toward top

with a new gasket and sealer. Tighten the bolts uniformly.

Thermostat

REMOVAL AND INSTALLATION

All Engines

1. Drain the engine coolant into a clean container so that the coolant remaining in the engine block is below the thermostat hous-

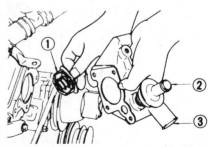

1. Thermostat 2. Air check valve 3. Water outlet
A-series thermostat removal

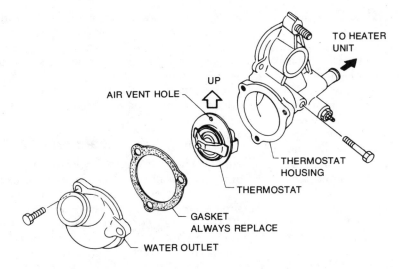

E-series thermostat and housing

ing. Save the drained coolant for use again, if it is still a fresh mixture.

2. Disconnect the upper radiator hose at the water outlet.

3. Loosen the two securing nuts and remove the water outlet, gasket, and the thermostat from the thermostat housing.

4. Install the thermostat in the reverse order of removal, using a new gasket with sealer and with the thermostat spring toward the inside of the engine.

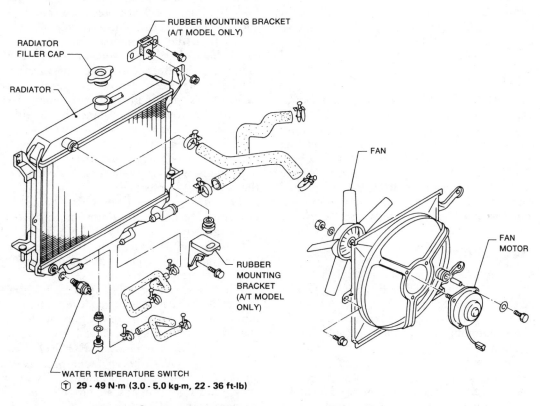

Sentra radiator and fan assembly, others similar

ENGINE REBUILDING

Most procedures involved in rebuilding an engine are fairly standard, regardless of the type of engine involved. This section is a guide to accepted rebuilding procedures. Examples of standard rebuilding practices are illustrated and should be used along with specific details concerning your particular engine, found earlier in this chapter.

The procedures given here are those used by any competent rebuilder. Obviously some of the procedures cannot be performed by the do-it-yourself mechanic, but are provided so that you will be familiar with the services that should be offered by rebuilding or machine shops. As an example, in most instances, it is more profitable for the home mechanic to remove the cylinder heads, buy the necessary parts (new valves, seals, keepers, keys, etc.) and deliver these to a machine shop for the necessary work. In this way you will save the money to remove and install the cylinder head and the mark-up on parts.

On the other hand, most of the work involved in rebuilding the lower end is well within the scope of the do-it-yourself mechanic. Only work such as hot-tanking, actually boring the block or Magnafluxing (invisible crack detection) need be sent to a machine shop.

Tools

The tools required for basic engine rebuilding should, with a few exceptions, be those included in a mechanic's tool kit. An accurate torque wrench, and a dial indicator (reading in thousandths) mounted on a universal base should be available. Special tools, where required, are available from the major tool suppliers. The services of a competent automotive machine shop must also be readily available.

Precautions

Aluminum has become increasingly popular for use in engines, due to its low weight and excellent heat transfer characteristics. The following precautions must be observed when handling aluminum (or any other) engine parts:
—Never hot-tank aluminum parts.
—Remove all aluminum parts (identification tags, etc.) from engine parts before hot-tanking (otherwise they will be removed during the process).

—Always coat threads lightly with engine oil or anti-seize compounds before installation, to prevent seizure.
—Never over-torque bolts or spark plugs in aluminum threads. Should stripping occur, threads can be restored using any of a number of thread repair kits available (see next section).

Inspection Techniques

Magnaflux and Zyglo are inspection techniques used to locate material flaws, such as stress cracks. Magnaflux is a magnetic process, applicable only to ferrous materials. The Zyglo process coats the matrial with a fluorescent dye penetrant, and any material may be tested using Zyglo. Specific checks of suspected surface cracks may be made at lower cost and more readily using spot check dye. The dye is sprayed onto the suspected area, wiped off, and the area is then sprayed with a developer. Cracks then will show up brightly.

Overhaul

The section is divided into two parts. The first, Cylinder Head Reconditioning, assumes that the cylinder head is removed from the engine, all manifolds are removed, and the cylinder head is on a workbench. The camshaft should be removed from overhead cam cylinder heads. The second section, Cylinder Block Reconditioning, covers the block, pistons, connecting rods and crankshaft. It is assumed that the engine is mounted on a work stand, and the cylinder head and all accessories are removed.

Procedures are identified as follows:
Unmarked—Basic procedures that must be performed in order to successfully complete the rebuilding process.
Starred (*)—Procedures that should be performed to ensure maximum performance and engine life.
Double starred (**)—Procedures that may be performed to increase engine performance and reliability.

When assembling the engine, any parts that will be in frictional contact must be pre-lubricated, to provide protection on initial start-up. Any product specifically formulated for this purpose may be used. NOTE: *Do not use engine oil. Where semi-permanent* (locked but removable) installation of bolts or nuts is desired, threads should be cleaned and located with Loctite ® or a similar product (non-hardening).

Repairing Damaged Threads

Several methods of repairing damaged threads are available. Heli-Coil® (shown here), Keenserts® and Microdot® are among the most widely used. All involve basically the same principle—drilling out stripped threads, tapping the hole and installing a pre-wound insert—making welding, plugging and oversize fasteners unnecessary.

Two types of thread repair inserts are usually supplied—a standard type for most Inch Coarse, Inch Fine, Metric Coarse and Metric Fine thread sizes and a spark plug type to fit most spark plug port sizes. Consult the individual manufacturer's catalog to determine exact applications. Typical thread repair kits will contain a selection of pre-wound threaded inserts, a tap (corresponding to the outside diameter threads of the insert) and an installation tool. Spark plug inserts usually differ because they require a tap equipped with pilot threads and a combined reamer/tap section. Most manufacturers also supply blister-packed thread repair inserts separately in addition to a master kit containing a variety of taps and inserts plus installation tools.

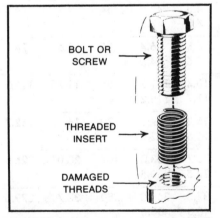

Damaged bolt holes can be repaired with thread repair inserts

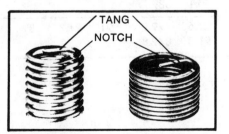

Standard thread repair insert (left) and spark plug thread insert (right)

Before effecting a repair to a threaded hole, remove any snapped, broken or damaged bolts or studs. Penetrating oil can be used to free frozen threads; the offending item can be removed with locking pliers or with a screw or stud extractor. After the hole is clear, the thread can be repaired, as follows:

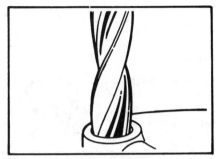

Drill out the damaged threads with specified drill. Drill completely through the hole or to the bottom of a blind hole

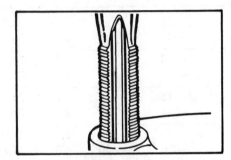

With the tap supplied, tap the hole to receive the thread insert. Keep the tap well oiled and back it out frequently to avoid clogging the threads

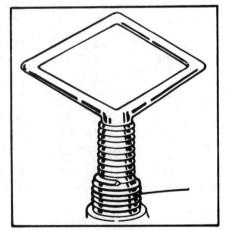

Screw the threaded insert onto the installation tool until the tang engages the slot. Screw the insert into the tapped hole until it is ¼–½ turn below the top surface. After installation break off the tang with a hammer and punch

Standard Torque Specifications and Fastener Markings

The Newton-metre has been designated the world standard for measuring torque and will gradually replace the foot-pound and kilogram-meter. In the absence of specific torques, the following chart can be used as a guide to the maximum safe torque of a particular size/grade of fastener.

- There is no torque difference for fine or coarse threads.
- Torque values are based on clean, dry threads. Reduce the value by 10% if threads are oiled prior to assembly.
- The torque required for aluminum components or fasteners is considerably less.

U. S. BOLTS

SAE Grade Number	1 or 2			5			6 or 7		

Bolt Markings

Manufacturer's marks may vary—number of lines always 2 less than the grade number.

Usage	Frequent			Frequent			Infrequent		
Bolt Size (inches)—(Thread)	Maximum Torque			Maximum Torque			Maximum Torque		
	Ft-Lb	kgm	Nm	Ft-Lb	kgm	Nm	Ft-Lb	kgm	Nm
¼—20	5	0.7	6.8	8	1.1	10.8	10	1.4	13.5
—28	6	0.8	8.1	10	1.4	13.6			
5⁄16—18	11	1.5	14.9	17	2.3	23.0	19	2.6	25.8
—24	13	1.8	17.6	19	2.6	25.7			
⅜—16	18	2.5	24.4	31	4.3	42.0	34	4.7	46.0
—24	20	2.75	27.1	35	4.8	47.5			
7⁄16—14	28	3.8	37.0	49	6.8	66.4	55	7.6	74.5
—20	30	4.2	40.7	55	7.6	74.5			
½—13	39	5.4	52.8	75	10.4	101.7	85	11.75	115.2
—20	41	5.7	55.6	85	11.7	115.2			
9⁄16—12	51	7.0	69.2	110	15.2	149.1	120	16.6	162.7
—18	55	7.6	74.5	120	16.6	162.7			
⅝—11	83	11.5	112.5	150	20.7	203.3	167	23.0	226.5
—18	95	13.1	128.8	170	23.5	230.5			
¾—10	105	14.5	142.3	270	37.3	366.0	280	38.7	379.6
—16	115	15.9	155.9	295	40.8	400.0			
⅞— 9	160	22.1	216.9	395	54.6	535.5	440	60.9	596.5
—14	175	24.2	237.2	435	60.1	589.7			
1— 8	236	32.5	318.6	590	81.6	799.9	660	91.3	894.8
—14	250	34.6	338.9	660	91.3	849.8			

METRIC BOLTS

NOTE: *Metric bolts are marked with a number indicating the relative strength of the bolt. These numbers have nothing to do with size.*

Description	Torque ft-lbs (Nm)			
Thread size x pitch (mm)	Head mark—4		Head mark—7	
6 x 1.0	2.2–2.9	(3.0–3.9)	3.6–5.8	(4.9–7.8)
8 x 1.25	5.8–8.7	(7.9–12)	9.4–14	(13–19)
10 x 1.25	12–17	(16–23)	20–29	(27–39)
12 x 1.25	21–32	(29–43)	35–53	(47–72)
14 x 1.5	35–52	(48–70)	57–85	(77–110)
16 x 1.5	51–77	(67–100)	90–120	(130–160)
18 x 1.5	74–110	(100–150)	130–170	(180–230)
20 x 1.5	110–140	(150–190)	190–240	(160–320)
22 x 1.5	150–190	(200–260)	250–320	(340–430)
24 x 1.5	190–240	(260–320)	310–410	(420–550)

NOTE: *This engine rebuilding section is a guide to accepted rebuilding procedures. Typical examples of standard rebuilding procedures are illustrated. Use these procedures along with the detailed instructions earlier in this chapter, concerning your particular engine.*

Cylinder Head Reconditioning

Procedure	Method
Remove the cylinder head:	See the engine service procedures earlier in this chapter for details concerning specific engines.
Identify the valves:	Invert the cylinder head, and number the valve faces front to rear, using a permanent felt-tip marker.
Remove the rocker arms (OHV engines only):	Remove the rocker arms with shaft(s) or balls and nuts. Wire the sets of rockers, balls and nuts together, and identify according to the corresponding valve.
Remove the camshaft (OHC engines only):	See the engine service procedures earlier in this chapter for details concerning specific engines.
Remove the valves and springs:	Using an appropriate valve spring compressor (depending on the configuration of the cylinder head), compress the valve springs. Lift out the keepers with needlenose pliers, release the compressor, and remove the valve, spring, and spring retainer. See the engine service procedures earlier in this chapter for details concerning specific engines.

Cylinder Head Reconditioning

Procedure	Method
Check the valve stem-to-guide clearance: 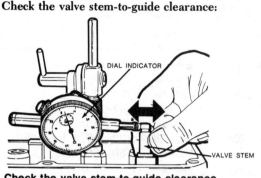 Check the valve stem-to-guide clearance	Clean the valve stem with lacquer thinner or a similar solvent to remove all gum and varnish. Clean the valve guides using solvent and an expanding wire-type valve guide cleaner. Mount a dial indicator so that the stem is at 90° to the valve stem, as close to the valve guide as possible. Move the valve off its seat, and measure the valve guide-to-stem clearance by rocking the stem back and forth to actuate the dial indicator. Measure the valve stems using a micrometer, and compare to specifications, to determine whether stem or guide wear is responsible for excessive clearance. **NOTE:** *Consult the Specifications tables earlier in this chapter.*
De-carbon the cylinder head and valves: 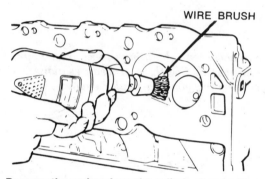 Remove the carbon from the cylinder head with a wire brush and electric drill	Chip carbon away from the valve heads, combustion chambers, and ports, using a chisel made of hardwood. Remove the remaining deposits with a stiff wire brush. **NOTE:** *Be sure that the deposits are actually removed, rather than burnished.*
Hot-tank the cylinder head (cast iron heads only): **CAUTION:** *Do not hot-tank aluminum parts.*	Have the cylinder head hot-tanked to remove grease, corrosion, and scale from the water passages. **NOTE:** *In the case of overhead cam cylinder heads, consult the operator to determine whether the camshaft bearings will be damaged by the caustic solution.*
Degrease the remaining cylinder head parts:	Clean the remaining cylinder head parts in an engine cleaning solvent. Do not remove the protective coating from the springs.
Check the cylinder head for warpage:  Check the cylinder head for warpage	Place a straight-edge across the gasket surface of the cylinder head. Using feeler gauges, determine the clearance at the center of the straight-edge. If warpage exceeds .003″ in a 6″ span, or .006″ over the total length, the cylinder head must be resurfaced. **NOTE:** *If warpage exceeds the manufacturer's maximum tolerance for material removal, the cylinder head must be replaced.* When milling the cylinder heads of V-type engines, the intake manifold mounting position is altered, and must be corrected by milling the manifold flange a proportionate amount.

Cylinder Head Reconditioning

Procedure	Method

*Knurl the valve guides:

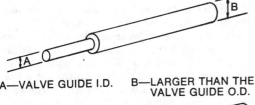

Cut-away view of a knurled valve guide

*Valve guides which are not excessively worn or distorted may, in some cases, be knurled rather than replaced. Knurling is a process in which metal is displaced and raised, thereby reducing clearance. Knurling also provides excellent oil control. The possibility of knurling rather than replacing valve guides should be discussed with a machinist.

Replace the valve guides:
NOTE: *Valve guides should only be replaced if damaged or if an oversize valve stem is not available.*

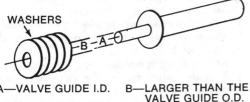

A—VALVE GUIDE I.D.   B—LARGER THAN THE VALVE GUIDE O.D.

WASHERS

A—VALVE GUIDE I.D.   B—LARGER THAN THE VALVE GUIDE O.D.

Valve guide installation tool using washers for installation

See the engine service procedures earlier in this chapter for details concerning specific engines. Depending on the type of cylinder head, valve guides may be pressed, hammered, or shrunk in. In cases where the guides are shrunk into the head, replacement should be left to an equipped machine shop. In other cases, the guides are replaced using a stepped drift (see illustration). Determine the height above the boss that the guide must extend, and obtain a stack of washers, their I.D. similar to the guide's O.D., of that height. Place the stack of washers on the guide, and insert the guide into the boss.
NOTE: *Valve guides are often tapered or beveled for installation.* Using the stepped installation tool (see illustration), press or tap the guides into position. Ream the guides according to the size of the valve stem.

Replace valve seat inserts:

Replacement of valve seat inserts which are worn beyond resurfacing or broken, if feasible, must be done by a machine shop.

Resurface (grind) the valve face:

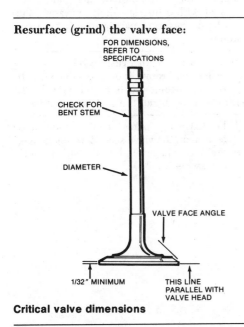

FOR DIMENSIONS, REFER TO SPECIFICATIONS

CHECK FOR BENT STEM

DIAMETER

VALVE FACE ANGLE

1/32″ MINIMUM   THIS LINE PARALLEL WITH VALVE HEAD

Critical valve dimensions

Using a valve grinder, resurface the valves according to specifications given earlier in this chapter.
CAUTION: *Valve face angle is not always identical to valve seat angle.* A minimum margin of

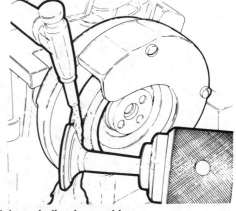

Valve grinding by machine

Cylinder Head Reconditioning

Procedure	Method
	$^1/_{32}''$ should remain after grinding the valve. The valve stem top should also be squared and resurfaced, by placing the stem in the V-block of the grinder, and turning it while pressing lightly against the grinding wheel. **NOTE:** *Do not grind sodium filled exhaust valves on a machine. These should be hand lapped.*

Resurface the valve seats using reamers or grinder:

Valve seat width and centering

Reaming the valve seat with a hand reamer

Select a reamer of the correct seat angle, slightly larger than the diameter of the valve seat, and assemble it with a pilot of the correct size. Install the pilot into the valve guide, and using steady pressure, turn the reamer clockwise.

CAUTION: *Do not turn the reamer counterclockwise.* Remove only as much material as necessary to clean the seat. Check the concentricity of the seat (following). If the dye method is not used, coat the valve face with Prussian blue dye, install and rotate it on the valve seat. Using the dye marked area as a centering guide, center and narrow the valve seat to specifications with correction cutters.

NOTE: *When no specifications are available, minimum seat width for exhaust valves should be $^5/_{64}''$, intake valves $^1/_{16}''$.*

After making correction cuts, check the position of the valve seat on the valve face using Prussian blue dye.

To resurface the seat with a power grinder, select a pilot of the correct size and coarse stone of the proper angle. Lubricate the pilot and move the stone on and off the valve seat at 2 cycles per second, until all flaws are gone. Finish the seat with a fine stone. If necessary the seat can be corrected or narrowed using correction stones.

Check the valve seat concentricity:

Check the valve seat concentricity with a dial gauge

Coat the valve face with Prussian blue dye, install the valve, and rotate it on the valve seat. If the entire seat becomes coated, and the valve is known to be concentric, the seat is concentric.

*Install the dial gauge pilot into the guide, and rest of the arm on the valve seat. Zero the gauge, and rotate the arm around the seat. Run-out should not exceed .002″.

Cylinder Head Reconditioning

Procedure	Method

*Lap the valves:
NOTE: *Valve lapping is done to ensure efficient sealing of resurfaced valves and seats.*

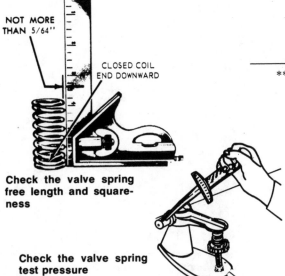

Lapping the valves by hand

Home-made valve lapping tool

HAND DRILL

ROD

SUCTION CUP

* Invert the cylinder head, lightly lubricate the valve stems, and install the valves in the head as numbered. Coat valve seats with fine grinding compound, and attach the lapping tool suction cup to a valve head.
NOTE: *Moisten the suction cup.* Rotate the tool between the palms, changing position and lifting the tool often to prevent grooving. Lap the valve until a smooth, polished seat is evident. Remove the valve and tool, and rinse away all traces of grinding compound.

** Fasten a suction cup to a piece of drill rod, and mount the rod in a hand drill. Proceed as above, using the hand drill as a lapping tool.
CAUTION: *Due to the higher speeds involved when using the hand drill, care must be exercised to avoid grooving the seat.* Lift the tool and change direction of rotation often.

Check the valve springs:

NOT MORE THAN 5/64"

CLOSED COIL END DOWNWARD

Check the valve spring free length and squareness

Check the valve spring test pressure

Place the spring on a flat surface next to a square. Measure the height of the spring, and rotate it against the edge of the square to measure distortion. If spring height varies (by comparison) by more than $1/16''$ or if distortion exceeds $1/16''$, replace the spring.

** In addition to evaluating the spring as above, test the spring pressure at the installed and compressed (installed height minus valve lift) height using a valve spring tester. Springs used on small displacement engines (up to 3 liters) should be ∓ 1 lb of all other springs in either position. A tolerance of ∓ 5 lbs is permissible on larger engines.

Cylinder Head Reconditioning

Procedure	Method

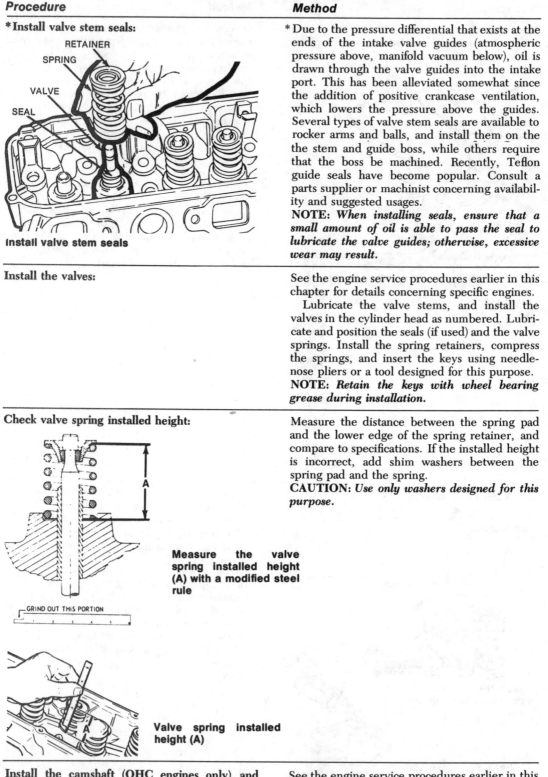

*Install valve stem seals:

RETAINER
SPRING
VALVE
SEAL

Install valve stem seals

* Due to the pressure differential that exists at the ends of the intake valve guides (atmospheric pressure above, manifold vacuum below), oil is drawn through the valve guides into the intake port. This has been alleviated somewhat since the addition of positive crankcase ventilation, which lowers the pressure above the guides. Several types of valve stem seals are available to rocker arms and balls, and install them on the the stem and guide boss, while others require that the boss be machined. Recently, Teflon guide seals have become popular. Consult a parts supplier or machinist concerning availability and suggested usages.

NOTE: *When installing seals, ensure that a small amount of oil is able to pass the seal to lubricate the valve guides; otherwise, excessive wear may result.*

Install the valves:

See the engine service procedures earlier in this chapter for details concerning specific engines.

Lubricate the valve stems, and install the valves in the cylinder head as numbered. Lubricate and position the seals (if used) and the valve springs. Install the spring retainers, compress the springs, and insert the keys using needle-nose pliers or a tool designed for this purpose.

NOTE: *Retain the keys with wheel bearing grease during installation.*

Check valve spring installed height:

Measure the distance between the spring pad and the lower edge of the spring retainer, and compare to specifications. If the installed height is incorrect, add shim washers between the spring pad and the spring.

CAUTION: *Use only washers designed for this purpose.*

A

GRIND OUT THIS PORTION

Measure the valve spring installed height (A) with a modified steel rule

A

Valve spring installed height (A)

Install the camshaft (OHC engines only) and check end-play:

See the engine service procedures earlier in this chapter for details concerning specific engines.

Cylinder Head Reconditioning

Procedure	Method

Inspect the rocker arms, balls, studs, and nuts (OHV engines only):

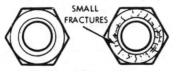

Stress cracks in the rocker nuts

Visually inspect the rocker arms, balls, studs, and nuts for cracks, galling, burning, scoring, or wear. If all parts are intact, liberally lubricate the rocker arms and balls, and install them on the cylinder head. If wear is noted on a rocker arm at the point of valve contact, grind it smooth and square, removing as little material as possible. Replace the rocker arm if excessively worn. If a rocker stud shows signs of wear, it must be replaced (see below). If a rocker nut shows stress cracks, replace it. If an exhaust ball is galled or burned, substitute the intake ball from the same cylinder (if it is intact), and install a new intake ball.

NOTE: *Avoid using new rocker balls on exhaust valves.*

Replacing rocker studs (OHV engines only):

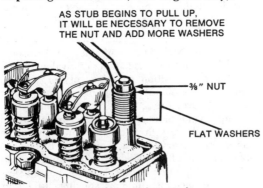

AS STUB BEGINS TO PULL UP,
IT WILL BE NECESSARY TO REMOVE
THE NUT AND ADD MORE WASHERS

⅜" NUT

FLAT WASHERS

Extracting a pressed-in rocker stud

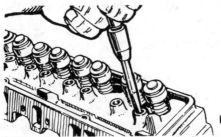

Ream the stud bore for oversize rocker studs

In order to remove a threaded stud, lock two nuts on the stud, and unscrew the stud using the lower nut. Coat the lower threads of the new stud with Loctite, and install.

Two alternative methods are available for replacing pressed in studs. Remove the damaged stud using a stack of washers and a nut (see illustration). In the first, the boss is reamed .005–.006" oversize, and an oversize stud pressed in. Control the stud extension over the boss using washers, in the same manner as valve guides. Before installing the stud, coat it with white lead and grease. To retain the stud more positively drill a hole through the stud and boss, and install a roll pin. In the second method, the boss is tapped, and a threaded stud installed.

Inspect the rocker shaft(s) and rocker arms (OHV engines only)

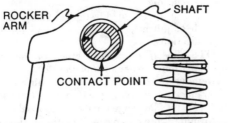

ROCKER ARM

SHAFT

CONTACT POINT

Check the rocker arm-to-rocker shaft contact area

Remove rocker arms, springs and washers from rocker shaft.

NOTE: *Lay out parts in the order as they are removed.* Inspect rocker arms for pitting or wear on the valve contact point, or excessive bushing wear. Bushings need only be replaced if wear is excessive, because the rocker arm normally contacts the shaft at one point only. Grind the valve contact point of rocker arm smooth if necessary, removing as little material as possible. If excessive material must be removed to smooth and square the arm, it should be replaced. Clean out all oil holes and passages in rocker shaft. If shaft is grooved or worn, replace it. Lubricate and assemble the rocker shaft.

Cylinder Head Reconditioning

Procedure	Method
Inspect the pushrods (OHV engines only):	Remove the pushrods, and, if hollow, clean out the oil passages using fine wire. Roll each pushrod over a piece of clean glass. If a distinct clicking sound is heard as the pushrod rolls, the rod is bent, and must be replaced.
	*The length of all pushrods must be equal. Measure the length of the pushrods, compare to specifications, and replace as necessary.
Inspect the valve lifters (OHV engines only): 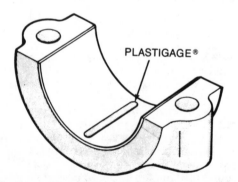 CHECK FOR CONCAVE WEAR ON FACE OF TAPPET USING TAPPET FOR STRAIGHT EDGE **Check the lifter face for squareness**	Remove lifters from their bores, and remove gum and varnish, using solvent. Clean walls of lifter bores. Check lifters for concave wear as illustrated. If face is worn concave, replace lifter, and carefully inspect the camshaft. Lightly lubricate lifter and insert it into its bore. If play is excessive, an oversize lifter must be installed (where possible). Consult a machinist concerning feasibility. If play is satisfactory, remove, lubricate, and reinstall the lifter.
*Testing hydraulic lifter leak down (OHV engines only):	Submerge lifter in a container of kerosene. Chuck a used pushrod or its equivalent into a drill press. Position container of kerosene so pushrod acts on the lifter plunger. Pump lifter with the drill press, until resistance increases. Pump several more times to bleed any air out of lifter. Apply very firm, constant pressure to the lifter, and observe rate at which fluid bleeds out of lifter. If the fluid bleeds very quickly (less than 15 seconds), lifter is defective. If the time exceeds 60 seconds, lifter is sticking. In either case, recondition or replace lifter. If lifter is operating properly (leak down time 15–60 seconds), lubricate and install it.

Cylinder Block Reconditioning

Procedure	Method
Checking the main bearing clearance: PLASTIGAGE® **Plastigage® installed on the lower bearing shell**	Invert engine, and remove cap from the bearing to be checked. Using a clean, dry rag, thoroughly clean all oil from crankshaft journal and bearing insert. NOTE: *Plastigage® is soluble in oil; therefore, oil on the journal or bearing could result in erroneous readings.* Place a piece of Plastigage along the full length of journal, reinstall cap, and torque to specifications. NOTE: *Specifications are given in the engine specifications earlier in this chapter.* Remove bearing cap, and determine bearing clearance by comparing width of Plastigage to the scale on Plastigage envelope. Journal taper is determined by comparing width of the Plastigage strip near its ends. Rotate crankshaft 90° and retest, to determine journal eccentricity. NOTE: *Do not rotate crankshaft with Plastigage*

Cylinder Block Reconditioning

Procedure	Method

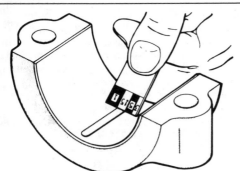

Measure Plastigage® to determine main bearing clearance

installed. If bearing insert and journal appear intact, and are within tolerances, no further main bearing service is required. If bearing or journal appear defective, cause of failure should be determined before replacement.

* Remove crankshaft from block (see below). Measure the main bearing journals at each end tiwce (90° apart) using a micrometer, to determine diameter, journal taper and eccentricity. If journals are within tolerances, reinstall bearing caps at their specified torque. Using a telescope gauge and micrometer, measure bearing I.D. parallel to piston axis and at 30° on each side of piston axis. Subtract journal O.D. from bearing I.D. to determine oil clearance. If crankshaft journals appear defective, or do not meet tolerances, there is no need to measure bearings; for the crankshaft will require grinding and/or undersize bearings will be required. If bearing appears defective, cause for failure should be determined prior to replacement.

Check the connecting rod bearing clearance:

Connecting rod bearing clearance is checked in the same manner as main bearing clearance, using Plastigage. Before removing the crankshaft, connecting rod side clearance also should be measured and recorded.

* Checking connecting rod bearing clearance, using a micrometer, is identical to checking main bearing clearance. If no other service is required, the piston and rod assemblies need not be removed.

Remove the crankshaft:

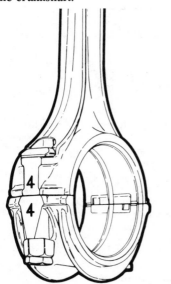

Using a punch, mark the corresponding main bearing caps and saddles according to position (i.e., one punch on the front main cap and saddle, two on the second, three on the third, etc.). Using number stamps, identify the corresponding connecting rods and caps, according to cylinder (if no numbers are present). Remove the main and connecting rod caps, and place sleeves of plastic tubing or vacuum hose over the connecting rod bolts, to protect the journals as the crankshaft is removed. Lift the crankshaft out of the block.

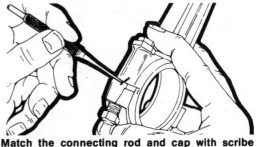

Match the connecting rod to the cylinder with a number stamp

Match the connecting rod and cap with scribe marks

Cylinder Block Reconditioning

Procedure	Method
Remove the ridge from the top of the cylinder: 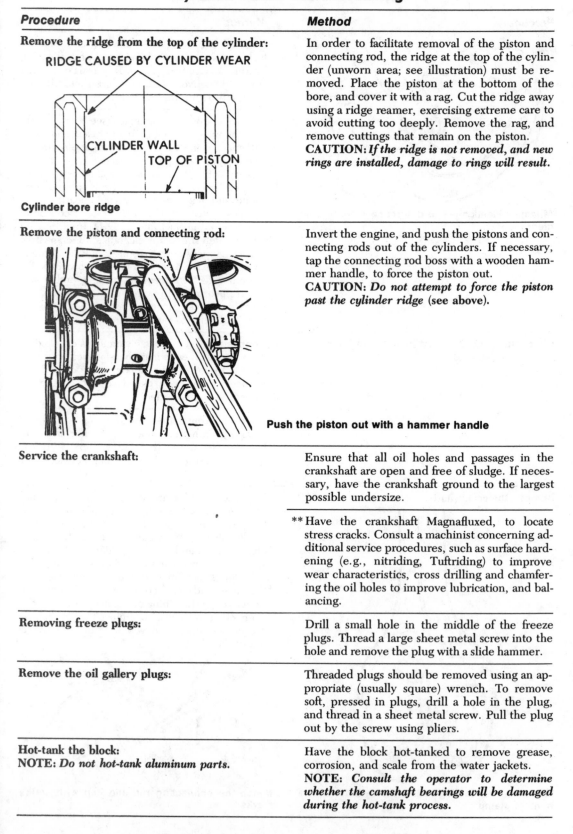 RIDGE CAUSED BY CYLINDER WEAR CYLINDER WALL TOP OF PISTON **Cylinder bore ridge**	In order to facilitate removal of the piston and connecting rod, the ridge at the top of the cylinder (unworn area; see illustration) must be removed. Place the piston at the bottom of the bore, and cover it with a rag. Cut the ridge away using a ridge reamer, exercising extreme care to avoid cutting too deeply. Remove the rag, and remove cuttings that remain on the piston. **CAUTION:** *If the ridge is not removed, and new rings are installed, damage to rings will result.*
Remove the piston and connecting rod: **Push the piston out with a hammer handle**	Invert the engine, and push the pistons and connecting rods out of the cylinders. If necessary, tap the connecting rod boss with a wooden hammer handle, to force the piston out. **CAUTION:** *Do not attempt to force the piston past the cylinder ridge* (see above).
Service the crankshaft:	Ensure that all oil holes and passages in the crankshaft are open and free of sludge. If necessary, have the crankshaft ground to the largest possible undersize.
	**Have the crankshaft Magnafluxed, to locate stress cracks. Consult a machinist concerning additional service procedures, such as surface hardening (e.g., nitriding, Tuftriding) to improve wear characteristics, cross drilling and chamfering the oil holes to improve lubrication, and balancing.
Removing freeze plugs:	Drill a small hole in the middle of the freeze plugs. Thread a large sheet metal screw into the hole and remove the plug with a slide hammer.
Remove the oil gallery plugs:	Threaded plugs should be removed using an appropriate (usually square) wrench. To remove soft, pressed in plugs, drill a hole in the plug, and thread in a sheet metal screw. Pull the plug out by the screw using pliers.
Hot-tank the block: NOTE: *Do not hot-tank aluminum parts.*	Have the block hot-tanked to remove grease, corrosion, and scale from the water jackets. **NOTE:** *Consult the operator to determine whether the camshaft bearings will be damaged during the hot-tank process.*

Cylinder Block Reconditioning

Procedure	Method
Check the block for cracks:	Visually inspect the block for cracks or chips. The most common locations are as follows: Adjacent to freeze plugs. Between the cylinders and water jackets. Adjacent to the main bearing saddles. At the extreme bottom of the cylinders. Check only suspected cracks using spot check dye (see introduction). If a crack is located, consult a machinist concerning possible repairs.
	**Magnaflux the block to locate hidden cracks. If cracks are located, consult a machinist about feasibility of repair.
Install the oil gallery plugs and freeze plugs:	Coat freeze plugs with sealer and tap into position using a piece of pipe, slightly smaller than the plug, as a driver. To ensure retention, stake the edges of the plugs. Coat threaded oil gallery plugs with sealer and install. Drive replacement soft plugs into block using a large drift as driver.
	*Rather than reinstalling lead plugs, drill and tap the holes, and install threaded plugs.
Check the bore diameter and surface: **Measure the cylinder bore with a dial gauge**	Visually inspect the cylinder bores for roughness, scoring, or scuffing. If evident, the cylinder bore must be bored or honed oversize to eliminate imperfections, and the smallest possible oversize piston used. The new pistons should be given to the machinist with the block, so that the cylinders can be bored or honed exactly to the piston size (plus clearance). If no flaws are evident, measure the bore diameter using a telescope gauge and micrometer, or dial gauge, parallel and perpendicular to the engine centerline, at the top (below the ridge) and bottom of the bore. Subtract the bottom measurements from the top to determine taper, and the parallel to the centerline measurements from the perpendicular measurements to determine eccentricity. If the measurements are not within specifications, the cylinder must be bored or honed, and an oversize piston installed. If the measurements are within specifications the cylinder may be used as is, with only finish honing (see below).

◄—CENTERLINE OF ENGINE—►

A—AT RIGHT ANGLE TO CENTERLINE OF ENGINE
B—PARALLEL TO CENTERLINE OF ENGINE

Cylinder bore measuring points

TELESCOPE GAUGE 90°
FROM PISTON PIN

Measure the cylinder bore with a telescope gauge

TELESCOPE GAUGE

MICROMETER

Measure the telescope gauge with a micrometer to determine the cylinder bore

Cylinder Block Reconditioning

Procedure	Method
	NOTE: *Prior to submitting the block for boring, perform the following operation(s).*
Check the cylinder block bearing alignment: **Check the main bearing saddle alignment**	Remove the upper bearing inserts. Place a straightedge in the bearing saddles along the centerline of the crankshaft. If clearance exists between the straightedge and the center saddle, the block must be alignbored.
*Check the deck height:	The deck height is the distance from the crankshaft centerline to the block deck. To measure, invert the engine, and install the crankshaft, retaining it with the center main cap. Measure the distance from the crankshaft journal to the block deck, parallel to the cylinder centerline. Measure the diameter of the end (front and rear) main journals, parallel to the centerline of the cylinders, divide the diameter in half, and subtract it from the previous measurement. The results of the front and rear measurements should be identical. If the difference exceeds .005″, the deck height should be corrected. NOTE: *Block deck height and warpage should be corrected at the same time.*
Check the block deck for warpage:	Using a straightedge and feeler gauges, check the block deck for warpage in the same manner that the cylinder head is checked (see Cylinder Head Reconditioning). If warpage exceeds specifications, have the deck resurfaced. NOTE: *In certain cases a specification for total material removal (Cylinder head and block deck) is provided. This specification must not be exceeded.*
Clean and inspect the pistons and connecting rods: RING EXPANDER **Remove the piston rings**	Using a ring expander, remove the rings from the piston. Remove the retaining rings (if so equipped) and remove piston pin. NOTE: *If the piston pin must be pressed out, determine the proper method and use the proper tools; otherwise the piston will distort.* Clean the ring grooves using an appropriate tool, exercising care to avoid cutting too deeply. Thoroughly clean all carbon and varnish from the piston with solvent. CAUTION: *Do not use a wire brush or caustic solvent on pistons.* Inspect the pistons for scuffing, scoring, cracks, pitting, or excessive ring groove wear. If wear is evident, the piston must be replaced. Check the connecting rod length by measuring the rod from the inside of the large end to the

Cylinder Block Reconditioning

Procedure	Method

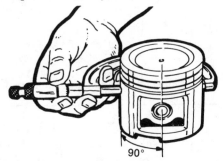

RING GROOVE
CLEANER

Clean the piston ring grooves

inside of the small end using calipers (see illustration). All connecting rods should be equal length. Replace any rod that differs from the others in the engine.

* Have the connecting rod alignment checked in an alignment fixture by a machinist. Replace any twisted or bent rods.

* Magnaflux the connecting rods to locate stress cracks. If cracks are found, replace the connecting rod.

Check the connecting rod length (arrow)

Fit the pistons to the cylinders:

Measure the piston prior to fitting

90°

Using a telescope gauge and micrometer, or a dial gauge, measure the cylinder bore diameter perpendicular to the piston pin, 2½″ below the deck. Measure the piston perpendicular to its pin on the skirt. The difference between the two measurements is the piston clearance. If the clearance is within specifications or slightly below (after boring or honing), finish honing is all that is required. If the clearance is excessive, try to obtain a slightly larger piston to bring clearance within specifications. Where this is not possible, obtain the first oversize piston, and hone (or if necessary, bore) the cylinder to size.

Assemble the pistons and connecting rods:

Install the piston pin lock-rings (if used)

Inspect piston pin, connecting rod small end bushing, and piston bore for galling, scoring, or excessive wear. If evident, replace defective part(s). Measure the I.D. of the piston boss and connecting rod small end, and the O.D. of the piston pin. If within specifications, assemble piston pin and rod.
CAUTION: *If piston pin must be pressed in, determine the proper method and use the proper tools; otherwise the piston will distort.*
Install the lock rings; ensure that they seat properly. If the parts are not within specifications, determine the service method for the type of engine. In some cases, piston and pin are serviced as an assembly when either is defective. Others specify reaming the piston and connecting rods for an oversize pin. If the connecting rod bushing is worn, it may in many cases be replaced. Reaming the piston and replacing the rod bushing are machine shop operations.

Cylinder Block Reconditioning

Procedure	Method

Clean and inspect the camshaft:

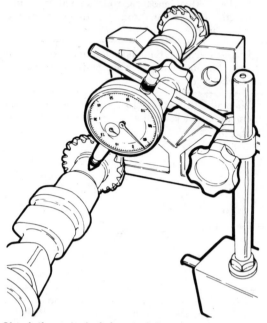

Check the camshaft for straightness

Degrease the camshaft, using solvent, and clean out all oil holes. Visually inspect cam lobes and bearing journals for excessive wear. If a lobe is questionable, check all lobes as indicated below. If a journal or lobe is worn, the camshaft must be reground or replaced.

NOTE: *If a journal is worn, there is a good chance that the bushings are worn.* If lobes and journals appear intact, place the front and rear journals in V-blocks, and rest a dial indicator on the center journal. Rotate the camshaft to check straightness. If deviation exceeds .001″, replace the camshaft.

*Check the camshaft lobes with a micrometer, by measuring the lobes from the nose to base and again at 90° (see illustration). The lift is determined by subtracting the second measurement from the first. If all exhaust lobes and all intake lobes are not identical, the camshaft must be reground or replaced.

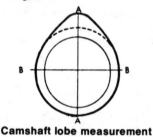

Camshaft lobe measurement

Replace the camshaft bearings (OHV engines only):

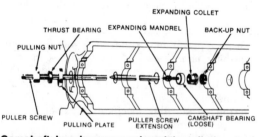

Camshaft bearing removal and installation tool (OHV engines only)

If excessive wear is indicated, or if the engine is being completely rebuilt, camshaft bearings should be replaced as follows: Drive the camshaft rear plug from the block. Assemble the removal puller with its shoulder on the bearing to be removed. Gradually tighten the puller nut until bearing is removed. Remove remaining bearings, leaving the front and rear for last. To remove front and rear bearings, reverse position of the tool, so as to pull the bearings in toward the center of the block. Leave the tool in this position, pilot the new front and rear bearings on the installer, and pull them into position: Return the tool to its original position and pull remaining bearings into position.

NOTE: *Ensure that oil holes align when installing bearings.* Replace camshaft rear plug, and stake it into position to aid retention.

Finish hone the cylinders:

Chuck a flexible drive hone into a power drill, and insert it into the cylinder. Start the hone, and move it up and down in the cylinder at a rate which will produce approximately a 60° crosshatch pattern.

NOTE: *Do not extend the hone below the cylin-*

Cylinder Block Reconditioning

Procedure	Method

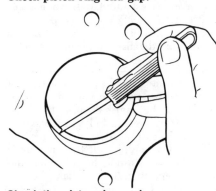

CROSS HATCH PATTERN

50°-60°

Cylinder bore after honing

der bore. After developing the pattern, remove the hone and recheck piston fit. Wash the cylinders with a detergent and water solution to remove abrasive dust, dry, and wipe several times with a rag soaked in engine oil.

Check piston ring end-gap:

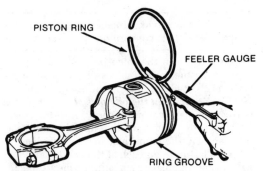

Check the piston ring end gap

Compress the piston rings to be used in a cylinder, one at a time, into that cylinder, and press them approximately 1″ below the deck with an inverted piston. Using feeler gauges, measure the ring end-gap, and compare to specifications. Pull the ring out of the cylinder and file the ends with a fine file to obtain proper clearance.
CAUTION: *If inadequate ring end-gap is utilized, ring breakage will result.*

Install the piston rings:

PISTON RING

FEELER GAUGE

RING GROOVE

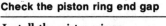
Check the piston ring side clearance

Inspect the ring grooves in the piston for excessive wear or taper. If necessary, recut the grooves(s) for use with an overwidth ring or a standard ring and spacer. If the groove is worn uniformly, overwidth rings, or standard rings and spacers may be installed without recutting. Roll the outside of the ring around the groove to check for burrs or deposits. If any are found, remove with a fine file. Hold the ring in the groove, and measure side clearance. If necessary, correct as indicated above.
NOTE: *Always install any additional spacers above the piston ring.*
The ring groove must be deep enough to allow the ring to seat below the lands (see illustration). In many cases, a "go-no-go" depth gauge will be provided with the piston rings. Shallow grooves may be corrected by recutting, while deep grooves require some type of filler or expander behind the piston. Consult the piston ring sup-

Cylinder Block Reconditioning

Procedure	Method
	plier concerning the suggested method. Install the rings on the piston, lowest ring first, using a ring expander. NOTE: *Position the ring as specified by the manufacturer.* Consult the engine service procedures earlier in this chapter for details concerning specific engines.
Install the camshaft (OHV engines only):	Liberally lubricate the camshaft lobes and journals, and install the camshaft. CAUTION: *Exercise extreme care to avoid damaging the bearings when inserting the camshaft.* Install and tighten the camshaft thrust plate retaining bolts. See the engine service procedures earlier in this chapter for details concerning specific engines.
Check camshaft end-play (OHV engines only): Check the camshaft end-play with a feeler gauge	Using feeler gauges, determine whether the clearance between the camshaft boss (or gear) and backing plate is within specifications. Install shims behind the thrust plate, or reposition the camshaft gear and retest endplay. In some cases, adjustment is by replacing the thrust plate. See the engine service procedures earlier in this chapter for details concerning specific engines.
DIAL INDICATOR CAMSHAFT Check the camshaft end-play with a dial indicator	*Mount a dial indicator stand so that the stem of the dial indicator rests on the nose of the camshaft, parallel to the camshaft axis. Push the camshaft as far in as possible and zero the gauge. Move the camshaft outward to determine the amount of camshaft endplay. If the endplay is not within tolerance, install shims behind the thrust plate, or reposition the camshaft gear and retest. See the engine service procedures earlier in this chapter for details concerning specific engines.
Install the rear main seal:	See the engine service procedures earlier in this chapter for details concerning specific engines.
Install the crankshaft: INSTALLING BEARING SHELL REMOVING BEARING SHELL Remove or install the upper bearing insert using a roll-out pin	Thoroughly clean the main bearing saddles and caps. Place the upper halves of the bearing inserts on the saddles and press into position. NOTE: *Ensure that the oil holes align.* Press the corresponding bearing inserts into the main bearing caps. Lubricate the upper main bearings, and lay the crankshaft in position. Place a strip of Plastigage on each of the crankshaft journals, install the main caps, and torque to specifications. Remove the main caps, and compare the Plastigage to the scale on the Plastigage envelope. If clearances are within tolerances, remove the Plastigage, turn the crankshaft 90°, wipe off all oil and retest. If all clearances are correct, re-

Cylinder Block Reconditioning

Procedure	Method

Home-made bearing roll-out pin

move all Plastigage, thoroughly lubricate the main caps and bearing journals, and install the main caps. If clearances are not within tolerance, the upper bearing inserts may be removed, without removing the crankshaft, using a bearing roll out pin (see illustration). Roll in a bearing that will provide proper clearance, and retest. Torque all main caps, excluding the thrust bearing cap, to specifications. Tighten the thrust bearing cap finger tight. To properly align the thrust bearing, pry the crankshaft the extent of its axial travel several times, the last movement held toward the front of the engine, and torque the thrust bearing cap to specifications. Determine the crankshaft end-play (see below), and bring within tolerance with thrust washers.

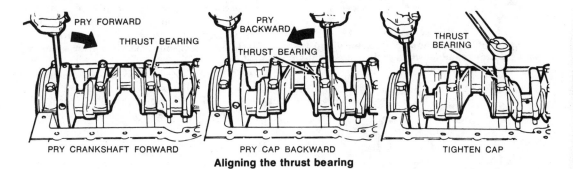

Aligning the thrust bearing

Measure crankshaft end-play:

Mount a dial indicator stand on the front of the block, with the dial indicator stem resting on the nose of the crankshaft, parallel to the crankshaft axis. Pry the crankshaft the extent of its travel rearward, and zero the indicator. Pry the crankshaft forward and record crankshaft end-play.
NOTE: *Crankshaft end-play also may be measured at the thrust bearing, using feeler gauges* (see illustration).

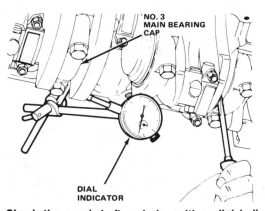

Check the crankshaft end-play with a dial indicator

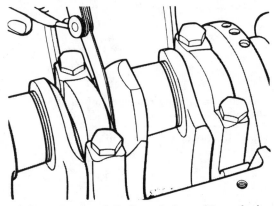

Check the crankshaft end-play with a feeler gauge

Cylinder Block Reconditioning

Procedure	Method

Install the pistons:

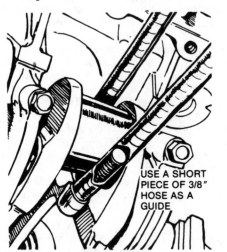

USE A SHORT PIECE OF 3/8" HOSE AS A GUIDE

Use lengths of vacuum hose or rubber tubing to protect the crankshaft journals and cylinder walls during piston installation

RING COMPRESSOR

Install the piston using a ring compressor

Press the upper connecting rod bearing halves into the connecting rods, and the lower halves into the connecting rod caps. Position the piston ring gaps according to specifications (see car section), and lubricate the pistons. Install a ring compresser on a piston, and press two long (8") pieces of plastic tubing over the rod bolts. Using the tubes as a guide, press the pistons into the bores and onto the crankshaft with a wooden hammer handle. After seating the rod on the crankshaft journal, remove the tubes and install the cap finger tight. Install the remaining pistons in the same manner. Invert the engine and check the bearing clearance at two points (90° apart) on each journal with Plastigage.

NOTE: *Do not turn the crankshaft with Plastigage installed.* If clearance is within tolerances, remove *all* Plastigage, thoroughly lubricate the journals, and torque the rod caps to specifications. If clearance is not within specifications, install different thickness bearing inserts and recheck.

CAUTION: *Never shim or file the connecting rods or caps.* Always install plastic tube sleeves over the rod bolts when the caps are not installed, to protect the crankshaft journals.

Check connecting rod side clearance:

Check the connecting rod side clearance with a feeler gauge

Determine the clearance between the sides of the connecting rods and the crankshaft, using feeler gauges. If clearance is below the minimum tolerance, the rod may be machined to provide adequate clearance. If clearance is excessive, substitute an unworn rod, and recheck. If clearance is still outside specifications, the crankshaft must be welded and reground, or replaced.

Inspect the timing chain (or belt):

Visually inspect the timing chain for broken or loose links, and replace the chain if any are found. If the chain will flex sideways, it must be replaced. Install the timing chain as specified. Be sure the timing belt is not stretched, frayed or broken.

NOTE: *If the original timing chain is to be reused, install it in its original position.*

Cylinder Block Reconditioning

Procedure	Method
Check timing gear backlash and runout (OHV engines):  Check the camshaft gear backlash	Mount a dial indicator with its stem resting on a tooth of the camshaft gear (as illustrated). Rotate the gear until all slack is removed, and zero the indicator. Rotate the gear in the opposite direction until slack is removed, and record gear backlash. Mount the indicator with its stem resting on the edge of the camshaft gear, parallel to the axis of the camshaft. Zero the indicator, and turn the camshaft gear one full turn, recording the runout. If either backlash or runout exceed specifications, replace the worn gear(s). 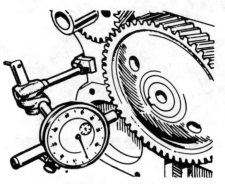 Check the camshaft gear run-out

Completing the Rebuilding Process

Following the above procedures, complete the rebuilding process as follows:

Fill the oil pump with oil, to prevent cavitating (sucking air) on initial engine start up. Install the oil pump and the pickup tube on the engine. Coat the oil pan gasket as necessary, and install the gasket and the oil pan. Mount the flywheel and the crankshaft vibration damper or pulley on the crankshaft. NOTE: *Always use new bolts when installing the flywheel.* Inspect the clutch shaft pilot bushing in the crankshaft. If the bushing is excessively worn, remove it with an expanding puller and a slide hammer, and tap a new bushing into place.

Position the engine, cylinder head side up. Lubricate the lifters, and install them into their bores. Install the cylinder head, and torque it as specified. Insert the pushrods (where applicable), and install the rocker shaft(s) (if so equipped) or position the rocker arms on the pushrods. Adjust the valves.

Install the intake and exhaust manifolds, the carburetor(s), the distributor and spark plugs. Adjust the point gap and the static ignition timing. Mount all accessories and install the engine in the car. Fill the radiator with coolant, and the crankcase with high quality engine oil.

Break-in Procedure

Start the engine, and allow it to run at low speed for a few minutes, while checking for leaks. Stop the engine, check the oil level, and fill as necessary. Restart the engine, and fill the cooling system to capacity. Check the point dwell angle and adjust the ignition timing and the valves. Run the engine at low to medium speed (800–2500 rpm) for approximately ½ hour, and retorque the cylinder head bolts. Road test the car, and check again for leaks.

Follow the manufacturer's recommended engine break-in procedure and maintenance schedule for new engines.

Emission Controls and Fuel System

EMISSION CONTROLS

There are three types of automotive pollutants; crankcase fumes, exhaust gases and gasoline evaporation. The equipment that is used to limit these pollutants is commonly called emission control equipment.

Crankcase Emission Controls

The crankcase emission control equipment consists of a positive crankcase ventilation valve (PCV), a closed or open oil filler cap and hoses to connect this equipment.

When the engine is running, a small portion of the gases which are formed in the combustion chamber during combustion leak by the piston rings and enter the crankcase. Since these gases are under pressure they tend to escape from the crankcase and enter into the atmosphere. If these gases were allowed to remain in the crankcase, they would contaminate the engine oil and cause sludge to build up. If the gases are allowed to escape into the atmosphere, they would pollute the air, as they contain unburned hydrocarbons. The crankcase emission control equipment recycles these gases back into the engine combustion chamber where they are burned.

Crankcase gases are recycled in the following manner: while the engine is running, clean filtered air is drawn into the crankcase through the carburetor air filter and then through a hose leading to the rocker cover. As the air passes through the crankcase it picks up the combustion gases and carries them out of the crankcase, up through the PCV valve and into the intake manifold. After they enter the intake manifold they are drawn into the combustion chamber and burned.

The most critical component in the system is the PCV valve. This vacuum controlled valve regulates the amount of gases which are recycled into the combustion chamber. At low engine speeds the valve is partially closed, limiting the flow of gases into the intake manifold. As engine speed increases, the valve opens to admit greater quantities of the gases into the intake manifold. If the valve should become blocked or plugged, the gases will be prevented from escaping from the crankcase by the normal route. Since these gases are under pressure, they will find their own way out of the crankcase. This alternate route is usually a weak oil seal or gasket in the engine. As the gas escapes by the gasket, it also creates an oil leak. Besides causing oil leaks, a clogged PCV valve also allows these gases to remain in the crankcase, promoting the formation of sludge in the engine.

The above explanation and the trouble-

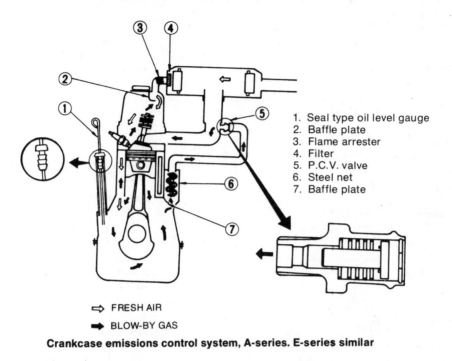

1. Seal type oil level gauge
2. Baffle plate
3. Flame arrester
4. Filter
5. P.C.V. valve
6. Steel net
7. Baffle plate

⇨ FRESH AIR

➡ BLOW-BY GAS

Crankcase emissions control system, A-series. E-series similar

shooting procedure which follows applies to all engines with PCV systems.

TESTING

Check the PCV system hoses and connections, to see that there are no leaks; then replace or tighten, as necessary.

To check the valve, remove it and blow through both of its ends. When blowing from the side which goes toward the intake manifold, very little air should pass through it. When blowing from the crankcase (valve cover) side, air should pass through freely.

Replace the valve with a new one, if the valve fails to function as outlined.

NOTE: *Do not attempt to clean or adjust the valve; replace it with a new one.*

REMOVAL AND INSTALLATION

To remove the PCV valve, simply loosen the hose clamp and remove the valve from the manifold-to-crankcase hose and intake manifold. Install the PCV valve in the reverse order of removal.

PCV FILTER

Replace the PCV filter inside the air cleaner when you replace the PCV valve, or more frequently if operating in dusty or smoggy conditions.

Evaporative Emission Control System

When raw fuel evaporates, the vapors contain hydrocarbons. To prevent these nasties from escaping into the atmosphere, the fuel evaporative emission control system was developed.

There are two different evaporative emission control systems used on Datsuns.

The system used through 1974 consists of a sealed fuel tank, a vapor-liquid separator, a flow guide (check) valve, and all of the hoses connecting these components, in the above order, leading from the fuel tank to the PCV

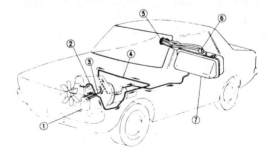

1. Carbon canister
2. Vacuum signal line
3. Canister vent line
4. Vapor vent line
5. Fuel filler cap with vacuum relief valve
6. Fuel check valve
7. Fuel tank

Evaporative emission control system schematic

hose, which connects the crankcase to the PCV valve.

In operation, the vapor formed in the fuel tank passes through the vapor separator, onto the flow guide valve and the crankcase. When the engine is not running, if the fuel vapor pressure in the vapor separator goes above 0.4 in. Hg, the flow guide valve opens and allows the vapor to enter the engine crankcase. Otherwise the flow guide valve is closed to the vapor separator while the engine is not running. When the engine is running, and a vacuum is developed in the fuel tank or in the engine crankcase and the difference of pressure between the relief side and the fuel tank or crankcase becomes 2 in. Hg, the relief valve opens and allows ambient air from the air cleaner into the fuel tank or the engine crankcase. This ambient air replaces the vapor within the fuel tank or crankcase, bringing the fuel tank or crankcase back into a neutral or positive pressure range.

The system used on 1975 and later models consists of sealed fuel tank, vapor-liquid separator (certain models only), vapor-liquid separator (certain models only), vapor vent line, carbon canister, vacuum signal line and a canister purge line.

In operation, fuel vapors and/or liquid are routed to the liquid/vapor separator or check valve where liquid fuel is directed back into the fuel tank as fuel vapors flow into the charcoal filled canister. The charcoal absorbs and stores the fuel vapors when the engine is not running or is at idle. When the throttle valves in the carburetor (or air intakes for fuel injection) are opened, vacuum from above the throttle valves is routed through a vacuum signal line to the purge control valve on the canister. The control valve opens and allows the fuel vapors to be drawn from the canister through a purge line and into the intake manifold and the combustion chambers.

INSPECTION AND SERVICE

Check the hoses for proper connections and damage. Replace as necessary. Check the vapor separator tank for fuel leaks, distortion and dents, and replace as necessary.

Flow Guide Valve—Through 1974

Remove the flow guide valve and inspect it for leakage by blowing air into the ports in the valve. When air is applied from the fuel tank side, the flow guide valve is normal if the air passes into the check side (crankcase side), but not into the relief side (air cleaner side). When air is applied from the check side, the valve is normal if the passage of air is restricted. When air is applied from the relief side (air cleaner side). When air is applied from the check side, the valve is normal if the passage of air is restricted. When air is applied from the relief side (air cleaner side), the valve is normal if air passes into the fuel tank side or into the check side.

Carbon Canister and Purge Control Valve—1975 and Later

To check the operation of the carbon canister purge control valve, disconnect the rubber hose between the canister control valve and the T-fitting, at the T-fitting. Inhale air on the hose leading to the control valve. Make sure there are no leaks. If the control valve leaks, remove the top cover of the valve and check for a dislocated or cracked diaphragm. If the diaphragm is damaged, a repair kit containing a new diaphragm, retainer, and spring is available and should be installed.

The carbon canister has an air filter in the bottom of the canister. The filter element should be checked once a year or every 12,000 miles; more frequently if the car is operated in dusty areas. Replace the filter by pulling it out of the bottom of the canister and installing a new one.

Applying vacuum to carbon canister

REMOVAL AND INSTALLATION

Removal and installation of the various evaporative emission control-system components consists of disconnecting the hoses, loosening retaining screws, and removing the part which is to be replaced or checked. Install in the reverse order. When replacing hose, make sure that it is fuel and vapor resistant.

Spark Timing Control System

The spark timing control system has been used in different forms on Datsuns since 1972.

The first system, Transmission Controlled Spark System (TCS) was used on most Datsuns through 1979. This system consists of a thermal vacuum valve, a vacuum switching valve, a high gear detecting switch, and a number of vacuum hoses. Basically, the system is designed to retard full spark advance except when the car is in high gear and the engine is at normal operating temperature. At all other times, the spark advance is retarded to one degree or another.

The 1980 and later Spark Timing Control System replaces the TCS system. The major difference is that it works solely from engine water temperature changes rather than a transmission-mounted switch. The system includes a thermal vacuum valve, a vacuum delay valve, and attendant hoses. It performs the same function as the earlier TCS system; to retard full spark advance at times when high levels of pollutants would otherwise be given off.

INSPECTION AND ADJUSTMENTS

Normally the TCS and Spark Timing Control systems should be trouble-free. However, if you suspect a problem in the system, first check to make sure all wiring (if so equipped) and hoses are connected and free from dirt. Also check to make sure the distributor vacuum advance is working properly. If everything appears all right, connect a timing light to the engine and make sure the initial timing is correct. On vehicles with the TCS system, run the engine until it reaches normal operating temperature, and then have an assistant sit in the car and shift the transmission through all the gears slowly. If the system is functioning properly, the timing will be 10 to 15 degrees advanced in high gear (compared to the other gear positions). If the system is still not operating correctly, you will have to check for continuity at all the connections with a test light.

To test the Spark Timing Control System, connect a timing light and check the ignition timing while the temperature gauge is in the "cold" position. Write down the reading. Allow the engine to run with the timing light attached until the temperature needle reaches the center of the gauge. As the engine is warming up, check with the timing light to make sure the ignition timing retards. When the temperature needle is in the middle of the gauge, the ignition timing should advance from its previous position. If the igni-

tion timing does not change, replace the thermal vacuum valve.

Early Fuel Evaporation System

The Early Fuel Evaporation System is used on the A-series engines. The system's purpose is to heat the air/fuel mixture when the engine is below normal operating temperature. The 1973–79 engines use a system much akin to the old style exhaust manifold heat riser. The only adjustment necessary is to occasionally lubricate the counterweight, with a spray-type heat riser lubricant. Other than that, the system should be trouble-free.

The 1980 and later engines use coolant water instead of exhaust gas heat to pre-warm the fuel mixture. This system should be trouble-free.

Throttle Opener Control System (TOCS)

The Throttle Opener Control System (TOCS) used on the A-series engines (except 1980 and later California cars) and Canadian Sentras is designed to reduce hydrocarbon emissions during coasting conditions.

During coasting, high manifold vacuum prevents the complete combustion of the air/fuel mixture because of the reduced amount of air. This condition will result in a large amount of hydrocarbon (HC) emission. Enriching the air/fuel mixture for a short time (during the high vacuum condition) will reduce the emission of the HC. However, enriching the air/fuel mixture with only the mixture adjusting screw will cause poor engine idle or invite an increase in the carbon monoxide (CO) content of the exhaust gases.

The TOCS system used on the 1980 and later A-series non-California cars and Canadian Sentras consists of a servo diaphragm, vacuum control valve, throttle opener solenoid valve, speed detecting switch and amplifier (on manual transmission models). Automatic transmission models use the speed detecting switch and amplifier. At the moment when manifold vacuum increases, as during deceleration, the vacuum control valve opens to transfer the manifold vacuum to the servo diaphragm chamber, and the carburetor throttle valve opens slightly. Under this condition, the proper amount of fresh air is sucked into the combustion chamber, resulting in a more thorough ignition and more complete burning of the HC in the exhaust gases.

ADJUSTMENT—TOCS

1. Connect a tachometer to the engine.
2. Connect a quick-response vacuum gauge to the intake manifold.
3. Disconnect the solenoid valve electrical leads.
4. Start and warm up the engine until it reaches normal operating temperature.
5. Adjust the idle speed to the proper specification (see Tune Up Specifications chart).
6. Raise the engine speed to 3,000–3,500 rpm under no-load (transmission in Neutral or Park), then allow the throttle to snap closed

Adjusting the TOCS pressure

Connect a quick response vacuum gauge to intake manifold when checking Throttle Opener Control System (TOCS)

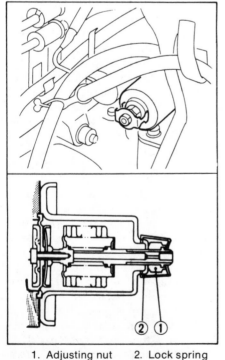

1. Adjusting nut   2. Lock spring
TOCS location and adjustment

quickly. Take notice as to whether or not the engine rpm returns to idle speed and if it does, how long the fall in rpm is interrupted before it reaches idle speed.

At the moment the throttle is snapped shut at high engine rpm, the vacuum in the intake manifold reaches between −23.6 in. Hg or above, then gradually decreases to idle level.

The pressure of the TOCS while operating should be −22.05± 0.79 in. Hg.

Turning the adjusting screw clockwise raises the vacuum level. Turning the screw counterclockwise lowers the vacuum level.

NOTE: *When adjusting the TOCS, turn the adjusting nut in or out with the lock spring in place. Always set the lock spring properly to prevent changes in the set pressure.*

Automatic Temperature Controlled Air Cleaner

The rate of fuel atomization (the process where the liquid gasoline is changed into a very fine mist) varies with the temperature of the air with which the fuel is being mixed. Because your car operates in a wide range of air temperatures, this air/fuel ratio cannot be held constant for efficient fuel combustion. Cold air drawn into the engine causes a denser and richer air/fuel mixture, inefficient fuel atomization, and thus, more hydrocarbons in the exhaust gas. Hot air drawn into the engine causes a leaner air/fuel mixture and more efficient atomization and combustion for less hydrocarbons in the exhaust gases.

The automatic temperature controlled air cleaner is designed so that the temperature of the ambient air being drawn into the engine is automatically controlled, to hold the temperature of the air and, consequently, the fuel/air ratio at a constant rate for efficient fuel combustion.

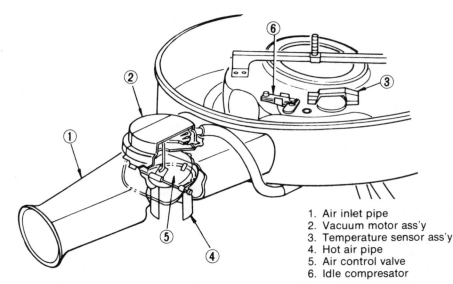

1. Air inlet pipe
2. Vacuum motor ass'y
3. Temperature sensor ass'y
4. Hot air pipe
5. Air control valve
6. Idle compresator

Automatic temperature controlled air cleaner, B210 and 210. Sentra similar

A temperature sensing vacuum switch controls vacuum applied to a vacuum motor operating a valve in the intake snorkle of the air cleaner. When the engine is cold or the air being drawn into the engine is cold, the vacuum motor opens the valve, allowing air heated by the exhaust manifold to be drawn into the engine. As the engine warms up, the temperature sensing unit shuts off the vacuum applied to the vacuum motor which allows the valve to close, shutting off the heated air and allowing cooler, outside (under hood) air to be drawn into the engine.

TESTING

When the air around the temperature sensor of the unit mounted inside the air cleaner housing reaches 100°F, the sensor should block the flow of vacuum to the air control valve vacuum motor. When the temperature around the temperature sensor is below 100°F, the sensor should allow vacuum to pass onto the air valve vacuum motor thus blocking off the air cleaner snorkle to under hood (unheated) air.

When the temperature around the sensor is above 118°F, the air control valve should be completely open to under hood air.

If the air cleaner fails to operate correctly, check for loose or broken vacuum hoses. If the hoses are not the cause, replace the vacuum motor in the air cleaner.

Exhaust Gas Recirculation (EGR)

The EGR system is used on all 1974 and later B210 and 210 model Datsuns and Nissan Sentras. Exhaust gas recirculation is used to reduce combustion temperatures in the engine, thereby reducing the oxides of nitrogen emissions.

An EGR valve is mounted on the center of the intake manifold. The recycled exhaust gas is drawn into the bottom of the intake manifold riser portion through the exhaust manifold heat stove and EGR valve. A vacuum diaphragm is connected to a timed signal port at the carburetor flange.

As the throttle valve is opened, vacuum is applied to the EGR valve vacuum diaphragm. When the vacuum reaches about 2 in. Hg, the diaphragm moves against spring pressure and is in a fully up position at 8 in. Hg of vacuum. As the diaphragm moves up, it opens the exhaust gas metering valve which allows exhaust gas to be pulled into the engine intake manifold. The system does not operate when the engine is idling because the

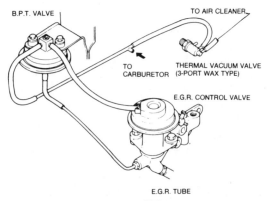

1980 210 Thermal Vacuum Valve

E-series EGR location on side of intake manifold

exhaust gas recirculation would cause a rough idle.

On 1975 and later models, a thermal vacuum valve inserted in the engine thermostat housing controls the application of the vacuum to the EGR valve. When the engine coolant reaches a predetermined temperature, the thermal vacuum valve opens and allows vacuum to be routed to the EGR valve. Below the predetermined temperature, the thermal vacuum valve closes and blocks vacuum to the EGR valve.

All 1978–80 B210 and 210 models have a B.P.T. (Back Pressure Transducer) valve installed between the EGR valve and the thermal vacuum valve. The B.P.T. valve monitors exhaust pressure in order to control, through its diaphragm, carburetor throttle vacuum applied to the EGR valve. The diaphragm opens and closes an air bleed, which is connected into the EGR vacuum line. High pressure results in higher levels of exhaust recirculation, because the diaphragm is raised, closing off the air bleed, and allowing more vacuum to reach and open the EGR valve. Thus, the amount of recirculated exhaust gas varies with exhaust pressure.

The 1980 California 210 and all 1981 and later U.S. 210s and Nissan Sentras use a V.V.T. valve (venturi vacuum transducer) in place of the B.P.T. valve. the V.V.T. monitors exhaust pressure and carburetor vacuum in order to activate the diaphragm which controls the throttle vacuum applied to the EGR control valve. This system expands the operating range of the EGR unit, as well as increasing the EGR flow rate as compared to the B.P.T. unit.

Many 1975 and later Datsuns are equipped with an EGR warning system which signals via a light in the dashboard that the EGR system may need service. The EGR warning light should come on every time the starter is engaged as a test to make sure the bulb is

not blown. The system uses a counter which works in conjunction with the odometer, and lights the warning signal after the vehicle has traveled a pre-determined number of miles.

To reset the counter, which is mounted in the engine compartment, remove the grommet installed in the side of the counter and insert the tip of a small screwdriver into the hole. Press down on the knob inside the hole. Reinstall the grommet.

TESTING—PRE-1975

Check the operation of the EGR system as follows:

1. Visually inspect the entire EGR control system. Clean the mechanism free of oil and dirt. Replace any rubber hoses found to be cracked or broken.

2. Make sure that the EGR solenoid valve is properly wired.

3. Increase the engine speed from idling to 2,000–3,500 rpm. The plate of the EGR control valve diaphragm and the valve shaft should move upward as the engine speed is increased.

4. Disconnect the EGR solenoid valve electrical leads and connect them directly to the vehicle's 12-volt electrical supply (battery). Race the engine again with the EGR solenoid valve connected to a 12-volt power source. The EGR control valve should remain stationary.

5. With the engine running at idle, push up on the EGR control valve diaphragm with your finger. When this is done, the engine idle should become rough and uneven.

Inspect the two components of the EGR system as necessary in the following manner:

a. Remove the EGR control valve from the intake manifold;

b. Apply 4.7–5.1 in. Hg of vacuum to the EGR control valve by sucking on a tube attached to the outlet on top of the valve. The valve should move to the full up position. The valve should remain open for more than 30 seconds after the application of vacuum is discontinued and the vacuum hose is blocked;

c. Inspect the EGR valve for any signs of warpage or damage;

d. Clean the EGR valve seat with a brush and compressed air to prevent clogging;

e. Connect the EGR solenoid valve to a 12-volt DC power source and notice if the valve clicks when intermittently electrified. If the valve clicks, it is considered to be working properly;

f. Check the EGR temperature sensing switch by removing it from the engine and placing it in a container of water together with a thermometer. Connect a self-powered test light to the two electrical leads of the switch;

g. Heat the container of water;

h. The switch should conduct current when the water temperature is below 77°F and stop conducting current when the water reaches a temperature somewhere between 88°–106°F. Replace the switch if it functions otherwise.

1975 and Later

1. Remove the EGR valve and apply enough vacuum to the diaphragm to open the valve.

2. The valve should remain open for over 30 seconds after the vacuum is removed.

3. Check the valve for damage, such as warpage, cracks, and excessive wear around the valve and seat.

4. Clean the seat with a brush and compressed air and remove any deposits from around the valve and port (seat).

5. To check the operation of the thermal vacuum valve, remove the valve from the engine and apply vacuum to the ports of the valve. The valve should not allow vacuum to pass.

6. Place the valve in a container of water with a thermometer and heat the water. When the temperature of the water reaches 134°–145°F, remove the valve and apply vacuum to the ports; the valve should allow vacuum to pass through it.

7. To test the B.P.T. valve installed on 1978 and later models, disconnect the two vacuum hoses from the valve. Plug one of the ports. While applying pressure to the bottom of the valve, apply vacuum to the unplugged port and check for leakage. If any exists, replace the valve.

8. To test the check valve installed in some 1978 and later models, remove the valve and blow into the side which connects to the EGR valve. Air should flow. When air is applied to the other side, air flow resistance should be greater. If not, replace the valve.

9. To check the V.V.T. valve which replaces the B.T.P. valve on some 1980 and later models, disconnect the top and bottom center hoses and apply a vacuum to the top

hose. Check for leaks. If a leak is present, replace the valve.

Mixture Ratio Rich-Lean and EGR Large-Small Exchange Systems

1980 California and all 1981 and later models; California Sentra

These systems control the air-fuel mixture ratio and the amount of recirculated exhaust gas (manual transmission models only) in accordance with the engine coolant temperature and speed of the car. The systems consist of a vacuum switching valve, a power valve, a speed detecting switch amplifier and a water temperature switch.

When the coolant temperature is above 122°F and the car is traveling at least 40 mph, the vacuum switching valve is on and acts to lean down the fuel mixture. It also allows a small amount of EGR to be burned on manual transmission cars. When the coolant temperature is above 122°F but the vehicle is traveling less than 40 miles per hour, the vacuum switching valve is off and allows the mixture to richen. It also allows a large amount of EGR to be burned in manual transmission models. When coolant temperature is below 122°F the vacuum switching valve is always on and acts to lean down the fuel mixture.

TESTING

1. Warm the engine up to operating temperature.

2. Shut off the engine and jack up the drive wheels of the vehicle just far enough that they clear the ground.

CAUTION: *Make sure the front wheels are chocked when raising the rear end of the car. When you have jacked the car to the desired height, support it with jackstands—DO NOT get in the car and attempt the following procedure with the car on a jack.*

3. Start the engine and shift the transmission into HIGH (top) gear and maintain the indicated speed above 50 mph.

4. Pinch the hose running from the vacuum switching valve to the air cleaner and see if the engine speed decreases and operates erratically.

5. Shift the transmission into the next lowest gear and run the indicated speed lower than 30 mph.

6. Disconnect the vacuum hose running between the vacuum switching valve and the

power valve, by detaching it at the power valve and blocking its open end with your finger. The engine should operate erratically. If the expected engine reaction in both of these tests does not happen, check all wiring connections and hoses for breaks and blockage.

Air Injection System

It is difficult for an engine to completely burn the air/fuel mixture through the normal combustion in the combustion chambers. Under certain operating conditions, unburned fuel is exhausted into the atmosphere. Air injection is one answer to the pollution problem of unburned exhaust gases.

The air injection system used on 1975–80 B210 and 210 Datsuns is designed so that ambient air, pressurized by a belt-driven air pump, is injected through the injection nozzles into the exhaust ports near each of the four exhaust valves. The exhaust gases are at high temperatures and ignite when brought into contact with the oxygen. The unburned fuel is then burned in the exhaust ports and manifold.

California B210 models began utilizing a secondary system in 1976 consisting of an air control valve which limits injection of secondary air and an emergency relief valve which controls the supply of secondary air. This system protects the catalytic converter from overheating. In 1977 through 1980, the function of these two valves was taken by a single combined air control (C.A.C.) valve.

All engines with the air pump system have a series of minor alterations to accommodate the system. These are:

1. Special close-tolerance carburetor. Most engines require a slightly rich idle mixture adjustment.

2. Distributor with special advance curve. Ignition timing is retarded about 10° at idle in most cases.

3. Cooling system changes such as larger fan, higher fan speed, and thermostatic fan clutch. This is required to offset the increase in temperature caused by retarded timing at idle.

4. Faster idle speed.

5. Heated air intake on some engines.

The only periodic maintenance required on the air pump system is replacement of the air filter element and adjustment of the drive belt.

TESTING

Air Pump

If the air pump makes an abnormal noise and cannot be corrected without removing the pump from the car, the following check is the only one the owner/mechanic should make. Disassembly of the pump and replacement of

Air pump (arrow)

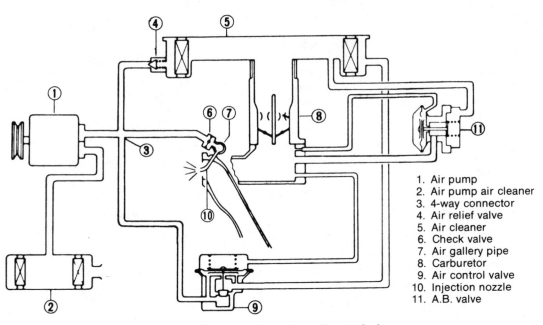

Air injection system schematic—typical

1. Air pump
2. Air pump air cleaner
3. 4-way connector
4. Air relief valve
5. Air cleaner
6. Check valve
7. Air gallery pipe
8. Carburetor
9. Air control valve
10. Injection nozzle
11. A.B. valve

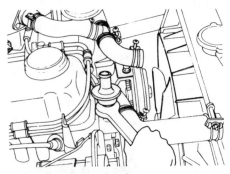

Air pump system check valve

any internal parts requires (in most cases) special tools, and knowledge generally outside the realm of the owner/mechanic. Major pump problems should be handled by a professional.

Check belt tension on the air pump drive belt. There should be about ¼″ inch play in the belt at its center point; too tight a belt will wear out the pump bearings quickly (and cause a noise), and a belt too loose will slip around on the pulley (causing the pump to operate inefficiently).

Turn the pump pulley ¾ of a turn in the clockwise direction and ¼ of a turn in the counterclockwise direction. If the pulley is binding and if rotation is not smooth, this could indicate a defective bearing.

Check Valve

Remove the check valve from the air pump discharge line. Test it for leakage by blowing

air into the valve from the air pump side and from the manifold side. Air should only pass through the valve from the air pump side if the valve is functioning normally. A small amount of air leakage from the manifold side can be overlooked. Replace the check valve if it is found to be defective.

Anti-Backfire Valve

Disconnect the rubber hose connecting the mixture control valve with the intake manifold and plug the hose. If the mixture control valve is operating correctly, air will continue to blow out the mixture control valve for a few seconds after the accelerator pedal is fully depressed (engine running) and released quickly. If air continues to blow out for more than five seconds, replace the mixture control valve.

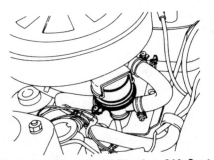

Removing anti-backfire (AB) valve, 210. Sentra location similar

Air Pump Relief Valve

Disconnect the air pump discharge hose leading to the exhaust manifold. With the engine running, restrict the air-flow coming from the pump. The air pump relief valve should vent the pressurized air to the atmosphere if it is working properly.

NOTE: *When performing this test do not completely block the discharge line of the air pump as damage may result if the relief valve fails to function properly.*

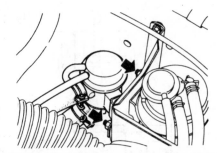

Combined Air Control valve mounting, California models

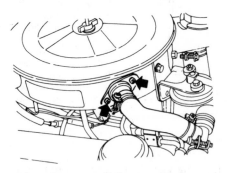

Removing air pump relief valve, B210 and 210 to 1980

Air Injection Nozzles

Check around the air manifold for air leakage with the engine running at 2,000 rpm. If air is leaking from the eye joint bolt, retighten or replace the gasket. Check the air nozzles for restrictions by blowing air into the nozzles.

Hoses

Check and replace hoses if they are found to be weakened or cracked. Check all hose connections and clips. Be sure that the hoses are not in contact with other parts of the engine.

Emergency Air Relief Valve

1. Warm up the engine.
2. Check all hoses for leaks, kinks, improper connections, etc.
3. Run the engine up to 2000 rpm under no load. No air should be discharged from the valve.
4. Disconnect the vacuum hose from the valve. This is the hose which runs to the intake manifold. Run the engine up to 2000 rpm. Air should be discharged from the valve. If not, replace it.

Combined Air Control Valve

1. Check all hoses for leaks, kinks, and improper connections.

2. Thoroughly warm up the engine.
3. With the engine idling, check for air discharge from the relief opening in the air cleaner case.
4. Disconnect and plug the vacuum hose from the valve. Air should be discharged from the valve with the engine idling. If the disconnected vacuum hose is not plugged, the engine will stumble.
5. Connect a hand-operated vacuum pump to the vacuum fitting on the valve and apply 7.8–9.8 in. Hg. of vacuum. Run the engine speed up to 3000 rpm. No air should be discharged from the valve.
6. Disconnect and plug the air hose at the check valve, with the conditions as in the preceding step. This should cause the valve to discharge air. If not, or if any of the conditions in this procedure are not met, replace the valve.

Air Induction System (A.I.S.)

The air induction system (A.I.S.) is designed to send secondary air to the exhaust manifold, utilizing a vacuum caused by exhaust pulsation in the exhaust manifold.

The exhaust pressure in the exhaust manifold usually pulsates in response to the opening and closing of the exhaust valve and it decreases below atmospheric pressure periodically.

If a secondary air intake is opened to the atmosphere under vacuum conditions, secondary air can be drawn into the exhaust manifold in proportion to the vacuum. Therefore, the A.I.S. system reduces carbon monoxide (CO) and HC emissions in exhaust gases.

The A.I.S. system has been used in conjunction with the air injection (air pump) system in B210 and 210 Datsuns from the mid 1970s up until 1979. In 1980, only the California model 210s used both systems together, the air pump having been dropped

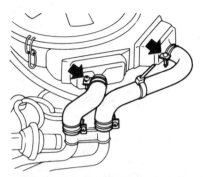

Sentra Air Induction connections. A-series similar

from the non-California cars. The 1981 and later model 210s and Nissan Sentras use just the A.I.S. system, as they employ no air pump.

Electric Choke

Gasoline engines produce most of their hydrocarbon (HC) emissions during warm-up and at low rpm running. The purpose of the electric choke is to shorten the time the choke is in operation, thus shortening the time of greatest HC output.

An electric heater warms the bimetal spring (typical spring found on most chokes) which controls the opening and closing of the choke valve. The heater begins to heat as soon as the engine starts.

Electric choke (arrow)

Catalytic Converter

This system is used on all 1975 (California) and later models. In addition to the air injection system, EGR and the engine modifications, the catalyst further reduces pollutants. Through catalytic action, it changes residual

hydrocarbons and carbon monoxide in the exhaust gas into carbon dioxide and water before the exhaust gas is discharged into the atmosphere.

> NOTE: *Only unleaded fuel must be used with catalytic converters; lead in fuel will quickly pollute the catalyst and render it useless.*

The emergency air relief valve is used as a catalyst protection device. When the temperature of the catalyst goes above maximum operating temperature, the temperature sensor signals the switching module to activate the emergency air relief valve. This stops air injection into the exhaust manifold and lowers the temperature of the catalyst.

Certain late 1970's catalyst-equipped models have a floor temperature warning system which emits a warning if the catalytic converter or engine becomes overly hot or malfunctions, causing floor temperature to rise.

Vacuum Hoses of Emission Control System
1982 AND LATER SENTRA

The following show the various color coding for connecting emission control vacuum hoses and air hoses. Careful attention should be paid to the proper location and hook-up of the hoses.

- Yellow: Vacuum line to distributor
- White: Vacuum line for EGR system
- Green: Manifold vacuum line
- Pink: Atmospheric pressure
- Blue: Venturi vacuum line to VVT valve

FUEL SYSTEM

Fuel Pump

The fuel pump is a mechanically-operated, diaphragm-type pump driven by the fuel pump eccentric on the camshaft. It is mounted on the side of the engine block.

Design of the fuel pump permits disassembly, cleaning, and repair or replacement of defective parts.

TESTING

1. Disconnect the line between the carburetor and the pump at the carburetor.

2. Connect a rubber hose to each open end of the T-connector, and connect this connec-

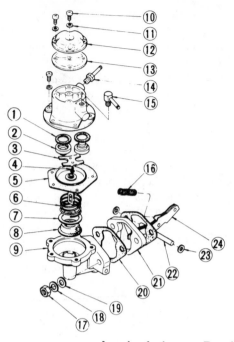

1. Packing
2. Valve assembly
3. Retainer
4. Screw
5. Diaphragm assembly
6. Diaphragm spring
7. Retainer
8. Diaphragm assembly
9. Complete-body lower
10. Screw
11. Washer-spring
12. Fuel pump cap
13. Cap gasket
14. Connector-inlet
15. Connector-outlet
16. Rocker arm spring
17. Nut
18. Washer-spring
19. Washer-plain
20. Gasket
21. Spacer
22. Rocker pin
23. Spacer
24. Rocker arm

A-series fuel pump. E-series similar type

tor-hose assembly between carburetor and fuel pump.

NOTE: *Locate this T-connector as close to the carburetor as possible.*

3. Connect a suitable pressure gauge to the opening of the T-connector, and fasten the hose between the carburetor and T-connector securely with a hose clamp.

4. Start the engine and run at various speeds.

5. The pressure gauge indicates static fuel pressure in the line. The gauge reading should be within 3.0 to 3.9 psi. There is usually enough gas in the float bowl to perform this test.

CAPACITY TEST

The capacity test is conducted if the static pressure of the pump is ok.

1. Disconnect the pressure gauge from the line. In place of the gauge, install a container suitable to collect the fuel (a graduated container works well here, as you can measure tye amount of fuel immediately).

2. Make sure the carburetor float bowl is full of gas. Start the engine and run at about 1,000 rpm for one minute.

3. The fuel pump should deliver 450 cc (15.2 US fl. oz.) of fuel per minute for all 1973–81 1200, B210 and 210 models. The delivery rate for 1982 210 fuel pumps is 1300 cc (44.0 U.S. fl. oz.) per minute at 1000 rpm;

1982 and later Sentra pumps deliver the same amount at 600 rpm.

REMOVAL AND INSTALLATION

1. Disconnect the two fuel lines from the fuel pump. Be sure to keep the line leading from the fuel tank up high to prevent the excess loss of fuel.

2. Remove the two fuel pump mounting nuts and remove the fuel pump assembly from the side of the engine.

3. Install the fuel pump in the reverse order of removal, using a new gasket and sealer on the mating surface.

Carburetor

The carburetor used on all models is a two-barrel down-draft type with a low-speed (primary) side and a high-speed (secondary) side.

All models have an electrically-operated anti-dieseling solenoid. As the ignition switch is turned off, the valve is energized and shuts off the supply of fuel to the idle circuit of the carburetor.

REMOVAL AND INSTALLATION

1. Remove the air cleaner.

2. Disconnect the fuel and vacuum lines from the carburetor.

3. Remove the throttle lever.

Carburetor Specifications

Year	Engine	Vehicle Model	Carb Model	Main Jet # Primary	Main Jet # Secondary	Main Air Bleed # Primary	Main Air Bleed # Secondary	Slow Jet # Primary	Slow Jet # Secondary	Float Level (in.)	Power Jet #
1973	A12	1200	DCH 306-4 ① / DCH 306-5 ②	95	140	80	80	43③	50③	0.709 / 0.748	60
1974	A13	B210	DCH 306-6 ① / DCH 306-7 ②	140	145	65	80	43④	50④	0.709 / 0.748	55
1975	A14 (Federal)	B210	DCH 306-10 ① / DCH 306-14 ②	102	150	95	80	45	50	0.75	45
	A14 (California)	B210	DCH 306-11 ① / DCH 306-15 ②	104	150	95	80	45	50	0.75	43
1976–77	A14 (Federal)	B210	DCH 306-10A ① / DCH 306-14A ②	102	145	95	80	45	50	0.75	45
1978	A14 (Federal)	B210	DCH 306-60 ① / DCH 306-14 ②	104	145	110 / 95	80	45	50	0.75	48 / 40
	A14 (California)	B210	DCH 306-11 ① / DCH 306-15 ②	105 / 104	145	95	80	45	50	0.75	40 / 48
	A14 (FU Model)	B210	DCH 306-37	107	145	65	60	46	50	0.75	48
1979	A14, A15 (Federal)	210	DCH-306 60E ① / DCH 306-68 ②	106 / 105	145	110 / 95	80	45	50	0.75	43
	A14, A15 (California)	210	DCH 306-61 ① / DCH 306-63 ②	107	145	95	80	45	50	0.75	43
	A14 (FU Model)	210	DCH 306-67	107	145	65	60	46	50	0.75	48

Carburetor Specifications (cont.)

Year	Engine	Vehicle Model	Carb Model	Main Jet #		Main Air Bleed #		Slow Jet #		Float Level (in.)	Power Jet #
				Primary	Secondary	Primary	Secondary	Primary	Secondary		
1980	A14, A15 (Federal)	210	DCH 306-100 ① DCH 306-101 ②	107	143	65	60	45	50	0.75	43
	A12A (Federal)	210	DCH 306-105	95	138	65	60	45	50	0.75	35
	A14, A15 (California)	210	DCH 306-110 ① DCH 306-111 ②	107	145	80	80	45	50	0.75	38
	A12A (California)	210	DCH 306-115	94	145	95	80	45	50	0.75	38
	A12A (Canada)	210	DCH 306-70 ①	96	140	70	60	43	50	0.75	50
	A14, A15 (Canada)	210	DCH 306-60 ① DCH 306-12 ②	104	145	110 95	80	45	50	0.75	48 50
1981	A12A (Federal)	210	DCR 306-100	105	125	95	80	45	50	0.75	35
	A14, A15 (Federal)	210	DCR 306-104 ① DCR 306-101 ① DCR 306-102 ②	115	125	80	80	45	50	0.75	35
	A12A (California)	210	DCR 306-110	103	125	60	80	45	50	0.75	35
	A15 (California)	210	DCR 306-111 ① DCR 306-112 ②	114	125	60	80	45	50	0.75	35

Year	Engine	Carburetor								
	A12A ⑤ (Canada)	210	DCR 306-120	100	145	70	80	43	50	0.75	35
	A15 ⑤ (Canada)	210	DCR 306-121 ① DCR 306-122 ②	100	145	70	80	43	70	0.75	35
1982	A12A (Federal)	210	DCR 306-106	105	125	95	80	45	50	0.75	35
	A14 ② (MPG)	210	DCR 306-109	117	125	80	80	45	50	0.75	35
	A15 (Federal)	210	DCR 306-107 ① DCR 306-108 ②	115 116	125	80	80	45	50	0.75	35
	A12A (California)	210	DCR 306-116	103	125	60	80	45	50	0.75	35
	A15 (California)	210	DCR 306-117 DCR 306-118	115 116	125	80	80	45	50	0.75	35
1982–83	E15 (Federal)	Sentra	DCR-306-132 ① DCR-306-133 ②	117 115	125 125	60 60	80 80	45 45	50 50	N.A.	38 38
	E15 (California)	Sentra	DCR-306-142 ① DCR-306-143 ②	115 114	125 125	80 80	80 80	45 45	50 50	N.A.	38 35
	E15 (Canada)	Sentra	DCR-306-152 ① DCR-306-153 ②	100 100	130 130	70 70	60 60	43 43	80 80	N.A.	40 40
	E15 (MPG)	Sentra	DFP-306-2	98	135	60	80	43	55	N.A.	—

NOTE: FU models are 5-speed Hatchbacks sold in the United States except California.
① Manual transmission
② Automatic transmission
③ Slow jet air bleed: Primary #215, Secondary #100
④ Slow jet air bleed: Primary #240, Secondary #100
⑤ 1982 Canada carburetors same specs and models as 1981

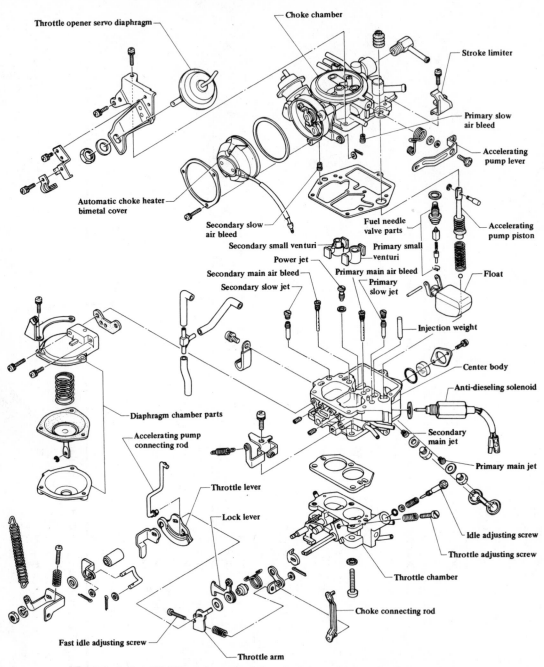

Throttle opener servo diaphragm

Choke chamber

Stroke limiter

Primary slow air bleed

Accelerating pump lever

Automatic choke heater bimetal cover

Secondary slow air bleed

Fuel needle valve parts

Accelerating pump piston

Secondary small venturi

Primary small venturi

Power jet

Secondary main air bleed

Primary main air bleed

Secondary slow jet

Primary slow jet

Float

Injection weight

Center body

Anti-dieseling solenoid

Secondary main jet

Primary main jet

Diaphragm chamber parts

Accelerating pump connecting rod

Throttle lever

Lock lever

Idle adjusting screw

Throttle adjusting screw

Throttle chamber

Choke connecting rod

Fast idle adjusting screw

Throttle arm

Exploded view '82 210 carburetor. Other A-series and E-series Sentra similar

4. Remove the four nuts and washers retaining the carburetor to the manifold.

5. Lift the carburetor from the manifold.

6. Remove and discard the gasket used between the carburetor and the manifold.

7. Install the carburetor in the reverse order of removal, using a new carburetor base gasket.

THROTTLE LINKAGE ADJUSTMENT

On all models, make sure the throttle is wide open when the accelerator pedal is floored. Some models have an adjustable accelerator pedal stop to prevent strain on the linkage.

CHILTON'S
FUEL ECONOMY
& TUNE-UP TIPS

Tune-Up • Spark Plug Diagnosis • Emission Controls

Fuel System • Cooling System • Tires and Wheels

General Maintenance

CHILTON'S FUEL ECONOMY & TUNE-UP TIPS

Fuel economy is important to everyone, no matter what kind of vehicle you drive. The maintenance-minded motorist can save both money and fuel using these tips and the periodic maintenance and tune-up procedures in this Repair and Tune-Up Guide.

There are more than 130,000,000 cars and trucks registered for private use in the United States. Each travels an average of 10-12,000 miles per year, and, in total they consume close to 70 billion gallons of fuel each year. This represents nearly ⅔ of the oil imported by the United States each year. The Federal government's goal is to reduce consumption 10% by 1985. A variety of methods are either already in use or under serious consideration, and they all affect your driving and the cars you will drive. In addition to "down-sizing", the auto industry is using or investigating the use of electronic fuel delivery, electronic engine controls and alternative engines for use in smaller and lighter vehicles, among other alternatives to meet the federally mandated Corporate Average Fuel Economy (CAFE) of 27.5 mpg by 1985. The government, for its part, is considering rationing, mandatory driving curtailments and tax increases on motor vehicle fuel in an effort to reduce consumption. The government's goal of a 10% reduction could be realized — and further government regulation avoided — if every private vehicle could use just 1 less gallon of fuel per week.

How Much Can You Save?

Tests have proven that almost anyone can make at least a 10% reduction in fuel consumption through regular maintenance and tune-ups. When a major manufacturer of spark plugs sur-

TUNE-UP

1. Check the cylinder compression to be sure the engine will really benefit from a tune-up and that it is capable of producing good fuel economy. A tune-up will be wasted on an engine in poor mechanical condition.

2. Replace spark plugs regularly. New spark plugs alone can increase fuel economy 3%.

3. Be sure the spark plugs are the correct type (heat range) for your vehicle. See the Tune-Up Specifications.

Heat range refers to the spark plug's ability to conduct heat away from the firing end. It must conduct the heat away in an even pattern to avoid becoming a source of pre-ignition, yet it must also operate hot enough to burn off conductive deposits that could cause misfiring.

The heat range is usually indicated by a number on the spark plug, part of the manufacturer's designation for each individual spark plug. The numbers in bold-face indicate the heat range in each manufacturer's identification system.

Manufacturer	Typical Designation
AC	R **45** TS
Bosch (old)	WA **145** T30
Bosch (new)	HR **8** Y
Champion	RBL **15** Y
Fram/Autolite	**415**
Mopar	P-**62** PR
Motorcraft	BR**F-42**
NGK	BP **5** ES-15
Nippondenso	W **16** EP
Prestolite	14GR **5** 2A

Periodically, check the spark plugs to be sure they are firing efficiently. They are excellent indicators of the internal condition of your engine.

On AC, Bosch (new), Champion, Fram/Autolite, Mopar, Motorcraft and Prestolite, a higher number indicates a hotter plug. On Bosch (old), NGK and Nippondenso, a higher number indicates a colder plug.

4. Make sure the spark plugs are properly gapped. See the Tune-Up Specifications in this book.

5. Be sure the spark plugs are firing efficiently. The illustrations on the next 2 pages show you how to "read" the firing end of the spark plug.

6. Check the ignition timing and set it to specifications. Tests show that almost all cars

veyed over 6,000 cars nationwide, they found that a tune-up, on cars that needed one, increased fuel economy over 11%. Replacing worn plugs alone, accounted for a 3% increase. The same test also revealed that 8 out of every 10 vehicles will have some maintenance deficiency that will directly affect fuel economy, emissions or performance. Most of this mileage-robbing neglect could be prevented with regular maintenance.

Modern engines require that all of the functioning systems operate properly for maximum efficiency. A malfunction anywhere wastes fuel. You can keep your vehicle running as efficiently and economically as possible, by being aware of your vehicles operating and performance characteristics. If your vehicle suddenly develops performance or fuel economy problems it could be due to one or more of the following:

PROBLEM	POSSIBLE CAUSE
Engine Idles Rough	Ignition timing, idle mixture, vacuum leak or something amiss in the emission control system.
Hesitates on Acceleration	Dirty carburetor or fuel filter, improper accelerator pump setting, ignition timing or fouled spark plugs.
Starts Hard or Fails to Start	Worn spark plugs, improperly set automatic choke, ice (or water) in fuel system.
Stalls Frequently	Automatic choke improperly adjusted and possible dirty air filter or fuel filter.
Performs Sluggishly	Worn spark plugs, dirty fuel or air filter, ignition timing or automatic choke out of adjustment.

Check spark plug wires on conventional point type ignition for cracks by bending them in a loop around your finger.

Be sure that spark plug wires leading to adjacent cylinders do not run too close together. (Photo courtesy Champion Spark Plug Co.)

have incorrect ignition timing by more than 2°.

7. If your vehicle does not have electronic ignition, check the points, rotor and cap as specified.

8. Check the spark plug wires (used with conventional point-type ignitions) for cracks and burned or broken insulation by bending them in a loop around your finger. Cracked wires decrease fuel efficiency by failing to deliver full voltage to the spark plugs. One misfiring spark plug can cost you as much as 2 mpg.

9. Check the routing of the plug wires. Misfiring can be the result of spark plug leads to adjacent cylinders running parallel to each other and too close together. One wire tends to pick up voltage from the other causing it to fire "out of time".

10. Check all electrical and ignition circuits for voltage drop and resistance.

11. Check the distributor mechanical and/or vacuum advance mechanisms for proper functioning. The vacuum advance can be checked by twisting the distributor plate in the opposite direction of rotation. It should spring back when released.

12. Check and adjust the valve clearance on engines with mechanical lifters. The clearance should be slightly loose rather than too tight.

SPARK PLUG DIAGNOSIS

Normal

APPEARANCE: This plug is typical of one operating normally. The insulator nose varies from a light tan to grayish color with slight electrode wear. The presence of slight deposits is normal on used plugs and will have no adverse effect on engine performance. The spark plug heat range is correct for the engine and the engine is running normally.

CAUSE: Properly running engine.

RECOMMENDATION: Before reinstalling this plug, the electrodes should be cleaned and filed square. Set the gap to specifications. If the plug has been in service for more than 10-12,000 miles, the entire set should probably be replaced with a fresh set of the same heat range.

Oil Deposits

APPEARANCE: The firing end of the plug is covered with a wet, oily coating.

CAUSE: The problem is poor oil control. On high mileage engines, oil is leaking past the rings or valve guides into the combustion chamber. A common cause is also a plugged PCV valve, and a ruptured fuel pump diaphragm can also cause this condition. Oil fouled plugs such as these are often found in new or recently overhauled engines, before normal oil control is achieved, and can be cleaned and reinstalled.

RECOMMENDATION: A hotter spark plug may temporarily relieve the problem, but the engine is probably in need of work.

Incorrect Heat Range

APPEARANCE: The effects of high temperature on a spark plug are indicated by clean white, often blistered insulator. This can also be accompanied by excessive wear of the electrode, and the absence of deposits.

CAUSE: Check for the correct spark plug heat range. A plug which is too hot for the engine can result in overheating. A car operated mostly at high speeds can require a colder plug. Also check ignition timing, cooling system level, fuel mixture and leaking intake manifold.

RECOMMENDATION: If all ignition and engine adjustments are known to be correct, and no other malfunction exists, install spark plugs one heat range colder.

Photos Courtesy Champion Spark Plug Co.

Carbon Deposits

APPEARANCE: Carbon fouling is easily identified by the presence of dry, soft, black, sooty deposits.

CAUSE: Changing the heat range can often lead to carbon fouling, as can prolonged slow, stop-and-start driving. If the heat range is correct, carbon fouling can be attributed to a rich fuel mixture, sticking choke, clogged air cleaner, worn breaker points, retarded timing or low compression. If only one or two plugs are carbon fouled, check for corroded or cracked wires on the affected plugs. Also look for cracks in the distributor cap between the towers of affected cylinders.

RECOMMENDATION: After the problem is corrected, these plugs can be cleaned and reinstalled if not worn severely.

MMT Fouled

APPEARANCE: Spark plugs fouled by MMT (Methycyclopentadienyl Maganese Tricarbonyl) have reddish, rusty appearance on the insulator and side electrode.

CAUSE: MMT is an anti-knock additive in gasoline used to replace lead. During the combustion process, the MMT leaves a reddish deposit on the insulator and side electrode.

RECOMMENDATION: No engine malfunction is indicated and the deposits will not affect plug performance any more than lead deposits (see Ash Deposits). MMT fouled plugs can be cleaned, regapped and reinstalled.

High Speed Glazing

APPEARANCE: Glazing appears as shiny coating on the plug, either yellow or tan in color.

CAUSE: During hard, fast acceleration, plug temperatures rise suddenly. Deposits from normal combustion have no chance to fluff-off; instead, they melt on the insulator forming an electrically conductive coating which causes misfiring.

RECOMMENDATION: Glazed plugs are not easily cleaned. They should be replaced with a fresh set of plugs of the correct heat range. If the condition recurs, using plugs with a heat range one step colder may cure the problem.

Ash (Lead) Deposits

APPEARANCE: Ash deposits are characterized by light brown or white colored deposits crusted on the side or center electrodes. In some cases it may give the plug a rusty appearance.

CAUSE: Ash deposits are normally derived from oil or fuel additives burned during normal combustion. Normally they are harmless, though excessive amounts can cause misfiring. If deposits are excessive in short mileage, the valve guides may be worn.

RECOMMENDATION: Ash-fouled plugs can be cleaned, gapped and reinstalled.

Detonation

APPEARANCE: Detonation is usually characterized by a broken plug insulator.

CAUSE: A portion of the fuel charge will begin to burn spontaneously, from the increased heat following ignition. The explosion that results applies extreme pressure to engine components, frequently damaging spark plugs and pistons.

Detonation can result by over-advanced ignition timing, inferior gasoline (low octane) lean air/fuel mixture, poor carburetion, engine lugging or an increase in compression ratio due to combustion chamber deposits or engine modification.

RECOMMENDATION: Replace the plugs after correcting the problem.

Photos Courtesy Fram Corporation

EMISSION CONTROLS

13. Be aware of the general condition of the emission control system. It contributes to reduced pollution and should be serviced regularly to maintain efficient engine operation.

14. Check all vacuum lines for dried, cracked or brittle conditions. Something as simple as a leaking vacuum hose can cause poor performance and loss of economy.

15. Avoid tampering with the emission control system. Attempting to improve fuel econ-

FUEL SYSTEM

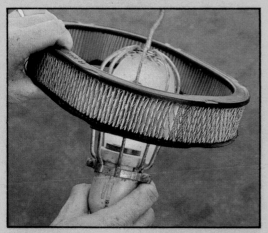

Check the air filter with a light behind it. If you can see light through the filter it can be reused.

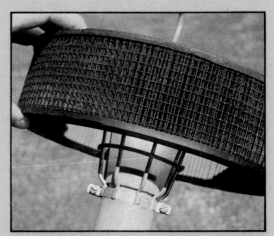

Extremely clogged filters should be discarded and replaced with a new one.

18. Replace the air filter regularly. A dirty air filter richens the air/fuel mixture and can increase fuel consumption as much as 10%. Tests show that ⅓ of all vehicles have air filters in need of replacement.

19. Replace the fuel filter at least as often as recommended.

20. Set the idle speed and carburetor mixture to specifications.

21. Check the automatic choke. A sticking or malfunctioning choke wastes gas.

22. During the summer months, adjust the automatic choke for a leaner mixture which will produce faster engine warm-ups.

COOLING SYSTEM

29. Be sure all accessory drive belts are in good condition. Check for cracks or wear.

30. Adjust all accessory drive belts to proper tension.

31. Check all hoses for swollen areas, worn spots, or loose clamps.

32. Check coolant level in the radiator or expansion tank.

33. Be sure the thermostat is operating properly. A stuck thermostat delays engine warm-up and a cold engine uses nearly twice as much fuel as a warm engine.

34. Drain and replace the engine coolant at least as often as recommended. Rust and scale

TIRES & WHEELS

38. Check the tire pressure often with a pencil type gauge. Tests by a major tire manufacturer show that 90% of all vehicles have at least 1 tire improperly inflated. Better mileage can be achieved by over-inflating tires, but never exceed the maximum inflation pressure on the side of the tire.

39. If possible, install radial tires. Radial tires deliver as much as ½ mpg more than bias belted tires.

40. Avoid installing super-wide tires. They only create extra rolling resistance and decrease fuel mileage. Stick to the manufacturer's recommendations.

41. Have the wheels properly balanced.

omy by tampering with emission controls is more likely to worsen fuel economy than improve it. Emission control changes on modern engines are not readily reversible.

16. Clean (or replace) the EGR valve and lines as recommended.

17. Be sure that all vacuum lines and hoses are reconnected properly after working under the hood. An unconnected or misrouted vacuum line can wreak havoc with engine performance.

23. Check for fuel leaks at the carburetor, fuel pump, fuel lines and fuel tank. Be sure all lines and connections are tight.

24. Periodically check the tightness of the carburetor and intake manifold attaching nuts and bolts. These are a common place for vacuum leaks to occur.

25. Clean the carburetor periodically and lubricate the linkage.

26. The condition of the tailpipe can be an excellent indicator of proper engine combustion. After a long drive at highway speeds, the inside of the tailpipe should be a light grey in color. Black or soot on the insides indicates an overly rich mixture.

27. Check the fuel pump pressure. The fuel pump may be supplying more fuel than the engine needs.

28. Use the proper grade of gasoline for your engine. Don't try to compensate for knocking or "pinging" by advancing the ignition timing. This practice will only increase plug temperature and the chances of detonation or pre-ignition with relatively little performance gain.

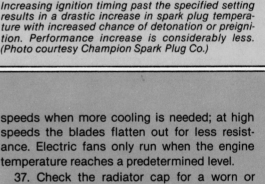

Increasing ignition timing past the specified setting results in a drastic increase in spark plug temperature with increased chance of detonation or preignition. Performance increase is considerably less. (Photo courtesy Champion Spark Plug Co.)

that form in the engine should be flushed out to allow the engine to operate at peak efficiency.

35. Clean the radiator of debris that can decrease cooling efficiency.

36. Install a flex-type or electric cooling fan, if you don't have a clutch type fan. Flex fans use curved plastic blades to push more air at low speeds when more cooling is needed; at high speeds the blades flatten out for less resistance. Electric fans only run when the engine temperature reaches a predetermined level.

37. Check the radiator cap for a worn or cracked gasket. If the cap does not seal properly, the cooling system will not function properly.

42. Be sure the front end is correctly aligned. A misaligned front end actually has wheels going in different directions. The increased drag can reduce fuel economy by .3 mpg.

43. Correctly adjust the wheel bearings. Wheel bearings that are adjusted too tight increase rolling resistance.

Check tire pressures regularly with a reliable pocket type gauge. Be sure to check the pressure on a cold tire.

GENERAL MAINTENANCE

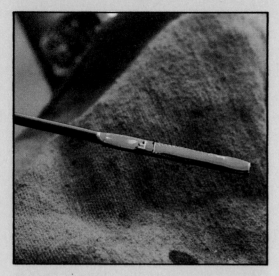

Check the fluid levels (particularly engine oil) on a regular basis. Be sure to check the oil for grit, water or other contamination.

A vacuum gauge is another excellent indicator of internal engine condition and can also be installed in the dash as a mileage indicator.

44. Periodically check the fluid levels in the engine, power steering pump, master cylinder, automatic transmission and drive axle.

45. Change the oil at the recommended interval and change the filter at every oil change. Dirty oil is thick and causes extra friction between moving parts, cutting efficiency and increasing wear. A worn engine requires more frequent tune-ups and gets progressively worse fuel economy. In general, use the lightest viscosity oil for the driving conditions you will encounter.

46. Use the recommended viscosity fluids in the transmission and axle.

47. Be sure the battery is fully charged for fast starts. A slow starting engine wastes fuel.

48. Be sure battery terminals are clean and tight.

49. Check the battery electrolyte level and add distilled water if necessary.

50. Check the exhaust system for crushed pipes, blockages and leaks.

51. Adjust the brakes. Dragging brakes or brakes that are not releasing create increased drag on the engine.

52. Install a vacuum gauge or miles-per-gallon gauge. These gauges visually indicate engine vacuum in the intake manifold. High vacuum = good mileage and low vacuum = poorer mileage. The gauge can also be an excellent indicator of internal engine conditions.

53. Be sure the clutch is properly adjusted. A slipping clutch wastes fuel.

54. Check and periodically lubricate the heat control valve in the exhaust manifold. A sticking or inoperative valve prevents engine warm-up and wastes gas.

55. Keep accurate records to check fuel economy over a period of time. A sudden drop in fuel economy may signal a need for tune-up or other maintenance.

SECONDARY THROTTLE LINKAGE ADJUSTMENT

All Datsun carburetors discussed in this book are two stage type carburetors. On this type of carburetor, the engine runs on the primary barrel most of the time, with the secondary barrel being used for acceleration purposes. When the throttle valve on the primary side opens to an angle of approximately 50 degrees (from its fully closed position), the secondary throttle valve is pulled open by the connecting linkage. The fifty degree angle of throttle valve opening works out to a clearance measurement of somewhere between 0.26–0.32 in. between the throttle valve and the carburetor body. The easiest way to measure this is to use a drill bit. Drill bits from size H to size P (standard letter size drill bits) should fit. Check the appendix in the back of the book for the exact size of the various drill bits. If an adjustment is necessary, bend the connecting link between the two linkage assemblies.

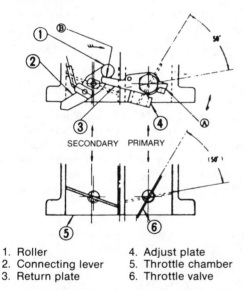

SECONDARY   PRIMARY

1. Roller
2. Connecting lever
3. Return plate
4. Adjust plate
5. Throttle chamber
6. Throttle valve

Secondary throttle linkage adjustment

DASHPOT ADJUSTMENT

A dashpot is used on carburetors ofr all cars with automatic transmissions and many late model manual transmission models. The dashpot slowly closes the throttle on automatic transmissions to prevent stalling and serves as an emission control device on all late model vehicles.

The dashpot should be adjusted to contact the throttle lever on deceleration at approximately 2,000–2,300 rpm for all models of the

LOCK NUT

THROTTLE LEVER

DASH POT

Dashpot adjustment

A-series engines, and 2,300 to 2,500 rpm for all E-series engines.

> NOTE: *Before attempting to adjust the dashpot, make sure the idle speed, timing and mixture adjustments are correct.*

FLOAT LEVEL ADJUSTMENT

The fuel level is normal if it is within the lines on the window glass of the float chamber (or the sight glass) when the vehicle is resting on level ground and the engine is off.

If the fuel level is outside the lines, remove the float housing cover. Have an absorbent cloth under the cover to catch the fuel from the fuel bowl. Adjust the float level by bending the needle seat on the float.

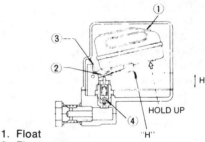

HOLD UP

"H"

1. Float
2. Float seat
3. Float stopper
4. Needle valve

1200 and B210 float level adjustment. 210 and Sentra similar

Close-up of float level sight window

The needle valve should have an effective stroke of about 0.0591 in. When necessary, the needle valve stroke can be adjusted by bending the float stopper.

NOTE: *Be careful not to bend the needle valve rod when installing the float and baffle plate, if removed.*

FAST IDLE ADJUSTMENT

1. With the carburetor removed from the vehicle, place the upper side of the fast idle cam and measure the clearance between the throttle valve and the wall of the throttle valve chamber at the center of the throttle valve. Check it against the following specifications:
- 1973 1200, 1974–76 B210:
    0.0315–0.0346 in. M/T
    0.0421–0.0461 in. A/T
- 1977–78 B210:
    0.0287–0.343 in. M/T
    0.0394–0.449 in. A/T
- 1979–82 210, A12A engine:
    0.0248–0.315 in. M/T
  A14 engine:
    0.0283–0.0350 in. M/T
  A15 engine:
    0.0386–0.461 in. A/T
- 1982–83 Sentra E15 engine:
    0.0315–0.343 in. M/T
    0.0421–0.0449 in. A/T

"M/T" means manual transmission. "A/T" means automatic transmission.

NOTE: *The first step of the fast idle adjustment procedure is not absolutely necessary.*

2. Install the carburetor on the engine.
3. Start the engine and measure the fast idle rpm with the engine at operating temperature. The cam should be on the 2nd step.
- 1973 1200, 1974 B210:
    M/T 1,720–2,050 rpm
    A/T 2,650–2,950 rpm
- 1975–76 B210:
    M/T 2,450–2,650 rpm
    A/T 2,700–2,900 rpm
- 1977–78 B210:
    M/T 1,900–2,700 rpm
    A/T 2,400–3,200 rpm
- 1980 and later 210, A12A, A14 engines:
    49 states M/T 2,400 and 3,200 rpm
    California M/T 2,300–3,100 rpm
  A15 engine:
    A/T 2,700–3,500 rpm
    M/T 2,300–3,100 rpm
- 1982–83 Sentra E-15 engine:
    California—2,300–3,100 rpm
    49 states—2,400–3,200 rpm
    Canada—1,900–2,700 rpm M/T
    2,400–3,200 A/T

4. To adjust the fast idle speed, turn the fast idle adjusting screw counterclockwise to increase the fast idle speed and clockwise to decrease the fast idle speed.

AUTOMATIC CHOKE ADJUSTMENT

1. With the engine cold, make sure the choke is fully closed (press the gas pedal all the way to the floor and release).
2. Check the choke linkage for binding. The choke plate should be easily opened and closed with your finger. If the choke sticks or binds, it can usually be freed with a liberal application of a spray-type carburetor cleaner made for the purpose. A couple of quick

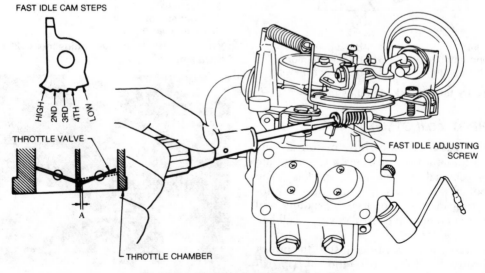

FAST IDLE CAM STEPS

HIGH 2ND 3RD 4TH LOW

THROTTLE VALVE

A

THROTTLE CHAMBER

FAST IDLE ADJUSTING SCREW

Fast idle adjustment, all models similar

squirts on the linkage and choke plate normally does the trick.

If not, the carburetor will have to be disassembled for repairs.

3. The choke is correctly adjusted when the index mark on the choke housing (notch) aligns with the center mark on the carburetor body. If the setting is incorrect, loosen the three screws clamping the choke body in place and rotate the choke cover left or right until the marks align. Tighten the screws carefully to avoid cracking the housing.

CHOKE UNLOADER ADJUSTMENT

1. Close the choke valve completely.
2. Hold the choke valve closed by stretching a rubber band between the choke piston lever and a stationary part of the carburetor.
3. Open the throttle lever fully.
4. Adjust the gap between the choke plate and the carburetor body to:
- A-series engines:
  - 1973–77: 0.0791 in.
  - 1978–80: 0.0929 in. except:
  - 1978 and later: Non-Cal. 5 speed hatchback 210, B210 and 1980 and later Canada manual trans. A12A: 0.0854 in.
- E-series engines:
  - 1982–83 (0.0929 in.)

OVERHAUL

Efficient carburetion depends greatly on careful cleaning and inspection during overhaul, since dirt, gum, water, or varnish in or on the carburetor parts are often responsible for poor performance.

Overhaul your carburetor in a clean, dust-free area. Carefully disassemble the carburetor, referring often to the exploded views. Keep all similar and look-alike parts segregated during disassembly and cleaning to avoid accidental interchange during assembly. Make a note of all jet sizes.

When the carburetor is disassembled, wash all parts (except diaphragms, electric choke units, pump plunger, and any other plastic, leather, fiber, or rubber parts) in clean carburetor solvent. Do not leave parts in the solvent any longer than is necessary to sufficiently loosen the deposits. Excessive cleaning may remove the special finish from the float bowl and choke valve bodies, leaving these parts unfit for service. Rinse all parts in clean solvent and blow them dry with compressed air to allow them to air dry. Wipe clean all cork, plastic, leather, and fiber parts with a clean, lint-free cloth.

NOTE: *Carburetor solvent is available in various-sized solvent cans, which are designed with a removable small parts basket in the top. The carburetor choke chamber and body, and all small parts can be soaked in this can until clean. These solvent cans are available at most auto parts stores, and are quite handy for soaking other small engine parts.*

Blow out all passages and jets with com-

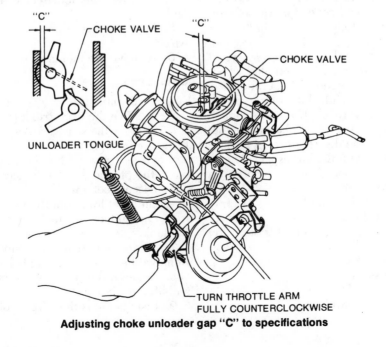

Adjusting choke unloader gap "C" to specifications

pressed air and be sure that there are no restrictions or blockages. Never use wire or similar tools to clean jets, fuel passages, or air bleeds. Clean all jets and valves separately to avoid accidental interchange.

Check all parts for wear or damage. If wear or damage is found, replace the defective parts. Especially check the following:

1. Check the float needle and seat for wear. If wear is found, replace the complete assembly.

2. Check the float hinge pin for wear and the float(s) for dents or distortion. Replace the float if fuel has leaked into it.

3. Check the throttle and choke shaft bores for wear or an out-of-round condition. Damage or wear to the throttle arm, shaft, or shaft bore will often require replacement of the throttle body. These parts require a close tolerance of fit; wear may allow air leakage, which could affect starting and idling.

NOTE: *Throttle shafts and bushings are not included in overhaul kits. They can be purchased separately.*

4. Inspect the idle mixture adjusting needles for burrs or grooves. Any such condition requires replacement of the needle, since you will not be able to obtain a satisfactory idle.

5. Test the accelerator pump check valves. They should pass air one way but not the other. Test for proper seating by blowing and sucking on the valve. Replace the valve if necessary. If the valve is satisfactory, wash the valve again to remove breath moisture.

6. Check the bowl cover for warped surfaces with a straightedge.

7. Closely inspect the valves and seats for wear and damage, replacing as necessary.

8. After the carburetor is assembled, check the choke valve for freedom of operation.

Carburetor overhaul kits are recommended for each overhaul. These kits contain all gaskets and new parts to replace those that deteriorate most rapidly. Failure to replace all parts supplied with the kit (especially gaskets) can result in poor performance and a leaky carburetor later.

Some carburetor manufacturers supply overhaul kits of three basic types: minor repair; major repair; and gasket kits. Basically, they contain the following:

• Minor Repair Kits:
    All gaskets
    Float needle valve
    Volume control screw

    All diaphragms
    Spring for the pump diaphragm
• Major Repair Kits:
    All jets and gaskets
    All diaphragms
    Float needle valve
    Volume control screw
    Pump ball valve
    Main jet carrier
    Float
• Gasket Kits:
    All gaskets

After cleaning and checking all components, reassemble the carburetor, using new parts and referring to the exploded view. When reassembling, make sure that all screws and jets are tight in their seats, but do not overtighten as the tips will be distorted. Tighten all screws gradually in rotation. Do not tighten needle valves into their seats; uneven jetting will result. Always use new gaskets. Be sure to adjust the float level when reassembling.

Fuel Tank
REMOVAL AND INSTALLATION
1200

1. Disconnect the battery. Remove the drain plug from the tank bottom and completely drain the tank into a suitable container.

2. Remove the fuel lines.

3. Remove the trunk finishing panel.

4. Remove the four bolts retaining the tank.

5. Disconnect the hose clamp and gauge wire.

6. Remove the fuel tank.

B210 Sedan

1. Disconnect the battery ground cable.

2. Remove the front trunk panel.

3. Remove the spare tire and the plug from the spare housing.

4. Place a pan under the drain plug, remove the plug and drain the gas.

5. Disconnect the filler hose, ventilation lines, and fuel line from the tank.

6. Disconnect the fuel gauge wires from the tank.

7. Remove the rear seat cushion and back. Remove the front mounting bolts.

8. Remove the other two retaining bolts, and lift out the tank.

9. Installation is the reverse of removal.

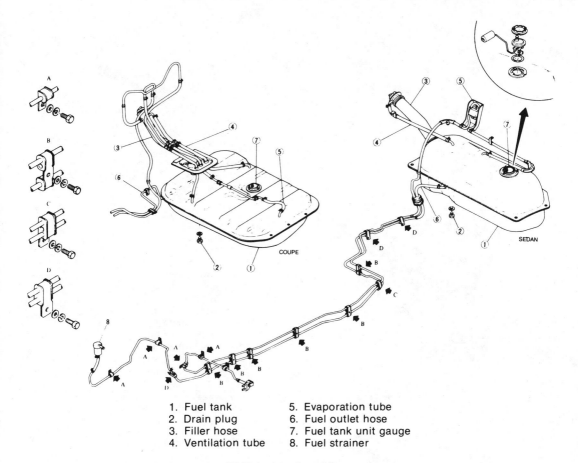

1. Fuel tank
2. Drain plug
3. Filler hose
4. Ventilation tube
5. Evaporation tube
6. Fuel outlet hose
7. Fuel tank unit gauge
8. Fuel strainer

B210 fuel tank and lines

B210 Coupe

1. Disconnect the battery ground cable.

2. Remove the finish panel from the right-side of the trunk.

3. Place a pan under the drain plug, remove the plug, and drain the gas.

4. Disconnect the filler hose, ventilation lines, and fuel line from the tank.

5. Disconnect the evaporative lines from the reservoir tank.

6. Remove the spare tire and then the inspection plate from the rear floor.

7. Disconnect the sending unit wires.

8. Remove the fuel tank mounting bolts and lift the tank out of the car.

9. Installation is the reverse of removal.

1979–and later 210 Sedan

NOTE: *Install fuel filler hose after fuel tank has been mounted in place. Failure to follow this rule could result in leakage from around the hose connections. Do not twist*

or smash vent hoses when they are routed. Be sure to retain them securely with clips.

1. Disconnect the battery ground cable.

2. Drain the fuel from the fuel tank, then disconnect the fuel hose.

3. Remove the filler hose protector and inspection cover in the luggage compartment.

4. Disconnect the fuel filler hose, vent hoses and the fuel tank gauge unit wire connector.

5. Remove the fuel tank protector.

6. Remove the fuel tank.

Installation is the reverse of removal.

1979–and later 210 Hatchback and Station Wagon

1. Disconnect the battery ground cable.

2. Drain the fuel from the fuel tank, then disconnect the fuel hose.

3. Remove the luggage carpet, luggage board, inspection cover and side finisher.

4. Disconnect the fuel filler hose, vent

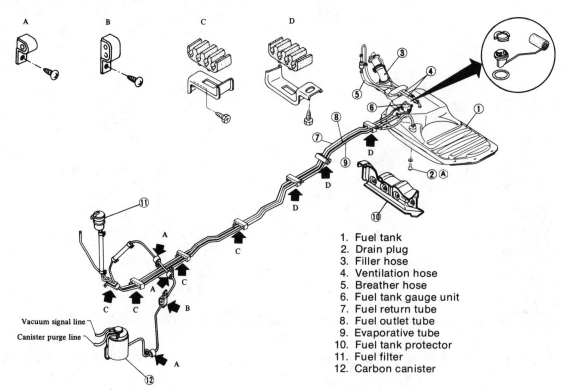

1. Fuel tank
2. Drain plug
3. Filler hose
4. Ventilation hose
5. Breather hose
6. Fuel tank gauge unit
7. Fuel return tube
8. Fuel outlet tube
9. Evaporative tube
10. Fuel tank protector
11. Fuel filter
12. Carbon canister

Vacuum signal line
Canister purge line

210 fuel tank and lines. Sentra similar

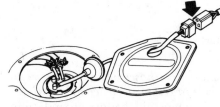

Removing fuel tank gauge unit and harness connection

hoses and the fuel tank gauge unit wire connector.

5. Remove the fuel tank protector.
6. Remove the fuel tank.
Installation is the reverse of removal.

1982 and Later Sentra

1. Drain fuel.
2. Remove inspection cover and disconnect fuel tank gauge unit harness connector.
3. Disconnect fuel filler and ventilation tubes.
NOTE: *Plug hose and pipe openings to prevent entry of dust and dirt.*
4. Disconnect fuel outlet, return and evaporation hoses.
5. Remove six bolts attaching fuel tank and then take out fuel tank.
6. Install in the reverse order of removal.

Chassis Electrical

UNDERSTANDING AND TROUBLESHOOTING ELECTRICAL SYSTEMS

For any electrical system to operate, it must make a complete circuit. This simply means that the power flow from the battery must make a complete circle. When an electrical component is operating, power flows from the battery to the component, passes through the component causing it to perform its function (lighting a light bulb, for example) and then returns to the battery through the ground of the circuit. This ground is usually (but not always) the metal part of the car on which the electrical component is mounted.

Perhaps the easiest way to visualize this is to think of connecting a light bulb with two wires attached to it to your car battery. The battery in your car has two posts (negative and positive). If one of the two wires attached to the light bulb was attached to the negative post of the battery and the other wire was attached to the positive post of the battery, you would have a complete circuit. Current from the battery would flow out one post, through the wire attached to it and then to the light bulb, causing it to light. It would then leave the light bulb, travel through the other wire, and return to the other post of the battery.

The normal automotive circuit differs from this simple example in two ways. First, instead of having a return wire from the bulb to the battery, the light bulb returns the current to the battery through the chassis of the vehicle. Since the negative battery cable is attached to the chassis and the chassis is made of electrically conductive metal, the chassis of the vehicle can serve as a ground wire to complete the circuit. Secondly, most automotive circuits contain switches to turn components on and off as required.

There are many types of switches, but the most common simply serves to prevent the passage of current when it is turned off. Since the switch is a part of the circle necessary for a complete circuit, it operates to leave an opening in the circuit, and thus an incomplete or open circuit, when it is turned off.

Some electrical components which require a large amount of current to operate also have a relay in their circuit. Since these circuits carry a large amount of current, the thickness of the wire (gauge size) in the circuit is also greater. If this large wire were connected from the component to the control switch on the instrument panel, and then back to the component, a voltage drop would occur in the circuit. To prevent this potential drop in voltage, an electromagnetic switch (relay) is used. The large wires in the circuit are connected from the car battery to one side of the relay, and from the opposite side of the relay to the component. The relay is normally open, preventing current from passing through the circuit. An additional, smaller, wire is connected from the relay to the control switch for the circuit. When the control switch is turned on, it grounds the smaller wire from the relay and completes the circuit. This closes the relay and allows current to flow from the battery to the component. The horn, headlight, and starter circuits are three which use relays.

You have probably noticed how the car's instrument panel lights get brighter the faster you rev the engine. This happens because your alternator (which supplies the battery) puts out more current at speeds above idle. This is normal. However, it is possible for larger surges of current to pass through the electrical system of your car. If this surge of current were to reach an electrical component, it could burn the component out. To prevent this from happening, fuses are connected into the current supply wires of most of the major electrical systems of your car. The fuse serves to head off the surge at the pass. When an electrical current of excessive power passes through the component's fuse, the fuse blows out and breaks the circuit, saving it from destruction.

The fuse also protects the component from damage if the power supply wire to the component is grounded before the current reaches the component.

There is another important rule to the complete circle circuit. *Every complete circuit from a power source must include a component which is using the power from the power source.* If you were to disconnect the light bulb (from the previous example of a light bulb being connected to the battery by two wires together (take our word for it—don't try it) the result would literally be shocking. A similar thing happens (on a smaller scale) when the power supply wire to a component or the electrical component itself becomes grounded before the normal ground connection for the circuit. To prevent damage to the system, the fuse for the circuit blows to interrupt the circuit—protecting the components from damage. Because grounding a wire from a power source makes a complete circuit—less the required component to use the power—this phenomenon is called a short circuit. The most common causes of short circuits are: the rubber insulation on a wire breaking or rubbing through to expose the

current carrying core of the wire to a metal part of the car, or a short switch.

Some electrical systems on the car are protected by a circuit breaker which is, basically, a self-repairing fuse. When either of the above-described events takes place in a system which is protected by a circuit breaker, the circuit breaker opens the circuit the same way a fuse does. However, when either the short is removed from the circuit or the surge subsides, the circuit breaker resets itself and does not have to be replaced as a fuse does.

The final protective device in the chassis electrical system is a fuse link. A fuse link is a wire that acts as a fuse. It is connected between the starter relay and the main wiring harness for the car. This connection is under the hood, very near a similar fuse link which protects all the chassis electrical components. It is the probable cause of trouble when none of the electrical components function, unless the battery is disconnected or dead.

Electrical problems generally fall into one of three areas:

1. The component that is not functioning is not receiving current.

2. The commponent itself is not functioning.

3. The component is not properly grounded.

Problems that fall into the first category are by far the most complicated. It is the current supply system to the component which contains all the switches, relays, fuses, etc.

The electrical system can be checked with a test light and a jumper wire. A test light is a device that looks like a pointed screwdriver with a wire attached to it. It has a light bulb in its handle. A jumper wire is a piece of insulated wire with an alligator clip attached to each end.

If a light bulb is not working, you must follow a systematic plan to determine which of the three causes is the villain.

1. Turn on the switch that controls the inoperable bulb.

2. Disconnect the power supply wire from the bulb.

3. Attach the ground wire on the test light to a good metal ground.

4. Touch the probe end of the test light to the end of the power supply wire that was disconnected from the bulb. If the bulb is receiving current, the test light will go on.

NOTE: *If the bulb is one which works only when the ignition key is turned on (turn signal), make sure the key is turned on.*

If the test light does not go on, then the problem is in the circuit between the battery and the bulb. As mentioned before, this includes all the switches, fuses, and relays in the system. The problem is an open circuit between the battery and the bulb. If the fuse is blown and, when replaced, immediately blows again, there is a short circuit in the system which must be located and repaired. If there is a switch in the system, bypass it with a jumper wire. This is done by connecting one end of the jumper wire to the power supply wire into the switch, and the other end of the jumper wire to the wire coming out of the switch. If the test light lights with the jumper wire installed, the switch or whatever was bypassed is defective.

NOTE: *Never substitute the jumper wire for the bulb, as the bulb is the component required to use the power from the power source.*

5. If the bulb in the test light goes on, then the current is getting to the bulb that is not working in the car. This eliminates the first of the three possible causes. Connect the power supply wire and connect a jumper wire from the bulb to a good metal ground. Do this with the switch which controls the bulb turned on, and also the ignition switch turned on if it is required for the light to work. If the bulb works with the jumper wire installed, then it has a bad ground. This is usually caused by the metal area on which the bulb mounts to the car being coated with some type of foreign matter or rust.

6. If neither test located the source of the trouble, then the light bulb itself is defective.

The above test procedure can be applied to any of the components of the chassis electrical system by substituting the component that is not working for the light bulb. Remember that for any electrical system to work, all connections must be clean and tight.

HEATER

Heater Assembly
REMOVAL AND INSTALLATION
1973 1200

1. Remove the package tray and ashtray.
2. Drain coolant. Disconnect the two hoses between the heater and engine.
3. Disconnect the cables from the heater unit and heater controls. Disconnect the wiring.
4. Disconnect the two control wires from the water cock and interior valve, and the control rod from the shut valve. Set the heater control upper lever to DEF and lower lever to OFF.
5. Pull off the right and left defroster hoses.
6. Remove the four screws holding the

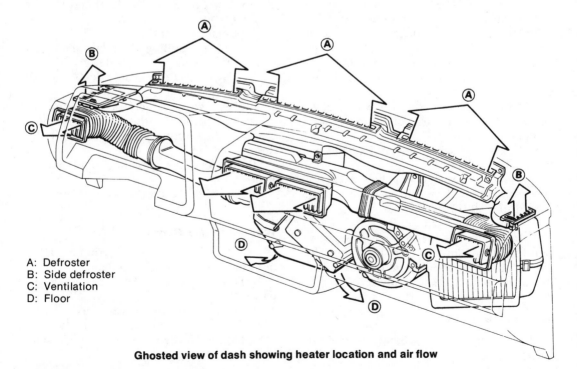

A: Defroster
B: Side defroster
C: Ventilation
D: Floor

Ghosted view of dash showing heater location and air flow

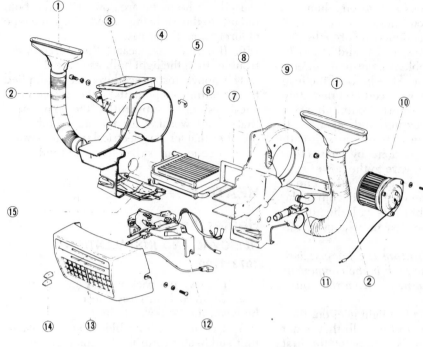

1. Defroster nozzle
2. Defroster hose
3. Air intake box
4. Heater box (L.H.)
5. Clip
6. Heater core
7. Ventilator valve
8. Resistor
9. Heater box (R.H.)
10. Fan and fan motor
11. Heater cock
12. Heater control
13. Center ventilator
14. Knob
15. Heat valve

B210 heater

heater unit to the firewall. Remove the control knob and remove the screws holding the control unit to the instrument panel. Remove the heater unit.

7. Reverse the procedure for installation.

B210

1. Disconnect the battery ground cable.
2. Drain all coolant from the radiator.
3. Disconnect the coolant inlet and outlet hoses.
4. Remove the heater duct hoses from both sides of the heater unit. Remove the defroster hose or hoses.
5. Disconnect the electrical wires of the heater unit (and air conditioner, if so equipped) at their connections.
6. Disconnect and remove the heater control cables.
8. Remove one attaching bolt from each side and one bolt from the top center of the heater unit (all B210 models).
8. Remove the heater unit.
9. Installation is the reverse of removal. Run the engine for a few minutes (don't forget to top up the radiator with coolant) with the heater on to make sure the system is filled with coolant.

1978 and later 210

1. Disconnect the ground cable at the battery. Drain the coolant.

2. Remove the package tray on the 210, if so equipped.
3. Remove the driver's side of the instrument panel. See the section below for instructions.
4. Remove the heater control assembly: remove the defroster ducts, vent door cables at the doors, harness connector and the control assembly.
5. Remove the radio.
6. On air conditioned models, disconnect cooler ducts at heater unit side.
7. Disconnect the heater ducts, side defrosters and the center vent duct.
8. Remove the screws attaching the defroster nozzle to the unit. Disconnect the blower wiring harness and the heater hoses.
9. Remove the retaining bolts and the heater unit.
10. Installation is the reverse of removal.

1982 and later Sentra

1. Set "TEMP" lever to maximum "HOT" position and drain engine coolant.
2. Disconnect heater hoses at engine compartment.
3. Remove instrument assembly.
4. Remove heater control assembly.
5. Remove heater unit assembly. Installation is the reverse of removal.

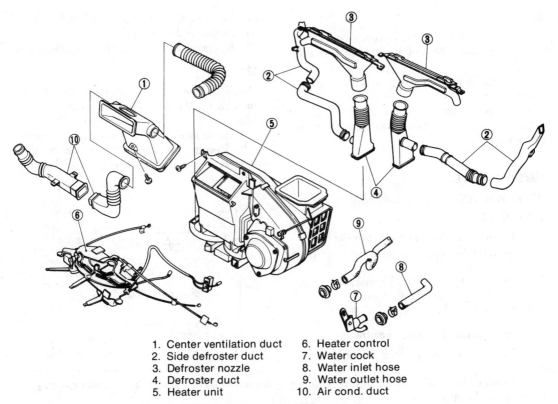

1. Center ventilation duct
2. Side defroster duct
3. Defroster nozzle
4. Defroster duct
5. Heater unit
6. Heater control
7. Water cock
8. Water inlet hose
9. Water outlet hose
10. Air cond. duct

210 heater assembly. Others similar

Heater Blower
REMOVAL AND INSTALLATION
210

1. Disconnect the battery ground cable.
2. Disconnect the heater blower harness connector.

3. Remove the three outer bolts holding the blower motor assembly in place and remove the motor with the fan attached.

NOTE: *Make sure you remove the outer bolts and not the bolts holding the motor to the backing plate.*

4. Installation is the reverse of removal.

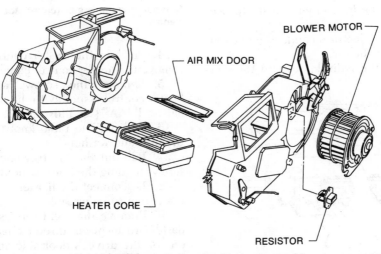

BLOWER MOTOR

AIR MIX DOOR

HEATER CORE

RESISTOR

Typical heater unit showing blower assembly

Sentra

1. Remove instrument lower cover.
2. Disconnect blower motor harness connector.
3. Remove lower casing attaching screws and drop casing.
4. Remove blower motor after removing retaining screws. Install in the reverse order of removal.

Heater Core

REMOVAL AND INSTALLATION
1200, B210

1. Remove the heater from the car.
2. Remove the clip and slide the hose from the heater core cock.
3. Remove the clips and separate the left and right sides of the heater case.
4. Lift out the heater core.

1978 and Later 210 and Sentra

1. Remove the heater unit as outlined earlier.
2. Loosen the hose clamps and disconnect the inlet and outlet hoses.
3. Remove the clips securing the case halves and separate the cases.
4. Remove the heater core.
5. Installation is in the reverse order of removal.

RADIO

REMOVAL AND INSTALLATION
1200, B210

1. Remove the instrument cluster (procedure follows).
2. Detach all electrical connections attaching the radio to the car.
3. Remove the radio knobs and their retaining nuts.

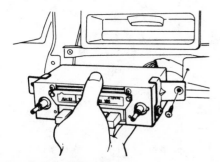

Radio removal, B210, 210

4. Remove the rear support bracket.
5. Remove the radio.
6. Reverse the procedure for installation.

210

NOTE: *The dashboard must be first removed on the 210 to gain access to the radio.*

1. Disconnect the battery ground cable.
2. Remove the steering column cover.
3. Remove the lighting control knob assembly.

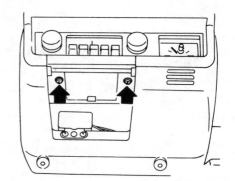

Sentra radio mounting screws under ash tray

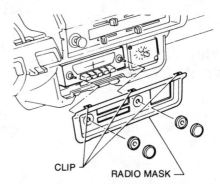

CLIP   RADIO MASK

Removing radio mask (cover) for radio access, Sentra

4. Pull out the heater control knob and remove the heater control panel facing.
5. Remove the screws attaching the heater control assembly to the dash panel, or cluster lid "A" (see illustration).
6. Pull out the radio knobs and remove the nuts and washers.
7. Pull out the ash tray and remove the screws holding the ash tray holder in place.
8. Disconnect the harness connector and the antenna feeder cable.
9. Remove the eight screws holding the dashboard in place: three along the bottom, one on the driver's door side and four along the windshield. Remove the dashboard.

10. Remove the radio bracket by loosening the retaining screws.

11. Remove the radio.

12. Installation is the reverse of removal.

Sentra

1. Remove ash tray and ash tray bracket.

2. Remove radio mounting bolts.

3. Remove radio mask (front cover) after removing tuning knobs.

4. Remove radio unit. Installation is the reverse of removal.

WINDSHIELD WIPER MOTOR AND LINKAGE

REMOVAL AND INSTALLATION

All Models

The wiper motor is on the firewall under the hood. The operating linkage is on the firewall inside the car.

1. Detach the motor wiring plug.

2. Inside the car, remove the nut connecting the linkage to the wiper shaft.

3. Unbolt and remove the wiper motor from the firewall.

4. Reverse the procedure for installation.

INSTRUMENT CLUSTER

REMOVAL AND INSTALLATION

1200

1. Disconnect the battery negative lead.

2. Depress the wiper, light switch, and

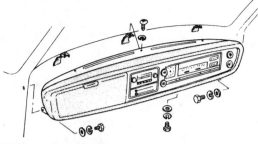

1200 dashboard removal

choke knobs, turning them counterclockwise to remove.

3. From the rear, disconnect the lighter wire. Turn and remove the lighter outer case.

4. Remove the radio and heater knobs.

5. Remove the shell cover from the steering column.

6. Remove the screws which hold the instrument cluster to the instrument panel. Pull out the cluster.

7. Disconnect the wiring connector. Disconnect the speedometer cable by unscrewing the nut at the back of the speedometer.

8. Individual instruments may be removed from the rear of the cluster.

B210

1. Disconnect the battery ground cable.

2. Remove the four screws and the steering column cover.

3. Remove the screws which attach the cluster face. Two are just above the steering column, and there is one inside each of the outer instrument recesses.

4. Pull the cluster lid forward.

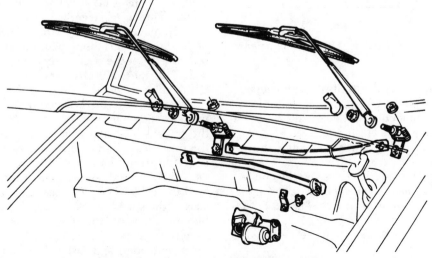

Wiper linkage and motor, 210. Others similar

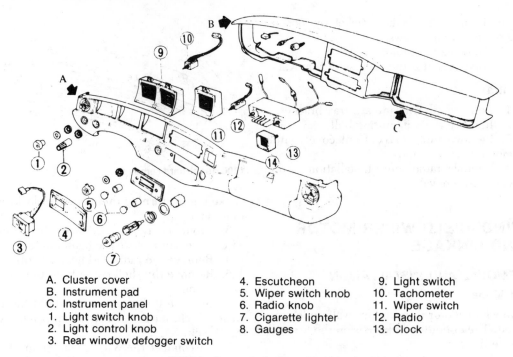

A. Cluster cover
B. Instrument pad
C. Instrument panel
1. Light switch knob
2. Light control knob
3. Rear window defogger switch

4. Escutcheon
5. Wiper switch knob
6. Radio knob
7. Cigarette lighter
8. Gauges

9. Light switch
10. Tachometer
11. Wiper switch
12. Radio
13. Clock

B210 instrument cluster removal

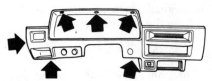

210 instrument panel left side attaching points

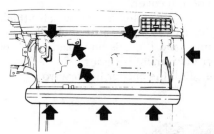

Right side attaching points, 210 instrument panel

5. Disconnect the multiple connector.
6. Disconnect the speedometer cable.
7. Disconnect any other wiring.
8. Remove the cluster face.
9. Remove the odometer knob if the vehicle has one.
10. Remove the six screws and the cluster.
NOTE: *To make removal of the cluster easier, remove the steering wheel and turn signal switch.*
11. Instruments may now be readily replaced.
12. Reverse the procedure for installation.

210

See 210 Radio Removal and Installation for instrument cluster removal and installation procedure.

Speedometer Cable Replacement

NOTE: *Cable routing varies slightly between the 1200, B210, 210 and Sentra models; cable replacement procedures for all models are basically the same. On some models it may be easier to remove the instrument cluster to gain access to the cable.*

1. Remove any lower dash covers that may be in the way and disconnect the speedometer cable from the back of the speedometer.
2. Pull the cable from the cable housing. If the cable is broken, the other half of the cable will have to be removed from the transmission end. Unscrew the retaining knob at the transmission and remove the cable from the transmission on extension housing.
3. Lubricate the cable with graphite powder (sold as speedometer cable lubricant) and feed the cable into the housing. It is best to start at the speedometer end and feed the cable down towards the transmission. It is also usually necessary to unscrew the transmission connection and install the cable end to the gear, then reconnect the housing to the

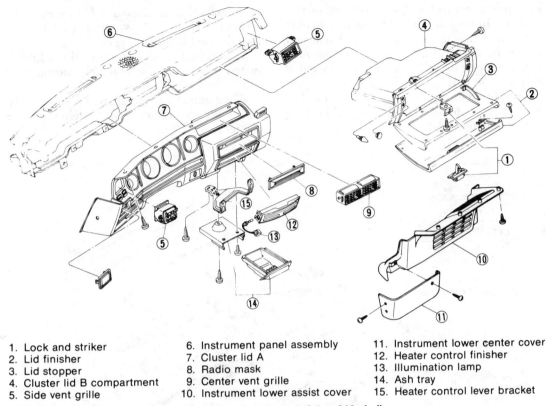

1. Lock and striker
2. Lid finisher
3. Lid stopper
4. Cluster lid B compartment
5. Side vent grille
6. Instrument panel assembly
7. Cluster lid A
8. Radio mask
9. Center vent grille
10. Instrument lower assist cover
11. Instrument lower center cover
12. Heater control finisher
13. Illumination lamp
14. Ash tray
15. Heater control lever bracket

1980 210 instrument panel. Other 210 similar

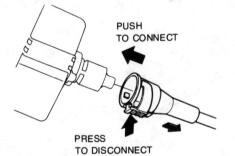

PUSH TO CONNECT

PRESS TO DISCONNECT

Sentra speedometer connection to speedometer. 210 similar

transmission. Slip the cable into the speedometer and reconnect the cable housing.

Ignition Switch

Ignition switch removal and installation procedures are covered in Chapter 8; Suspension and Steering.

Seatbelt System
WARNING BUZZER AND LIGHT

Since 1972, the federal government has required all cars to have a warning system designed to remind the driver to buckle his or her seat belt.

When the ignition switch is turned to the "ON" position, the warning lamp comes on and remains on for 4 to 8 seconds. At the same time, the chime (warning buzzer in 1980 and earlier models) sounds for 4 to 8 seconds intermittently if the driver's seat belt is not properly fastened. The chime or buzzer is also used as a theft warning alarm.

This warning system consists of an ignition switch, a timer unit, a warning lamp, a driver's seat belt switch and a buzzer or chime. The dash board seat belt lights and the buzzer

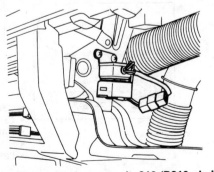

Seat belt warning buzzer unit, 210 (B210 similar). Sentra seat belt timer is under radio

or chime is controlled by pressure-sensitive switches hidden in the front bench or bucket seats. A switch in each of the front seat belt retractors turns off the warning system only when the belt or belts are pulled a specified distance out of their retractors.

Two different types of switches are used to control the system, depending upon the type of transmission used:

On manual-transmission equipped cars, the transmission neutral switch is used to activate the seat belt warning circuit.

Automatic transmissions use the inhibitor switch to activate the seat belt warning circuit.

When removing the seats, be sure to unplug the pressure-sensitive switches at their connections.

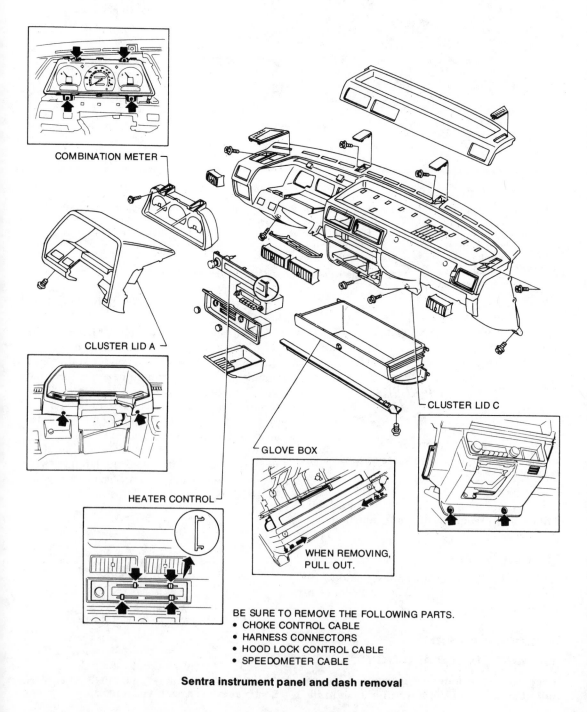

COMBINATION METER

CLUSTER LID A

CLUSTER LID C

GLOVE BOX

HEATER CONTROL

WHEN REMOVING, PULL OUT.

BE SURE TO REMOVE THE FOLLOWING PARTS.
- CHOKE CONTROL CABLE
- HARNESS CONNECTORS
- HOOD LOCK CONTROL CABLE
- SPEEDOMETER CABLE

Sentra instrument panel and dash removal

SEAT BELT SWITCH—DISCONNECTING

1. Disconnect battery ground cable.
2. Slide seat all the way forward.
3. Disconnect harness connector.
4. Remove inner seat belt by removing security bolt.
5. Install inner seat belt in the reverse order of removal.

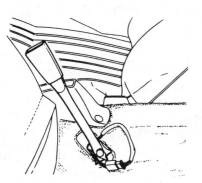

Seat belt warning switch

Seat Belt/Starter Interlock System

1974–75

As required by law, all 1974 and most 1975 Datsun passenger cars cannot be started until the front seat occupants are seated and have fastened their seat belts. If the proper sequence is not followed, e.g., the occupants fasten the seat belts and *then* sit on them, the engine cannot be started.

The shoulder harness and lap belt are permanently fastened together, so that they both must be worn. The shoulder harness uses an inertia-lock reel to allow freedom of movement under normal driving conditions.

NOTE: *This type of reel locks up when the car decelerates rapidly, as during a crash.*

The switches for the interlock system have been removed from the lap belt retractors and placed in the belt buckles. The seat sensors remain the same as those used in 1973.

For ease of service, the car may be started from outside, by reaching in and turning the key, but without depressing the seat sensors.

In case of system failure, an override switch is located under the hood. This is a "one start" switch and it must be reset each time it is used.

This system was discontinued after 1975.

LIGHTING

Headlights
REMOVAL AND INSTALLATION

NOTE: *The 1200 and B210 Datsun have radiator grilles which are unit-constructed to also serve as headlight frames. For these models it will be necessary to remove the grille to gain access to the headlights.*

1. Remove the grille, if necessary.
2. Remove the headlight retaining ring (frame) screws. These are the three or four short screws in the assembly; there are also two longer screws at the top and side of the headlight which are used to aim the headlight. *Do not tamper* with these or the headlight will have to be re-aimed.
3. Remove the ring around the round (pre-'81) headlights by turning it clockwise. The square headlamp assemblies should pull straight out without having to turn them.
4. Pull the headlight bulb from its socket and disconnect the electrical socket.

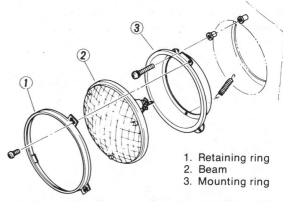

1. Retaining ring
2. Beam
3. Mounting ring

Exploded view of standard headlight. Square headlights similar

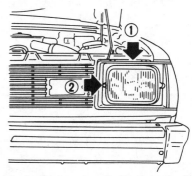

1. Vertical adjustment   2. Horizontal adjustment
210 headlight adjustment. Others similar except Sentra vertical adjustment screw is on bottom of unit

5. Connect the plug to the new bulb.

6. Position the new headlight in the shell. Make sure that the word "TOP" is, indeed, at the top and that the knobs in the headlight lens engage the slots in the mounting shell.

7. Place the retaining ring over the bulb and install the screws.

8. Install the grille, if removed.

CIRCUIT PROTECTION

Fusible Links

A fusible link is a protective device used in an electrical circuit. When current increases beyond a certain amperage, the fusible metal wire of the link melts, thus breaking the electrical circuit (like a fuse) and preventing further damage to the other components and wiring. Whenever a fusible link is melted because of a short circuit, correct the cause before installing a new link.

Use the following chart to locate the fusible link(s) on your Datsun.

All Datsun fusible links are the plug in kind. To replace them, simply unplug the bad link and insert the new one.

CAUTION: *Never wrap vinyl tape around a fusible link. Extreme care should be taken with this link to ensure that it does not come into contact with any other wiring harness, vinyl, or rubber parts.*

WIRING DIAGRAMS

Wiring diagrams have been left out of this book. As cars have become more complex, and as more and more options have been available on them, wiring diagrams have also grown in size and complexity. It has become

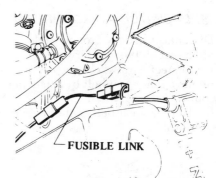

FUSIBLE LINK

Most fusible links are found beside the battery

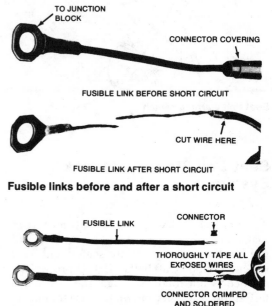

TO JUNCTION BLOCK

CONNECTOR COVERING

FUSIBLE LINK BEFORE SHORT CIRCUIT

CUT WIRE HERE

FUSIBLE LINK AFTER SHORT CIRCUIT

Fusible links before and after a short circuit

FUSIBLE LINK

CONNECTOR

THOROUGHLY TAPE ALL EXPOSED WIRES

CONNECTOR CRIMPED AND SOLDERED

New fusible links are spliced to the wire

impossible to reproduce wiring diagrams that are readable yet do not take up an unreasonable number of pages. Contact your Datsun dealer if you are in need of a wiring diagram.

Fusible Links

Year	Model	Number	Color/Protects	Location
1973	1200	1	Green/Charging system	At positive battery terminal
1974–78	B210	1	Green/Fuse block, electrical systems	At positive battery terminal
1979–82	210	2	Green/Starting, ignition, charging, headlights	At positive battery terminal
1982–83	Sentra	2	Green/Starting, ignition, charging, headlights	At positive battery terminal

Fuse Box and Flasher Location

Year	Model	Fuse Box Location	Flasher Location
1973	1200	Under instrument panel, right of steering wheel	Under dash
1974–78	B210	Below hood release knob	Turn signal: Behind radio Hazard: Under driver's side of dashboard
1979–82	210	Below hood release knob	Under driver's side dashboard ①
1982–83	Sentra	Below hood release knob	Under driver's side dashboard ①

NOTE: The original turn signal flasher unit is pink, and larger than the original hazard flasher unit, which is gold.
① Both the turn signal and the hazard flashers are side by side

Clutch and Transmission

MANUAL TRANSMISSION

Various four speed manual transmissions are standard equipment on all 1200, B210 and 210 models covered in this guide, except for the 1981 and later 210 MPG, which is equipped with a five speed transmission as standard. The front wheel drive Nissan Sentra uses either a four or five speed manual transaxle, which is actually a combination transmission and differential. All models feature integral shift linkage, which requires no adjustment.

The 1973 1200, 1974 B210 and 1980 210s use the F4W56 four speed transmission, which is constructed in two sections: a combined clutch and transmission housing, and an extension housing. There is a cast iron adaptor plate between the housings, and no case cover plates. The 1981 and later 210s use the F4W56 four speed.

The 1977–78 B210 uses the model FS5W63A five speed transmission. The 1979 210 has a FS5W60L five speed transmission, while the 1980 and later use the FS5W60A five speed transmission.

Front wheel drive Sentra models use either the RS5F30A five speed, or the RN4F30A four speed transaxle.

REMOVAL AND INSTALLATION
All 1200, B210 and 210 Models

1. Jack up the car and safely support it with jackstands. Disconnect the battery cables. Disconnect the backup light switch, neutral switch, Top gear, overdrive, and any other switches on the transmission after marking their positions with tape for later assembly.

2. On all models (1200, B210 and 210) disconnect the exhaust pipe from the exhaust manifold and bracket. Disconnect the speedometer cable from the speedometer cable drive on the transmission.

3. Scribe or paint matchmarks on the driveshaft flange and transmission flange so the driveshaft can be reinstalled with both

Clutch Specifications

Model	Pedal Height Above Floor (in.)	Pedal Free-Play (in.)
1200	5.6	0.12
B210	6.02	0.04–0.12
210	5.75	0.04–0.20
Sentra	7.9–8.1	0.43–0.83

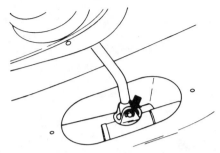

1200, B210 and 210 shift lever removal

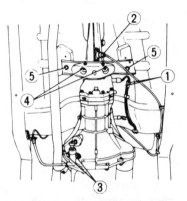

1200 and B210—disconnect the back-up light switch (1), speedometer cable (2), clutch slave cylinder (3), rear engine mount bolts (4), crossmember bolts (5). 210 similar

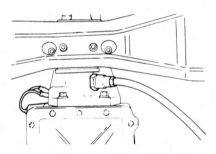

Disconnect speedometer and back-up light switch

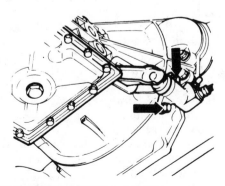

Remove the clutch slave cylinder

flanges in the exact same relationship. Unbolt the driveshaft at the rear of the transmission. Quickly plug the end of the transmission extension housing to prevent leakage of transmission oil (which will begin immediately when the driveshaft is unbolted).

4. Remove the shift lever.

5. Remove the clutch operating cylinder from the clutch housing.

6. Support the engine by placing a jack under the oil pan with a wooden block used between the oil pan and the jack.

CAUTION: *Do not place the jack under the oil pan drain plug.*

7. Support the transmission, preferably with a jack, and unbolt the transmission from the crossmember. Remove the crossmember.

8. Lower the rear of the engine slightly to allow a little clearance.

9. Remove the starter from the engine.

10. Remove the bolts securing the transmission to the engine and gusset.

11. With the engine and transmission still supported, lower the jack supporting the transmission (with the transmission on it) to the rear and away from the engine. Remove the transmission from underneath the car.

NOTE: *When removing the transmission, take care not to strike any adjacent parts, especially the main drive gear and spline.*

Install the transmission in the reverse order of removal, paying attention to the following points:

1. Before installing, clean all mating surfaces of the engine rear plate and transmission case. Clean the transmission rear flange and front driveshaft flange. Make sure the matchmarks on both flanges are lined up during assembly.

2. Before installing, lightly apply a multipurpose grease to the spline parts of the clutch disc and main drive gear. Also, apply the same grease to the moving surfaces of the gear control lever and striking rod.

3. Remove the transmission filler plug and fill the ttransmission with a gearbox lubricant rated API GL-5 to the level of the filler plug hole.

4. Check the clutch linkage adjustment after installing the transmission.

Sentra Front Wheel Drive Models

1. Remove battery and battery holding plate.

2. Jack up front of car and safely support with jackstands.

3. Remove the radiator reservoir tank.

4. Drain the transmission gear oil.

5. Draw out the drive halfshafts from the transaxle (refer to Chapter 7 "Drive Train" for procedure).

NOTE: *When removing halfshafts, use care not to damage the lip of the oil seal. After shafts are removed, insert a steel bar or wooden dowel of suitable diameter to prevent the side gears from rotating and falling into the differential case.*

6. Remove the wheel house protector.

7. Separate the control rod and support rod from the transaxle.

Temporarily insert a bar or dowel into the transaxle after halfshaft is removed

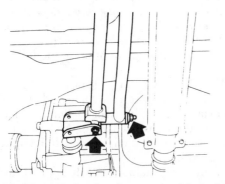

Separating control rod and support rod from Sentra transaxle

Removing Sentra wheel house protector

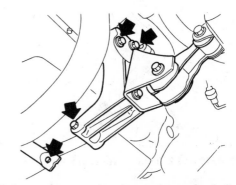

Sentra engine mount and gusset securing bolts

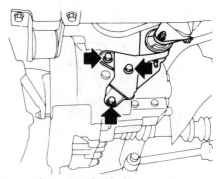

Sentra engine mounting bolts

8. Remove the engine gusset securing bolt and the engine mounting.

9. Remove the clutch control cable from the withdrawal lever.

10. Disconnect speedometer cable from the transaxle.

11. Disconnect the wires from the reverse (back-up) and neutral switches.

12. Support the engine by placing a jack under the oil pan, with a wooden block placed between the jack and pan for protection.

13. Support the transaxle with a hydraulic floor jack.

14. Remove the engine mounting securing bolts.

15. Remove the bolts attaching the transaxle to the engine.

16. Using the hydraulic floor jack as a carrier, carefully lower the transaxle down and away from the car.

CAUTION: *Be careful not to strike any adjacent parts or input shaft (the shaft protruding from the transaxle which fits into the clutch assembly) when removing the transaxle from the car.*

Installation of the Sentra transaxle is in the reverse order of removal, but pay attention to the following points:

1. Before installing, clean the mating sur-

faces on the engine rear plate and clutch housing.

2. Apply a light coat of a lithium-based grease (which includes molybdenum-disulfide) to the spline parts of the clutch disc and the transaxle input shaft.

3. Remove the filler plug and fill the transaxle with 4⅞ U.S. pints (four speed) and 5¾ U.S. pints (five speed) of a quality API GL-4 rating. Fill to the level of the plug hole.

4. Apply a thread sealant to the threads of the filler plug and install the plug in the transaxle case. Tighten the bolts securing the transaxle to the engine to 12–15 ft. lbs.

CLUTCH

The purpose of the clutch is to disconnect and connect engine power from the transmission. A car at rest requires a lot of engine torque to get all that weight moving. An internal-combustion engine does not develop a high starting torque (unlike steam engines for example), so it must be allowed to operate without any load until it builds up enough torque to move the car. Torque increases with engine rpm. The clutch allows the engine to build up torque by physically disconnecting the engine from the transmission, relieving the engine of any load or resistance. The transfer of engine power to the transmission (the load) must be smooth and gradual; if it isn't driveline components would wear out or break quickly. This gradual power transfer is made possible by gradually releasing the clutch pedal. The clutch disc and pressure plate are the connecting link between the engine and transmission. When the clutch pedal is released, the disc and plate contact each other (clutch engagement), physically joining the engine and transmission. When the pedal is pushed in, the disc and plate separate (the clutch is disengaged), disconnecting the engine from the transmission.

The clutch used in all 1200, B210 and 210 Datsun models covered in this guide is a hydraulic, single dry-disc, diaphragm spring type clutch. The Sentra clutch is conventional (non-hydraulic) singleplate, diaphragm spring type clutch. The major clutch components consist of the flywheel, the clutch disc, the pressure plate, diaphragm springs, the throwout (release) bearing and fork, the clutch master cylinder, slave cylinder and connecting line, and the pedal. The flywheel and the

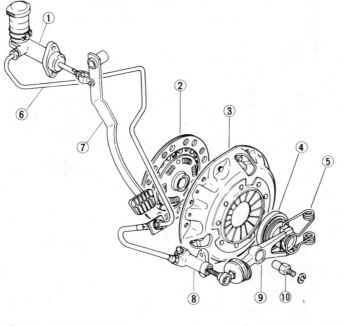

1. Clutch master cylinder
2. Clutch disc assembly
3. Clutch cover assembly
4. Release bearing and sleeve assembly
5. Return spring
6. Clutch line
7. Clutch pedal
8. Operating cylinder
9. Withdrawal lever
10. Withdrawal lever ball pin

1200 and B210 clutch control system. 210 similar

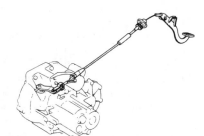

Sentra clutch control layout

clutch pressure plate (driving members) are connected to the engine crankshaft and rotate with it. The clutch disc is located between the flywheel and pressure plate, and is splined to the transmission shaft. A driving member is one that is attached to the engine and transfers engine power to a driven member (clutch disc) on the transmission shaft. A driving member (pressure plate) rotates (drives) a driven member (clutch disc) on contact, and in so doing, turns the transmission shaft. There is a circular diaphragm spring within the pressure plate cover (transmission side). In a relaxed state (when the clutch pedal is fully relased), this spring is convex; that is, it is dished outward toward the transmission. Pushing in the clutch pedal actuates the slave cylinder (only on hydraulic clutches), which is the smaller of the two hydraulic cylinders and the one that actually operates the clutch mechanism.

Connected to the other end of the slave cylinder rod is the throwout bearing fork, which is also found on the non-hydraulic Sentra clutch. When the clutch pedal is depressed, the slave cylinder (or the clutch cable on Sentra) pushes the fork and bearing forward to contact the diaphragm spring of the pressure plate. The outer edges of the spring are secured to the pressure plate and are pivoted on rings so that when the center of the spring is compressed by the throwout bearing, the outer edges bow outward, and, by so doing, pull the pressure plate in the same direction—away from the clutch disc. This action separates the disc from the plate, disengaging the clutch from the transmission and allowing the transmission to be shifted into another gear. Releasing the pedal allows the throwout bearing to pull away from the diaphragm spring resulting in a reversal of spring position. As bearing pressure is gradually released from the spring center, the outer edges of the spring bow inward, pushing the pressure plate into closer contact with the clutch disc. As the disc and plate move

closer together, friction between the two increases and slippage is reduced until, when full spring pressure is applied (by fully releasing the pedal), the speed of the disc and plate are the same. This stops all slipping, creating a direct connection between the plate and disc which results in the transfer of power from the engine to the transmission. The clutch disc is now rotating with the pressure plate at the engine speed and, because it is splined to the transmission shaft, the shaft now turns at the same engine speed.

ADJUSTMENT

Refer to the Clutch Specifications Chart for clutch pedal height above floor and pedal free play.

Since all 1200, B210 and 210 models have a hydraulically operated clutch, pedal height is usually adjusted with a stopper limiting the upward travel of the pedal. Pedal free-play is adjusted at the master cylinder pushrod. The Sentra clutch is adjusted with a pedal stopper and adjusting locknut.

1. Adjust pedal height on all models ("H" in illustration) with pedal stopper. Then tighten lock nut (see illustration).

2. Adjust 1200, B210 and 210 pedal free play with master cylinder pushrod. Then tighten lock nut.

3. Adjust Sentra withdrawal lever at the

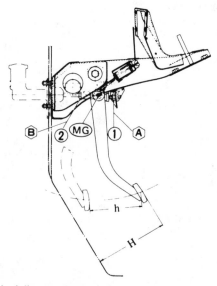

1. Adjust pedal height here
2. Adjust pedal free-play here
MG. Lubricate with multipurpose grease here
H. is pedal height
h. is free-play

Clutch adjusting points

lever tip end (on side of transaxle) with adjusting nut. Play in lever is 0.08–0.16 in.

Depress and release clutch pedal (on all models) over its entire stroke to ensure that the clutch linkage operates smoothly without squeak, noise, and interference, or binding.

REMOVAL AND INSTALLATION
1200, B210, 210 Hydraulic Clutch

1. Remove the transmission from the engine.
2. Loosen the bolts in sequence, a turn at a time. Remove the bolts.
3. Remove the pressure plate and clutch disc.
4. Remove the release mechanism. Apply multi-purpose grease to the bearing sleeve inside groove, the contact point of the withdrawal lever and bearing sleeve, the contact surface of the lever ball pin and lever. Replace the release mechanism.
5. Inspect the pressure plate for wear, scoring, etc., and reface or replace as necessary. Inspect the release bearing and replace as necessary. Apply a small amount of grease to the transmission splines. Install the disc on the splines and slide back and forth a few times. Remove the disc and remove excess grease on hub. *Be sure no grease contacts the disc or pressure plate.*
6. Install the disc, aligning it with a splined dummy shaft.
7. Install the pressure plate and torque the bolts to 11–16 ft. lbs.
8. Remove the dummy shaft.
9. Replace the transmission.

Sentra

1. Remove transaxle from engine.
2. Insert Nissan clutch aligning tool or a similar splined clutch tool (must fit the Sentra's clutch splines) into the clutch disc hub.
3. Loosen the bolts attaching the clutch cover to the flywheel, one turn each at a time, until the spring pressure is released.
   NOTE: *Be sure to turn them out in a crisscross pattern.*
4. Remove the clutch disc and cover assembly.
5. Inspect the pressure plate for scoring or roughness, and reface or replace as necessary (slight roughness can be smoothed with a fine emery cloth). Inspect the clutch disc for worn or oily facings, loose rivets and broken or loose springs, and replace. (You probably have the clutch out of the car to replace it anyway).

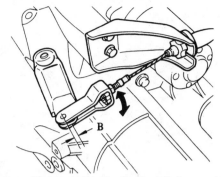

Sentra withdrawal lever adjustment. Arrow shows locknut adjustment

6. Apply a light coat of a molybdenum-disulfide grease to the transaxle input shaft spline. Slide the clutch disc on the input shaft several times to distribute the grease. Remove the clutch disc and wipe off the excess lubricant pushed off by the disc hub.
   CAUTION: *Take special care to prevent any grease or oil from getting on the clutch facing. During assembly, keep all disc facings, flywheel and pressure plate clean and dry. Grease, oil or dirt on these parts will result in a slipping clutch when assembled.*
7. Install the clutch cover assembly. Each bolt should be tightened one turn at a time in a crisscross pattern. Torque the bolts to 12–15 ft. lbs.
8. Remove the clutch aligning tool.
9. Reinstall the transaxle.

Clutch Master Cylinder
REMOVAL AND INSTALLATION
Hydraulic Clutch Models

1. Remove snap pin from clevis pin, and pull out clevis pin.
2. Disconnect the clutch pedal arm from the pushrod.
3. Disconnect the clutch hydraulic line from the master cylinder.
   NOTE: *Take precautions to keep brake fluid from coming in contact with any painted surfaces.*
4. Remove the nuts attaching the master cylinder and remove the master cylinder and pushrod toward the engine compartment side.
5. Install the master cylinder in the reverse order of removal and bleed the clutch hydraulic system.

OVERHAUL

1. Remove the master cylinder from the vehicle.

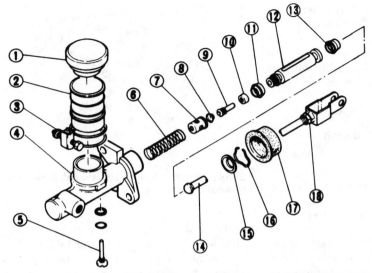

1. Reservoir cap
2. Reservoir
3. Reservoir band
4. Cylinder body
5. Supply valve stopper
6. Return spring
7. Spring seat
8. Valve spring
9. Supply valve rod
10. Supply valve
11. Primary cup
12. Piston
13. Secondary cup
14. Push rod
15. Stopper
16. Stopper ring
17. Dust cover
18. Lock nut

210 clutch master cylinder. 1200 and B210 similar

2. Drain the clutch fluid (same as brake fluid) from the master cylinder reservoir.

3. Remove the boot and circlip and remove the pushrod.

4. Remove the stopper, piston, cup and return spring.

5. Clean all of the parts in clean brake fluid.

6. Check the master cylinder and piston for wear, corrosion and scores and replace the parts as necessary. Light scoring and glaze can be removed with crocus cloth soaked in clean brake fluid.

7. The cup seal should be replaced each time the master cylinder is disasembled, if there is any evidence of wear, cracking, damage, or fatigue.

8. Check the clutch fluid reservoir, filler cap, dust cover and the pipe for distortion and damage and replace the parts as necessary.

9. Lubricate all new parts with clean brake fluid.

10. Reassemble the master cylinder parts in the reverse order of disassembly, taking note of the following:

   a. Reinstall the cup seal carefully to prevent damaging the lipped portions;

   b. Adjust the height of the clutch pedal after installing the master cylinder in position on the vehicle;

   c. Fill the master cylinder and clutch fluid reservoir and then bleed the clutch hydraulic system (see "Bleeding the Clutch Hydraulic System").

Clutch Slave Cylinder
REMOVAL AND INSTALLATION
Hydraulic Clutch Models

1. Remove the slave cylinder attaching bolts and the pushrod from the shift fork.

2. Disconnect the flexible fluid hose from the slave cylinder and remove the unit from the vehicle.

3. Install the slave cylinder in the reverse order of removal and bleed the clutch hydraulic system.

OVERHAUL

1. Remove the slave cylinder from the vehicle.

2. Remove the pushrod and boot.

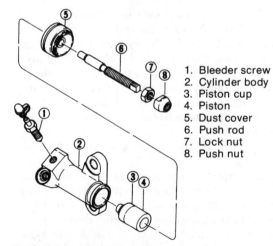

1. Bleeder screw
2. Cylinder body
3. Piston cup
4. Piston
5. Dust cover
6. Push rod
7. Lock nut
8. Push nut

Typical hydraulic clutch slave cylinder

3. Force out the piston by blowing compressed air into the slave cylinder at the hose connection.

NOTE: *Be careful not to apply excess air pressure to avoid possible injury.*

4. Clean all of the parts in clean brake fluid.

CAUTION: *Never use mineral solvents such as kerosene or gasoline to clean master cylinder and other brake parts. These solvents will ruin the rubber parts of the hydraulic system.*

5. Check and replace the slave cylinder bore and piston if wear or severe scoring exists. Light scoring and glaze can be removed with crocus cloth soaked in clean brake fluid.

6. Normally the piston cup should be replaced when the slave cylinder is disasembled. Check the piston cup and replace it if it is found to be worn, fatigued or scored.

7. Replace the rubber boot if it is cracked or broken.

8. Lubricate all of the new parts in clean brake fluid and reassemble in the reverse order of disassembly, taking note of the following:

   a. Use care when reassembling the piston cup to prevent damaging the lipped portion of the piston cup;

   b. Fill the master cylinder with brake fluid and bleed the clutch hydraulic system;

   c. Adjust the clearance between the pushrod and the shift fork to $5/64$ in.

Bleeding the Clutch Hydraulic System

1. Check and fill the clutch fluid reservoir to the specified level as necessary. During the bleeding process, continue to check and replenish the reservoir to prevent the fluid level from getting lower than ½ the specified level.

2. Remove the dust cap from the bleeder screw on the clutch slave cylinder and connect a tube to the bleeder screw and insert the other end of the tube into a clean glass or metal container.

NOTE: *Take precautionary measures to prevent the brake fluid from getting on any painted surfaces.*

3. Pump the clutch pedal several times, hold it down and loosen the bleeder screw slowly.

4. Tighten the bleeder screw and release the clutch pedal gradually. Repeat this operation until air bubbles disappear from the brake fluid being expelled out through the bleeder screw.

5. Repeat until all evidence of air bubbles completely disappears from the brake fluid being pumped out through the tube.

6. When the air is completely removed, securely tighten the bleeder screw and replace the dust cap.

7. Check and refill the master cylinder reservoir as necessary.

8. Depress the clutch pedal several times to check the operation of the clutch and check for leaks.

AUTOMATIC TRANSMISSION

All Datsun models covered in this guide are also available with a three-speed automatic transmission (Sentras have an automatic transaxle). Except for the various checks and maintenance procedures outlined here, it is recommended that major automatic transmission service be left to an automatic transmission specialist who has the expertise and special tools required to work on these units.

PAN REMOVAL

1. Jack up the front of the car and support it safely on stands.

2. Slide a drain pan under the transmission. Loosen the rear oil pan bolts first, to allow most of the fluid to drain off without making a mess on your garage floor.

3. Remove the oil pan guard on Sentra. Remove the remaining bolts and drop the pan.

4. Discard the old gasket, clean the pan, and reinstall the pan with a new gasket.

5. Tighten the retaining bolts in a crisscross pattern starting at the center.

CAUTION: *The transmission case is alu-*

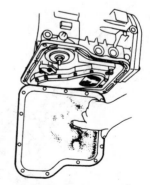

Automatic transmission pan removal

*minum and easily stripped, so don't put too
much torque on the bolts.*

6. Refill the transmission through the dipstick tube. Check the fluid level as described
in Chapter 1.

SHIFT LINKAGE ADJUSTMENT

The adjustment of the manual linkage (control cable on Sentra) is an important adjustment of the automatic transmission. Move the
shift lever from the "P" range into the "1"
range. You should be able to feel the detents
(stops) in each range.

If the detents cannot be felt or the pointer
indicating the range is improperly aligned, the
linkage (control cable) needs adjustment.

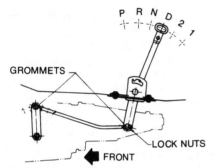

**Automatic transmission shift linkage adjustment,
1200, B210 and 210**

1200, B210 and 210

1. Place shift lever in "D" range.
2. Loosen locknuts (see illustration) and
move shift lever until "D" is properly aligned
and car is in "D" range.
3. Tighten locknuts when lever is in proper
position.

Recheck "P" and range "1" positions. As a
safety measure, be sure you can feel full de-
tent when shift lever is placed in "P". If you
are unable to make an adjustment, grommets

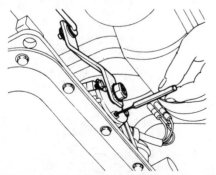

**Adjusting neutral (inhibitor) switch using align-
ment pin**

may be badly worn or damaged and should
be replaced.

Sentra Automatic Transaxle

1. Place gear lever in the "P" position.
2. Connect the control cable end to the
manual lever in the transaxle unit, and tighten
the control cable securing bolts.
3. Move the gear lever from the "P" position to the "1" position. Make sure that the
gear lever can move smoothly and without any
sliding noise.
4. Place the gear lever in the "P" range
again. Make sure that the control lever locks
at the "P" range.
5. Remove the control cable adjusting nut
A and loosen nut B, then connect the control
cable to the trunnion. Install nut A and B,
then tighten them.
6. Move the gear lever from "P" to "1" position again. Make sure the lever moves
smoothly without any sliding noise.
7. Apply a dab of grease to the spring
washer.
8. After properly adjusting the control cable, check the spring pin to see if it is assembled as shown in the illustration. If not, adjust the spring pin.

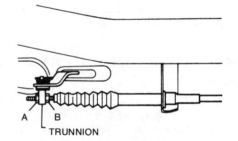

Sentra automatic transaxle cable adjustment

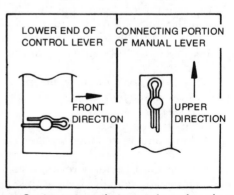

**Proper Sentra automatic transaxle spring pin po-
sition**

DOWNSHIFT SOLENOID/KICKDOWN SWITCH CHECK AND ADJUSTMENT

1200, B210 and 210 Models

The kickdown switch is located at the upper post of the accelerator pedal, inside the car. The downshift solenoid is screwed into the outside of the transmission case.

When the kickdown operation is not made properly or the speed changing point is too high, check the kickdown switch, downshift solenoid and the wiring connection between them.

1. Turn the ignition switch "ON" to the first position.

2. Push the accelerator pedal all the way down to actuate the downshift switch.

3. The downshift solenoid should click when actuated if working properly. If there is no click, loosen the locknut and extend the switch until the pedal lever makes contact with the switch and the switch clicks.

> CAUTION: *Do not allow the switch to make contact too soon. This would cause the transmission to downshift on part throttle.*

If the switch can be heard clicking even if the transmission is not kicking down, check the electrical continuity of the switch with a continuity tester. Also check to see if current is reaching the switch.

INHIBITOR SWITCH (NEUTRAL SAFETY AND BACKUP LIGHT) ADJUSTMENT

The switch unit is bolted to the left-side of the transmission case, behind the transmission shift lever. The switch prevents the engine from being started in any transmission position except Park or Neutral. It also controls the backup lights.

1200, B210 and 210 Models

1. Remove the transmission shift lever retaining nut and the lever.

2. Remove the switch.

3. Remove the machine screw in the case under the switch.

4. Align the switch to the case by inserting a 0.059 in. (1.5 mm) diameter pin through the hole in the switch into the screw hole. Mark the switch location.

5. Remove the pin, replace the machine screw, install the switch as marked, and replace the transmission shift lever and retaining nut.

6. Make sure, while holding the brakes and parking brake on, that the engine will start only in Park or Neutral. Check that the backup lights go on only in Reverse.

Sentra

1. Loosen the inhibitor attaching screws (three Phillips head screws).

2. Set the select lever (manual shaft) at the "N" position.

3. Insert a 2.5mm (0.098 in.) diameter pin into the adjustment holes in both the inhibitor switch and the switch lever as near vertical as possible.

4. Tighten the screws.

5. Check the inhibitor switch for continuity at the "N", "P" and "R" ranges. With the gear lever in neutral position, turn the manual lever an equal amount in both directions to see if the current flow ranges are nearly the same.

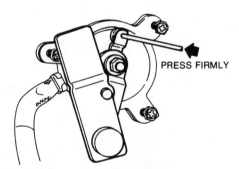

PRESS FIRMLY

Sentra inhibitor switch adjustment

REMOVAL AND INSTALLATION

1. Disconnect the battery cable.

2. Remove the accelerator linkage.

3. Detach the shift linkage.

4. Disconnect the neutral safety switch and downshift solenoid wiring.

5. Remove the drain plug and drain the torque converter. If there is no converter drain plug, drain the transmission. If there is no transmission drain plug, remove the pan to drain. Replace the pan to keep out dirt.

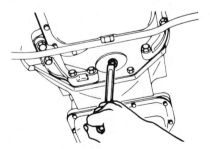

Disconnecting the torque converter bolts through access hole

6. Remove the front exhaust pipe.

7. Remove the vacuum tube and speedometer cable.

8. Disconnect the fluid cooler tubes.

9. Remove the driveshaft and starter.

10. Support the transmission with a jack and wood block under the oil pan and support the engine.

11. Remove the rear crossmember.

12. Mark the relationship between the torque converter and the drive plate with a scribe or grease pencil. Remove the four bolts holding the converter to the drive plate through the hole at the front, under the engine. Unbolt the transmission from the engine.

13. Reverse the procedure for installation. Make sure that the drive plate is warped no more than 0.020 in. Torque the drive plate-to-torque converter and converter housing-to-engine bolts to 29–36 ft. lbs. Drive plate-to-crankshaft bolt torque is 101–116 ft. lbs.

14. Refill the transmission and check the fluid level.

Drive Train

DRIVELINE

Driveshaft and Universal Joints

The driveshaft transfers power from the front-mounted engine and transmission to the differential and rear axles and then to the rear wheels to drive the car. All 1200, B210 and 210 Datsun models covered in this guide utilize a conventional rear wheel drive system.

The driveshafts in these models have two universal joints at each end, and a slip yoke at the front of the assembly which fits into the back of the transmission. These "U-joints" permit the driveshaft to both connect transmission and differential, which are not mounted on the same plane and to follow the rear axle up and down with the rear suspension movement as it also spins on its axis.

On the front wheel drive Sentras, the en-

1. Sleeve yoke
2. Spider with four bearing journals
3. Bearing race snap-ring
4. Bearing race with needle rollers
5. Spider with four bearing journals
6. Flange yoke
7. Bearing race snap-ring
8. Bearing race with needle rollers
9. Bolt
10. Lockwasher
11. Nut

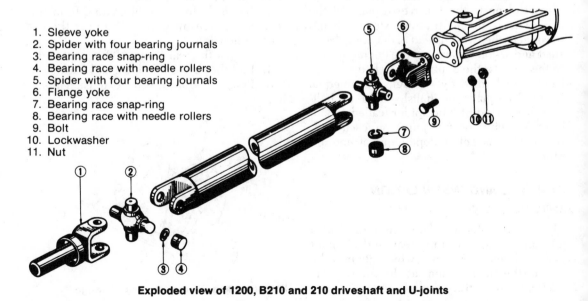

Exploded view of 1200, B210 and 210 driveshaft and U-joints

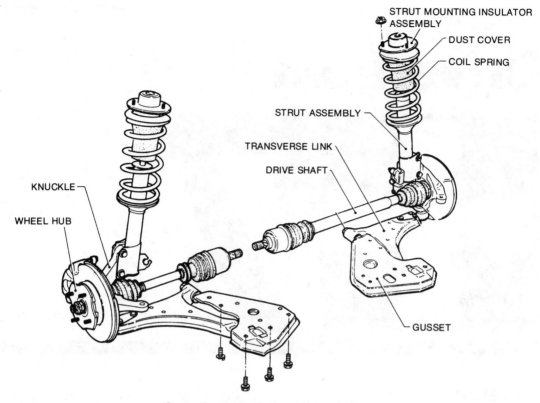

STRUT MOUNTING INSULATOR
ASSEMBLY

DUST COVER

COIL SPRING

STRUT ASSEMBLY

TRANSVERSE LINK

DRIVE SHAFT

KNUCKLE

WHEEL HUB

GUSSET

Sentra front drive train and suspension

tire drive train is bolted in unit with the engine up front. Since the Sentra engine is transversely mounted (across the chassis), its crankshaft is already spinning on the same plane as the front (drive) wheels. Compared to its Datsun cousins, the Sentra transaxle has an easy job—instead of having to change the direction of the engine torque from a longitudinal plane to the transverse plane of the drive wheels, the Sentra transaxle merely has to connect the two. Instead of one long driveshaft and U-joints carrying the engine torque to the wheels, the Sentra transaxle drives the front wheels directly through two unequal length driveshafts, or "halfshafts." Each halfshaft has a U-joint type spider (called a Constant Velocity, or CV joint) on each end, making the wheels independent of one another.

REMOVAL AND INSTALLATION
1200, B210, 210

These driveshafts are all one-piece units with a U-joint and flange at the rear, and a U-joint and a splined sleeve yoke which fits into the rear of the transmission, at the front. Early 1200 and some B210 models generally have

U-joints with grease fittings. U-joints without grease fittings must be disassembled for lubrication, usually at 24,000 mile intervals. The splines are lubricated by transmission oil.

1. Jack up car and safely support it with jackstands. Matchmark both the driveshaft and rear flange so that the shaft can be reinstalled in the same position.

2. Be ready to catcn oil coming from the rear of the transmission and to plug the extension housing.

3. Unbolt the rear flange (differential end).

4. Pull the driveshaft down and back.

5. Plug the transmission extension housing.

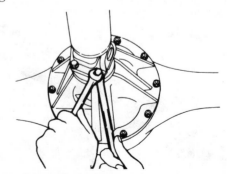

Disconnecting the rear driveshaft flange

6. Reverse the procedure to install, oiling the splines. Flange bolt torque is 15–20 ft. lbs. (1200), 17–24 ft. lbs. (B210-210).

Sentra

1. Jack up the car and safely support it with jackstands.

2. Remove the wheel and tire assembly.

3. Remove the brake caliper assembly (refer to Chapter 9 "Brakes" for this procedure).

4. Pry off the cotter pin from the castellated nut on the wheel hub.

5. Loosen, but do not remove, the wheel hub nut from the halfshaft while holding the wheel hub with a suitable tool.

6. Remove the tie rod ball joint (see Chapter 8 "Suspension" for this procedure). Remove the lower ball joint. Do not reuse the nut once it has been removed; install a new nut during assembly.

7. Drain the gear oil from the transaxle.

8. Remove the bolts holding the halfshaft flange to the transaxle. Remove the halfshaft, along with the wheel hub and knuckle.

9. Insert a suitable bar, wooden dowel or similar tool into the transaxle to prevent the sidegear from dropping inside (see Manual Transaxle Removal procedures for an illustration).

CAUTION: *When removing the transaxle, be very careful not to damage the grease seal on the transaxle side.*

10. Installation is the reverse of removal. Coat the transaxle-end halfshaft spline with a molybdenum-disulfide grease before insertion. Make sure the rubber gaiters on both ends of the halfshaft are in good shape; it not, replace them (use new metal bands to retain the gaiters).

U-JOINT OVERHAUL

All Rear Wheel Drive Models

DISASSEMBLY

1. Match mark the relationship of all components for reassembly.

2. Remove the snap-rings. On early units, the snap-rings are seated in the yokes. On later units, the snap-rings seat in the needle bearing races.

3. Tap the yoke with a rubber hammer to release one bearing cap. The needle rollers are lined up around the inside wall of the caps and may be loose if their grease packing has disappeared. Use care in disassembling the U-joint from this point, as the rollers are easily lost.

4. Remove the other bearing caps. Remove the U-joint spiders from the yokes.

INSPECTION

1. Spline backlash should not exceed 0.0197 in. (0.5 mm).

2. Driveshaft run-out should not exceed 0.015 in. (0.4 mm).

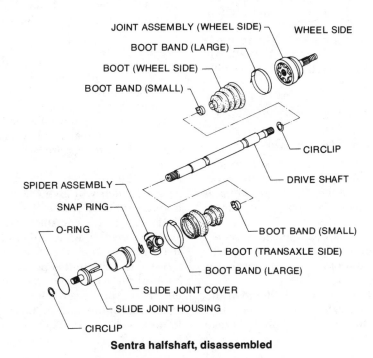

JOINT ASSEMBLY (WHEEL SIDE) — WHEEL SIDE
BOOT BAND (LARGE) —
BOOT (WHEEL SIDE) —
BOOT BAND (SMALL) —
CIRCLIP
DRIVE SHAFT
SPIDER ASSEMBLY —
SNAP RING —
O-RING —
BOOT BAND (SMALL)
BOOT (TRANSAXLE SIDE)
BOOT BAND (LARGE)
SLIDE JOINT COVER
SLIDE JOINT HOUSING
CIRCLIP

Sentra halfshaft, disassembled

3. On later models with snap-rings seated in the needle bearing races, different thicknesses of snap-rings are available for U-joint adjustment. Play should not exceed 0.0008 in. (0.02 mm).

4. U-joint spiders must be replaced if their bearing journals are worn more than 0.0059 in. (0.15 mm) from their original diameter.

ASSEMBLY

1. Grease the inside diameter of the cap races with enough grease to hold the rollers in place. Line the rollers up tightly, side by side inside the races.

2. Put the spider into place in its yokes.

3. Replace all seals.

4. Tap the races into position and secure them with snap-rings.

Sentra

The CV joints on the Sentra are a non-disassembling design. Special tools (a large press to remove the spider assembly from the shaft, for example) and experience are needed to disassemble and replace these joints. We recommend you take the halfshafts to a professional service facility for further repair.

Rear Axle

All 1200, B210 and 210 Datsun models covered in this guide utilize a solid (non-independent) rear axle. On the 1200 and B210 models, the rear axle assembly is attached to the frame through semi-elliptic leaf springs and telescopic shock absorbers. The rear axle of the 210 models is suspended through coil springs and links, and damped with telescopic shock absorbers.

Axle Shaft

REMOVAL AND INSTALLATION

NOTE: *Bearings must be pressed on and off the shaft with an arbor press. Unless you have access to one, it is inadvisable to attempt any repair work on the axle shaft and bearing assemblies.*

1. Remove the hub cap or wheel cover. Loosen the lug nuts.

2. Raise the rear of the car and support it safely on stands.

3. Remove the rear wheel. Remove the four brake backing plate retaining nuts. Detach the parking brake linkage from the brake backing plate.

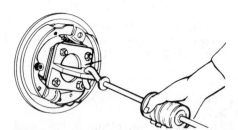

Removing axle on 1200, B210 and 210 models using a slide hammer

4. Attach a slide hammer to the axle shaft and remove it. Use the slide hammer and a two-pronged puller to remove the oil seal from the housing.

NOTE: *If a slide hammer is not available, the axle can sometimes be pried out using pry bars on opposing sides of the hub.*

If end-play is found to be excessive, the bearing should be replaced. Shimming the bearing is not recommended as this ignores end-play of the bearing itself and could result in improper seating of the bearing.

5. Using a chisel, carefully nick the bearing retainer in three or four places. The retainer does not have to be cut, only collapsed enough to allow the bearing retainer to be slid off the shaft.

6. Pull or press the old bearing off and install the new one by pressing it into position.

7. Install the outer bearing retainer with its raised surface facing the wheel hub, and then install the bearing and the inner bearing retainer in that order on the axle shaft.

8. With the smaller chamfered side of the inner bearing retainer facing the bearing, press on the retainer. The edge of the retainer should fully touch the bearing.

9. Clean the oil seal seat in the rear axle housing. Apply a thin coat of chassis grease.

10. Using a seal installation tool, drive the oil seal into the rear axle housing. Wipe a thin coat of bearing grease on the lips of the seal.

11. Determine the number of retainer gaskets which will give the correct bearing-to-outer retainer clearance of 0.01 in.

12. Insert the axle shaft assembly into the axle housing, being careful not to damage the seal. Ensure that the shaft splines engage those of the differential pinion. Align the vent holes of the gasket and the outer bearing retainer. Install the retaining bolts.

13. Install the nuts on the bolts and tighten them evenly, and in a criss-cross pattern, to 20 ft. lbs.

Troubleshooting the Rear Axle

BASIC REAR AXLE PROBLEMS

First, determine when the noise is most noticeable.

Drive Noise: Produced under vehicle acceleration.

Coast Noise: Produced while the car coasts with a closed throttle.

Float Noise: Occurs while maintaining constant car speed (just enough to keep speed constant) on a level road.

Road Noise

Brick or rough surfaced concrete roads produce noises that seem to come from the rear axle. Road noise is usually identical in Drive or Coast and driving on a different type of road will tell whether the road is the problem.

Tire Noise

Tire noises are often mistaken for rear axle problems. Snow treads or unevenly worn tires produce vibrations seeming to originate elsewhere. Temporarily inflating the tires to 40 lbs will significantly alter the tire noise, but will have no effect on rear axle noises (which normally cease below about 30 mph).

Engine/Transmission Noise

Determine at what speed the noise is most pronounced, then stop the car in a quiet place. With the transmission in Neutral, run the engine through speeds corresponding to road speeds where the noise was noticed. Noises produced with the car standing still are coming from the engine or transmission.

Front Wheel Bearings

While holding the car speed steady, lightly apply the footbrake; this will often decrease bearing noise, as some of the load is taken from the bearing.

Rear Axle Noises

Eliminating other possible sources can narrow the cause to the rear axle, which normally produces noise from worn gears or bearings. Gear noises tend to peak in a narrow speed range, while bearing noises will usually vary in pitch with engine speeds.

NOISE DIAGNOSIS

The Noise Is	*Most Probably Produced By*
1. Identical under Drive or Coast	Road surface, tires or front wheel bearings
2. Different depending on road surface	Road surface or tires
3. Lower as the car speed is lowered	Tires
4. Similar with car standing or moving	Engine or transmission
5. A vibration	Unbalanced tires, rear wheel bearing, unbalanced driveshaft or worn U-joint
6. A knock or click about every 2 tire revolutions	Rear wheel bearing
7. Most pronounced on turns	Damaged differential gears
8. A steady low-pitched whirring or scraping, starting at low speeds	Damaged or worn pinion bearing
9. A chattering vibration on turns	Wrong differential lubricant or worn clutch plates (limited slip rear axle)
10. Noticed only in Drive, Coast or Float conditions	Worn ring gear and/or pinion gear

Differential

NOTE: *All differential service should be performed by a professional mechanic, especially one well-versed in differential repair. A great deal of experience and many special tools are required in servicing a differential; this is not an area the owner/mechanic should tackle without experience.*

The rear axle on the 1200, B210 and 210 models must transmit power through a 90° bend. To accomplish this, straight cut bevel gears or spiral cut bevel gears were originally used. This type of gear drive is satisfactory for differential side gears, but since the centerline of the gears must intersect, they are not suitable for ring and pinion gears (main drive gears in all differentials). The lowering of the driveshaft brought about a variation of bevel gears called the hypoid gear. This type of gear does not require a meeting of the gear centerlines and can therefore be underslung, relative to the centerline of the ring gear.

OPERATION

The differential is an arrangement of gears which permits the rear wheels to turn at different speeds when cornering and divides the torque between the axle shafts. The differential gears are mounted on a pinion shaft and

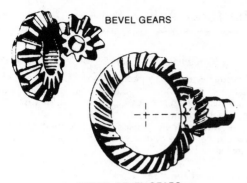

Bevel gears

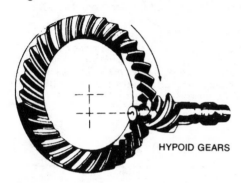

Hypoid gears

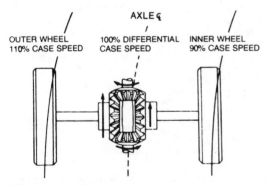

Differential action during cornering

the gears are free to rotate on this shaft. The pinion shaft is fitted in a bore in the differential case and is at right angles to the axle shafts.

Power flow through the differential is as follows. The drive pinion, which is turned by the driveshaft, turns the ring gear. The ring gear, which is bolted to the differential case, rotates the case. The differential pinion forces the pinion gears against the side gears. In cases where both wheels have equal traction, the pinion gears do not rotate on the pinion shaft, because the input force of the pinion gear is divided equally between the two side gears. Consequently the pinion gears revolve with the pinion shaft, although they do not

rotate on the pinion shaft itself. The side gears, which are splined to the axle shafts, and meshed with the pinion gears, rotate the axle shafts.

When it becomes necessary to turn a corner, the differential becomes effective and allows the axle shafts to rotate at different speeds. As the inner wheel slows down, the side gear splined to the inner wheel axle shaft also slows down. The pinion gears act as balancing levers by maintaining equal tooth loads to both gears while allowing unequal speeds of rotation at the axle shafts. If the vehicle speed remains constant, and the inner wheel slows down to 90 percent of vehicle speed, the outer wheel will speed up to 110 percent.

Determining Gear Ratio

Determining the axle ratio of any given axle can be a very useful "tool" to the contemporary car owner. Axle ratios are a major factor in a vehicle's fuel mileage, so the car buyer of today should know both what he or she is looking for, and what the salesperson is talking about. Knowledge of axle ratios is also valuable to the owner/mechanic who is shopping through salvage yards for a used axle, who is repairing his or her own rear axle, or who is changing rear axle ratios by changing rear axles.

The rear axle ratio is said to have a certain ratio, say 4.11. It is called a "4.11 rear" although the 4.11 actually means 4.11 to 1 (4.11:1). This means that the driveshaft will turn 4.11 times for every turn of the rear wheels. The number 4.11 is determined by dividing the number of teeth on the pinion gear into the number of teeth on the ring gear. In the case of a 4.11 rear, there could be 9 teeth on the pinion and 37 teeth on the ring gear ($37 \div 9 = 4.11$). This provides a sure way, although troublesome, of determining your rear axle's ratio. The axle must be drained and the rear cover removed to do this, and then the teeth counted.

A much easier method is to jack up the car and safely support it with jackstands, so BOTH rear wheels are off the ground. Block the front wheels, set the parking brake and put the transmission in Neutral. Make a chaulk mark on the rear wheel and the driveshaft. Turn the rear wheel one complete revolution and count the number of turns that the driveshaft makes (having an assistant here to count one or the other is helpful). The number of turns the driveshaft makes in one complete revolution of the rear wheel is an approximation of the rear axle ratio.

Suspension and Steering

FRONT SUSPENSION

All models covered in this book use Mac-Pherson strut front suspension. In this type of suspension, each strut combines the function of coil spring and shock absorber. The spindle is mounted to the lower part of the strut through a single ball joint. No upper suspension arm is required in this design. The lower suspension arm is required in this design. The lower suspension arm is bolted to the front subframe assembly.

Springs and Shock Absorbers
TESTING SHOCK ABSORBER ACTION

Shock absorbers require replacement if the vehicle fails to recover quickly after a large bump is encountered, if there is a tendency for the vehicle to sway or nose dive excessively, or, sometimes, if the suspension is overly susceptible to vibration.

A good way to test the shocks is to intermittently apply downward pressure to one corner of the vehicle until it is moving up and down for almost the full suspension travel, then release it and watch the recovery. If the vehicle bounces slightly about one more time and then comes to rest, the shock absorbers are serviceable. If the vehicle goes on bouncing, the shocks require replacement.

Strut
REMOVAL AND INSTALLATION

1. Jack up the car and support it safely. Remove the wheel.

2. Disconnect and plug the brake hose. Remove the brake caliper as outlined in Chapter 9. Remove the disc and hub as described in this chapter. On some 1200 models and early B210s with drum front brakes, loosen the brake tube connecting nut, remove the brake hose locking spring, withdraw the plate, and remove the brake hose from the strut assembly bracket.

3. Disconnect the tension rod and stabilizer bar from the transverse link.

4. Unbolt the steering arm. Pry the control arm down to detach it from the strut.

5. Place a jack under the bottom of the strut.

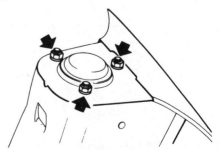

Front top strut mounting bolts. All models similar

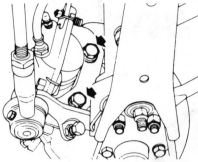

Brake caliper-to-strut mounting bolts

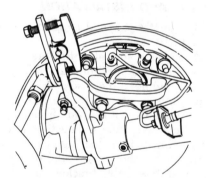

Disconnect brake hose before removing struts

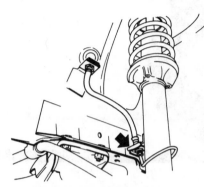

Removing side rod ball joint using ball joint puller. Forked ball joint tool may also be used

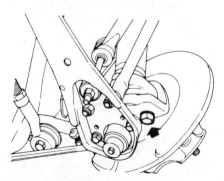

1200 and B210 strut-to-control arm/steering knuckle bolts. 210 similar

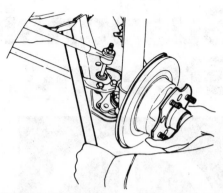

Pry the control arm down to separate the strut from the knuckle

6. Open the hood and remove the nuts holding the top of the strut.

7. Lower the jack slowly and cautiously until the strut assembly can be removed.

8. Reverse the procedure to install. The self-locking nuts holding the top of the strut must be replaced. Bleed the brakes.

Coil Spring and Shock Absorber
REMOVAL AND INSTALLATION

CAUTION: *The coil springs are under considerable tension, and can exert enough force to cause serious injury. Disassemble the struts only if the proper tools are available, and use extreme caution.*

Coil springs on all models must be removed with the aid of a coil spring compressor. If you don't have one, don't try to improvise by using something else: you could risk injury. The Datsun coil spring compressor is Special Tool ST3565S001 or variations of that number. Basically, they are all the same tool. These are the recommended compressors, although they are probably not the only spring compressors which will work. Always follow manufacturer's instructions when operating a spring compressor. You can now buy cartridge type shock absorbers for many Datsuns and Nissans: installation procedures are not the same as those given here. In the case of these aftermarket shocks, always follow the instructions that come with the shock absorbers.

To remove the coil spring(s), you must first remove the strut assembly from the vehicle. See above for procedures and follow the caution.

1. Secure the strut assembly in a vise.

2. Attach the spring compressor to the spring, leaving the top few coils free.

3. Remove the dust cap from the top of the

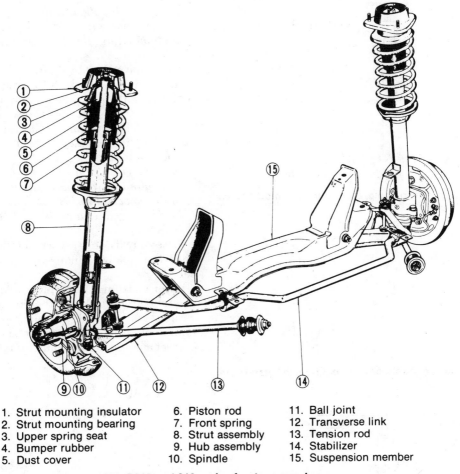

1. Strut mounting insulator
2. Strut mounting bearing
3. Upper spring seat
4. Bumper rubber
5. Dust cover
6. Piston rod
7. Front spring
8. Strut assembly
9. Hub assembly
10. Spindle
11. Ball joint
12. Transverse link
13. Tension rod
14. Stabilizer
15. Suspension member

1200, B210 and 210 series front suspension

strut to expose the center nut, if a dust cap is provided.

4. Compress the spring just far enough to permit the strut insulator to be turned by hand. Remove the self-locking center nut.

5. Take out the strut insulator, strut bearing, oil seal, upper spring seat and bound bumper rubber from the top of the strut. Note their sequence of removal and be sure to assemble them in the same order.

6. Remove the spring with the spring compressor still attached.

Assembly is the reverse of disassembly.

NOTE: *If replacement of any strut component parts is found to be necessary, make sure that parts are the same brand as those used in the strut assembly.*

Observe the following. Make sure you assemble the unit with the shock absorber piston rod fully extended. When assembling, take care that the rubber spring seats, both top and bottom, and the spring are posi-

tioned in their grooves before releasing the spring.

7. To remove the shock absorber: Remove the dust cap, if equipped, and push the pis-

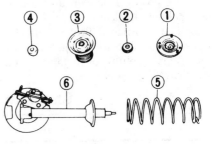

1. Strut mounting insulator
2. Bearing
3. Spring upper seat and dust cover
4. Damper rubber
5. Coil spring
6. Strut assembly

Exploded view of 1200 and B210 strut, others similar

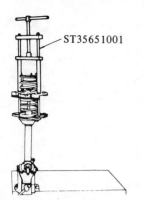

ST35651001

Datsun spring compressor correctly mounted on coil spring

Removing the shock absorber from the gland tube

Filling the shock assembly with oil

NOTE: *If the gland tube is dirty, clean it before removing it to prevent dirt from contaminating the fluid inside the strut tube.*

8. Remove the O-ring from the top of the piston rod guide and lift out the piston rod together with the cylinder. Drain all of the fluid from the strut and shock components into a suitable container. Clean all parts; *do not use* a mineral-based solvent on any of the rubber parts.

NOTE: *The piston rod, piston rod guide and cylinder are a matched set: single parts of this shock absorber assembly should not be exchanged with parts from other assemblies.*

Assembly is the reverse of disassembly, with the following notes to be closely observed:

After installing the cylinder and piston rod assembly (the shock absorber kit) in the outer casing, remove the piston rod guide, if equipped, from the cylinder and pour the correct amount of fresh fluid into the cylinder

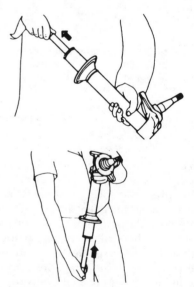

Bleeding air from strut unit

ton rod down until it bottoms. With the piston in this position, loosen and remove the gland packing shock absorber retainer. This calls for Datsun Special Tool ST35500001, but you should be able to loosen it with a pipe wrench (very carefully) or by tapping it around with a drift.

Shock Strut Refill Capacities

Year	Model	Shock Make	Capacity
1973	1200	AMPCO (ATSUGI)	280cc (17.1 cu. in.)
1974–78	B210	AMPCO (ATSUGI)	325cc (19.83 cu. in.)
1979–82	210 (U.S.) 210 (1.2L Canadian)	ATSUGI ATSUGI TOKICO	325cc (19.83 cu. in.) 260cc (16 cu. in.) 230cc (14.5 cu. in.)

and strut outer casing. Shock absorber kits list the correct amount of fluid to use, or check the following chart. Use only a high quality fluid made specifically for hydraulic struts (Nissan Strut Oil or equivalent).

NOTE: *It is crucial for correct shock absorber damping that the proper amount of fluid be used.*

Install the O-ring, fluid and any other cylinder components. Fit the gland packing and tighten it after greasing the gland packing-to-piston rod mating surfaces.

NOTE: *When tightening the gland packing, extend the piston rod about 3 to 5 inches from the end of the outer casing to expel most of the air from the strut.*

After the kit is installed, bleed the air from the system in the following mannner: hold the strut with its bottom end facing down. Pull the piston rod out as far as it will go. Turn the strut upside down and push the piston in as far as it will go. Repeat this procedure several times until an equal pressure is felt on both the pull out and the push in strokes of the piston rods. The remaining assembly is the reverse of disassembly.

Ball Joint
INSPECTION

The lower ball joint should be replaced when play becomes excessive. Datsun does not publish specifications on just what constitutes excessive play, relying instead on a method of determining the force (in inch pounds) required to keep the ball joint turning. This method is not very helpful to the owner mechanic since it involves removing the ball joint, which is what we are trying to avoid in the first place. An effective way to determine ball joint play is to jack up the car until the wheel is just a couple of inches off the ground and the ball joint is unloaded (meaning you can't jack directly underneath

Cross section of a ball joint. Note plug at the bottom for grease nipple

the ball joint). Place a long bar under the tire and move the wheel and tire assembly up and down. Keep one hand on top of the tire while you are doing this. If there is over ¼ inch of play at the top of the tire, the ball joint is probably bad. This is assuming that the wheel bearings are in good shape and properly adjusted. As a double check on this, have someone watch the ball joint while you move the tire up and down with the bar. If you can see considerable play, besides feeling play at the top of the wheel, the ball joint needs replacing.

REMOVAL AND INSTALLATION
All Models Except Sentra

The ball joint should be greased every 30,000 miles. There is a plugged hole in the bottom of the joint for the installation of grease fitting.

1. Raise and support the car so that the wheels hang free. Remove the wheel.
2. Unbolt the tension rod and stabilizer bar from the transverse link.
3. Unbolt the strut from the steering arm.
4. Remove the cotter pin and ball joint stud nut. Separate the ball joint and steering arm.
5. Unbolt the ball joint from the transverse link.
6. Reverse the procedure to install a new ball joint. Grease the joint after installation, forcing grease in until the old grease begins to squeeze out of the joint.

Sentra

The Sentra lower ball joints can be unbolted from the lower control arm. The ball joint is attached to the arm by a plate with three bolts through it, from the top of the lower arm. The nuts screw up onto these bolts from underneath the joint.

1. Remove the driveshaft (refer to Drive Shaft Removal for procedures).
2. Remove the lower ball joint by removing the three nuts and separating the ball joint from the steering knuckle using a ball joint removal tool.
3. Install the new ball joint in the reverse order of removal.
4. Lubricate the ball joint after assembly.

Lower Control Arm (Transverse Link) and Ball Joint
REMOVAL AND INSTALLATION

NOTE: *A ball joint removal tool of either the forked type (sometimes known as a*

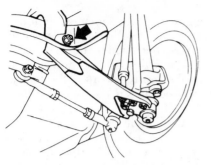

Removing bolt connecting control arm to crossmember—210

"knuckle buster," meaning the steering knuckles, not your knuckles) or the puller type is needed.

1. Jack up the vehicle and support it with jack stands; remove the wheel.

2. Remove the splash board, if so equipped.

3. Remove the cotter pin and castle nut from the side rod (steering arm) ball joint and separate the ball joint from the side rod.

4. Separate the steering knuckle arm from the MacPherson strut.

5. Remove the tension rod and stabilizer bar from the lower arm.

6. Remove the nuts and bolts connecting the lower control arm (transverse link) to the suspension crossmember on all models.

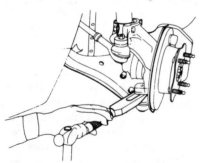

Separating ball joint from the knuckle using forked ball joint tool

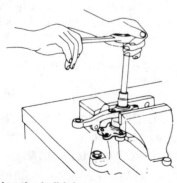

Removing the ball joint

7. Remove the lower control arm (transverse link) with the suspension ball joint and knuckle arm still attached.

8. Installation is the reverse of removal, with the following notes:

9. Check all rubber parts, such as tension rod and stabilizer bar bushings), to be sure they are not deteriorated or cracked, and replace if necessary. Also examine tension rod and stabilizer bar for evidence of damage and replace if necessary.

10. Be sure the stabilizer bar is not closer to either side, but is located at the middle.

11. When installing the control arm, temporarily tighten the nuts and/or bolts securing the control arm to the suspension crossmember. Tighten them fully only after the car is sitting on its wheels.

12. Lubricate the ball joints after assembly.

Tie-Rod Ends (Steering Side Rods)

REMOVAL AND INSTALLATION

You will need either type of ball joint remover for this operation.

1. Jack up the front of the vehicle and support it on jack stands.

2. Locate the faulty tie-rod end. It will have a lot of play in it and the dust cover will probably be ripped.

3. Remove the cotter key and nut from the tie-rod stud. Note the position of the tie-rod end in relation to the rest of the steering linkage.

4. Loosen the locknut holding the tie-rod to the rest of the steering linkage.

5. Free the tie-rod ball joint from either the relay rod or steering knuckle by using the ball joint remover.

6. Unscrew and remove the tie-rod end, counting the number of turns it takes to completely free it.

7. Install the new tie-rod end, turning it in exactly as far as you screwed out the old one. Make sure it is correctly positioned in relation to the rest of the steering linkage.

8. Fit the ball joint and nut, tighten them and install a new cotter pin.

Before finally tightening the tie-rod lock nut or clamp, adjust the toe-in of the vehicle.

Front End Alignment

The major front end adjustments for the Datsun are given here—caster/camber, toe, and

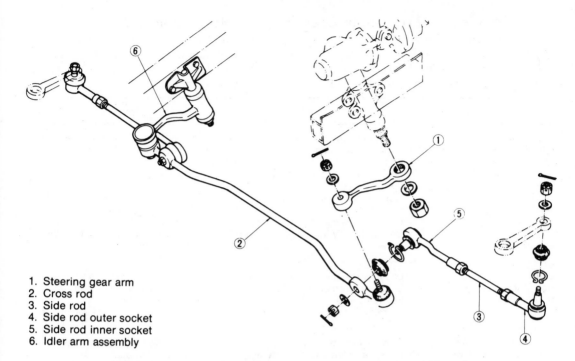

1. Steering gear arm
2. Cross rod
3. Side rod
4. Side rod outer socket
5. Side rod inner socket
6. Idler arm assembly

Steering linkage—toe-in adjustment is made at the side rod (tie rod)

steering angle. However, we recommend that a professional shop, specializing in front end alignment handle the work. Shops such as this are fully equipped for these procedures, and get the alignment correct the first time, which is something the average owner/mechanic may not do (especially if you do not have access to a hydraulic lift). The usually modest cost of a professional front end alignment job is well worth it when compared to the prospect of an improperly aligned (and unsafe) front end.

CASTER AND CAMBER

Caster is the forward or rearward tilt of the upper end of the kingpin, or the upper ball joint, which results in a slight tilt of the steering axis forward or backward. Rearward tilt is referred to as a positive caster, while forward tilt is referred to as negative caster.

Camber is the inward or outward tilt from the vertical, measured in degrees, of the front wheels at the top. An outward tilt gives the wheel positive camber. Proper camber is critical to assure even tire wear.

Since caster and camber are adjusted traditionally by adding or subtracting shims behind the upper control arms, and the Datsuns covered in this guide have replaced the upper control arm with the MacPherson strut, the only way to adjust caster and camber is to

replace bent or worn parts of the front suspension.

TOE

Toe is the amount, measured in a fraction of an inch, that the wheels are closer together at one end than the other. Toe-in means that the front wheels are closer together at the front than the rear; toe-out means the rears are closer than the front. Datsuns are adjusted to have a slight amount of toe-in. Toe-in is adjusted by turning the tie-rod, which has a right-hand thread on one end and a left-hand thread on the other.

You can check your vehicle's toe-in yourself without special equipment if you make careful measurements. The wheels must be straight ahead.

1. Toe-in can be determined by measuring the distance between the center of the tire treads, at the front of the tire and at the rear. If the tread pattern of your car's tires makes this impossible, you can measure between the edges of the wheel rims, but make sure to move the car forward and measure in a couple of places to void errors caused by bent rims or wheel runout.

2. If the measurement is not within specifications, loosen the locknuts at both ends of the tie-rod (the driver's side locknut is left-hand threaded).

Troubleshooting Basic Steering and Suspension Problems

Most problems in the front end and steering are caused by improperly maintained tires which you can correct yourself, or by incorrect wheel alignment, which requires the services of a professional mechanic. Get in the habit of checking tires frequently; this is usually the first place that problems in the front end or steering will show up.

The Condition	Is Caused By	What to Do
Hard steering (steering wheel is hard to turn)	• Low or uneven tire pressure • Loose power steering pump drive bolt • Low or incorrect power steering fluid • Incorrect front end alignment • Defective power steering pump • Bent or poorly lubricated front end parts	• Inflate tires to correct pressure • Adjust belt • Add fluid as necessary • Have front end alignment checked/adjusted • Have pump checked/repaired • Lubricate and/or have defective parts replaced
Loose steering (too much play in the steering wheel)	• Loose wheel bearings • Loose or worn steering linkage • Faulty shocks • Worn ball joints	• Adjust wheel bearings • Have worn parts serviced • Replace shocks • Have ball joints checked/serviced
Car veers or wanders (car pulls to one side with hands off the steering wheel)	• Incorrect tire pressure • Improper front end alignment • Loose wheel bearings • Loose or bent front end components • Faulty shocks	• Inflate tires to correct pressure • Have front end alignment checked/adjusted • Adjust wheel bearings • Have worn components checked/serviced • Replace shocks
Wheel oscillation or vibration transmitted through steering wheel	• Improper tire pressures • Tires out of balance • Loose wheel bearings • Improper front end alignement • Worn or bent front end components	• Inflate tires to correct pressure • Have tires balanced • Adjust wheel bearings • Have front end alignment checked/adjusted • Have front end checked/serviced
Uneven tire wear	• Incorrect tire pressure • Front end out of alignment • Tires out of balance	• Inflate tires to correct pressure • Have front end alignment checked/adjusted • Have tires balanced

3. Turn the top of the tie-rod toward the front of the car to reduce toe-in, or toward the rear to increase it. When the correct dimension is reached, tighten the locknuts and check the adjustment.

NOTE: *The length of the tie-rods must always be equal to each other.*

STEERING ANGLE ADJUSTMENT

The maximum steering angle is adjusted by stopper bolts on the steering arms. Loosen the locknut on the stopper bolt, turn the stopped bolt in or out as required to obtain the proper maximum steering angle and retighten the locknut.

SUSPENSION HEIGHT

Suspension height is adjusted by replacing the springs. Various springs are available for adjustment.

REAR SUSPENSION

There are two basic rear suepension types used on the Datsuns and Nissans covered in this guide. All 1200 and B210 models are equipped with solid (non-independent) rear axles suspended by leaf springs and telescopic shock absorbers. The 1979 and later 210s including wagons, are equipped with

Wheel Alignment Specifications

Year	Model	Caster Range (deg.)	Caster Preferred Setting (deg.)	Camber Range (deg.)	Camber Preferred Setting (deg.)	Toe-In (in.)	Steering Axis Inclination (deg.)	Wheel Pivot Ratio (deg.) Inner Wheel	Wheel Pivot Ratio (deg.) Outer Wheel
1973	1200	40'–1°40'	1°10'	35'–1°35'	1°05'	0.16–0.24	7°55'	42–44	35–37
1974	B210	1°15'–2°15'	—	40'–1°40'	—	0.079–0.157	7°47'–8°47'	37–39	31–33
1975–78	B210	1°00'–2°30'	1°45'	0°25'–1°55'	1°10'	0.08–0.16	7°32'–9°02'	37–39	31–33
1979–82	210 Sedan, Hatchback	1°40'–3°10'	—	0°–1°30'	—	0.04–0.12	7°50'–9°20'	38–42	31°30'–35°30'
	210 Station Wagon	1°55'–3°25'	—	0°–1°30'	—	0.04–0.12	7°50'–9°20'	38–42	31°30'–35°30'
1982–83	Sentra	45'–2°15'	—	–35'–1°05'	—	0.12–0.20	12°10'–13°40'	40–44	31–35

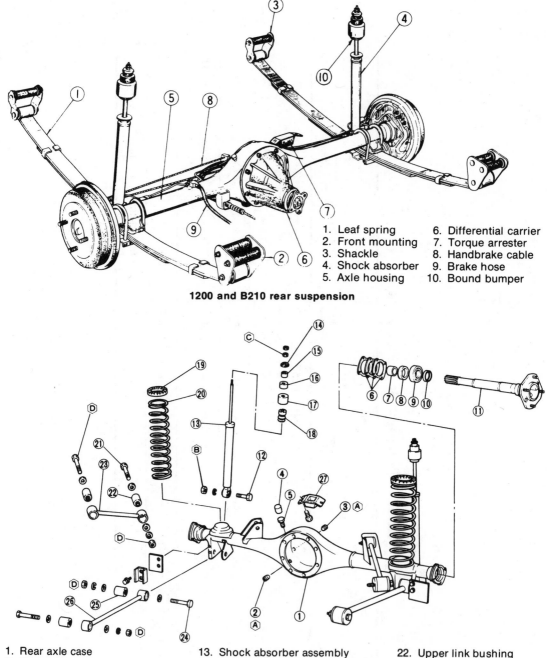

1. Leaf spring
2. Front mounting
3. Shackle
4. Shock absorber
5. Axle housing
6. Differential carrier
7. Torque arrester
8. Handbrake cable
9. Brake hose
10. Bound bumper

1200 and B210 rear suspension

1. Rear axle case
2. Drain plug
3. Filler plug
4. Breather cap
5. Breather
6. Rear axle case end shim
7. Bearing collar
8. Oil seal
9. Rear axle bearing (wheel bearing)
10. Bearing spacer
11. Rear axle shaft
12. Shock absorber lower end bolt
13. Shock absorber assembly
14. Special washer
15. Shock absorber mounting bushing A
16. Shock absorber mounting bushing B
17. Bound bumper cover
18. Bound bumper rubber
19. Shock absorber mounting insulator
20. Coil spring
21. Upper link bushing bolt
22. Upper link bushing
23. Upper link
24. Lower link bushing bolt
25. Lower link bushing
26. Lower link
27. Torque arrester

Tightening torque (ft-lb)
Ⓐ (43–72)
Ⓑ (51–58)
Ⓒ (11–14)
Ⓓ (51–58)

210 rear axle and suspension

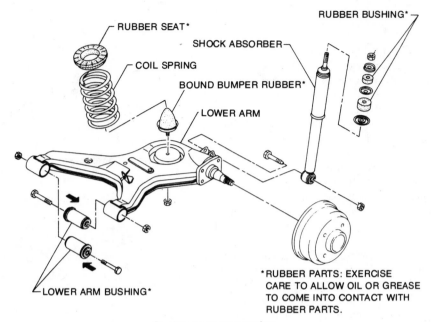

RUBBER SEAT*
SHOCK ABSORBER
COIL SPRING
BOUND BUMPER RUBBER*
LOWER ARM
RUBBER BUSHING*

*RUBBER PARTS: EXERCISE
CARE TO ALLOW OIL OR GREASE
TO COME INTO CONTACT WITH
RUBBER PARTS.

LOWER ARM BUSHING*

Sentra rear suspension

four-link type solid rear axles suspended by coil springs and telescopic shock absorbers. The 1982 and later Nissan Sentras utilize an independent rear suspension—one lower control arm on each side, damped by a telescopic shock absorber and coil spring.

CAUTION: *Before doing any rear suspension work, block both front wheels of the car to insure that it won't move or shift while you are under it. Always support the support the rear of the car with jackstands, NOT a jack. Also, remember you are dealing with spring steel that has enough force when compressed to injure you (when released) if you don't follow the removal and installation procedures exactly.*

Springs
REMOVAL AND INSTALLATION
Leaf Spring Type

1200 AND B210

1. Raise the rear axle until the wheels hang free. Support the car on stands. Support the rear axle with a hydraulic jack.
2. Unbolt the bottom end of shock absorber.
3. Unbolt the axle from the spring leaves. Unbolt and remove the front spring bracket. Lower the front of the spring to the floor.
4. Unbolt and remove the spring rear shackle.

5. Before reinstallation, coat the front bracket pin, bushing, shackle pin, and shackle bushing with a soap and water solution to serve as a lubricant.
6. Reverse the procedure to install. The front pin nut and the shock absorber mounting should be tightened before the vehicle is lowered to the floor.

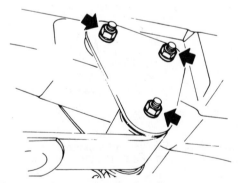

1200 and B210 front spring bracket

1200 and B210 rear spring shackle

Coil Spring Type
210 AND SENTRA

1. Block the front wheels.
2. Jack up the rear of the car high enough to permit working underneath, and place jackstands securely underneath the body members on both sides.
3. Place a floor jack under the center of the differential carrier (not necessary on Sentra).
4. Remove the rear wheels.
5. Remove the bolts securing the shock absorber lower ends on each side.
6. Lower the jack slowly and remove the coil springs on each side after they are fully extended.
7. Inspect the springs for yield, deformation or cracks.
8. Install the springs in the reverse order of removal. The bottom of the coil springs must sit squarely on each spring seat.

Shock Absorber
INSPECTION AND TESTING

Inspect and test the rear shock absorbers in the same manner as outlined for the front shock absorbers. Shocks should always be replaced in pairs.

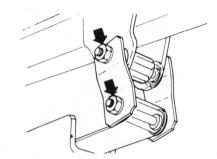

Remove the spring shackle

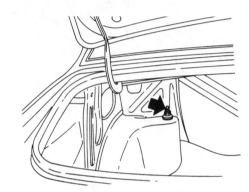

Rear shock absorber top mounting (sedans)

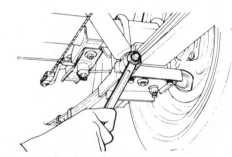

Removing the lower shock absorber nut

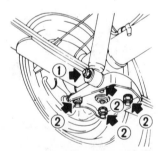

Detach lower shock absorber mount (1) and spring U-bolts (2)—1200 and B210 coupe shown

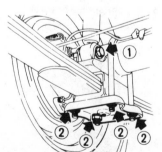

Detach lower shock absorber mount (1) and spring U-bolts (2)—1200 and B210 sedan shown

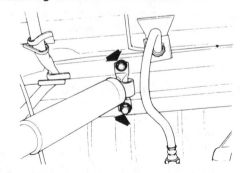

Upper shock absorber retaining bolts

REMOVAL AND INSTALLATION
Leaf Spring Type
1200 AND B210

1. Jack up the rear of the car and support the rear axle on two stands.

2. Disconnect the lower shock mounting bolt at the spring plate (plenty of pentrating oil is often useful here).

3. From inside the car, remove the rear seat back and disconnect the upper mounting nut.

4. Remove the shock absorber.

5. Install the replacement shock in the reverse of the removal procedure.

210 AND SENTRA

1. Open trunk and remove nuts securing shock absorber upper end to wheel house panel. Pry off the shock mount covers on the station wagon.

2. Remove bolt securing shock absorber lower end to lower control arm and remove shock absorber (using penetrating oil if necessary).

NOTE: *When removing shock absorber lower end from bracket, squeeze shock absorber and lift it out right above to accommodate the embossment inside bracket.*

3. Test shock absorber action by slowly pulling the piston rod out to full extension. Check for a steady pull with plenty of resistance and no sticking. Now begin to push the rod back, with a steady motion, until the shock is fully compressed. The feel of the damping should not be grabby, weak or loose. There should be no evidence of the shock leaking either air or oil (or both). Check the piston rod for straightness, and all rubber parts (including mount bushings) for wear, cracks, damage or deformation. Replace entire shock unit if necessary (usually replaced in pairs).

4. Install shock absorbers in the reverse order of removal.

NOTE: *Tighten shock absorber upper end nut to 11–14 ft. lbs. until it is fully tightened to thread end of piston rod. Then securely tighten lock nut. Tighten lower shock mounting nut to 51–58 ft. lbs.*

STEERING

Steering Wheel

REMOVAL AND INSALLATION

1. Piston the wheels in the straight-ahead direction. The steering wheel should be right-side up and level.

2. Disconnect the battery ground cable.

3. Look at the back of your steering wheel. If there are countersunk screws in the back

Removing horn pad—210

Using puller to remove the steering wheel

of the spokes, remove the screws and pull off the horn pad. Some models have a horn wire running from the pad to the steering wheel. Disconnect it. On the 3-spoke "sport" steering wheel on some 210s and the Sentra wheel, the central horn pad simply pulls off.

4. Remove the rest of the horn switching mechanism, noting the relative location of the parts. Remove the mechanism only if it hinders subsequent wheel removal procedures.

5. Match-mark the top of the steering column shaft and the steering wheel flange.

6. Remove the attaching nut and remove the steering wheel with a puller.

CAUTION: *Do not strike the shaft with a hammer, which may cause the column to collapse.*

7. Install the steering wheel in the reverse order of removal, aligning the punch marks. Do not drive or hammer the wheel into place, or you may cause the collapsible steering columns to collapse; in which case you'll have to buy a whole new steering column unit.

8. Tighten the steering wheel nut to 22–25 ft. lbs. on the 1200 and B210, and to 27–38 ft. lbs.

9. Reinstall the horn pad and button.

Turn Signal Switch

REMOVAL AND INSTALLATION

On the 1979 and later 210s, and 1982 and later Sentra, the turn signal switch is part of a combination switch (which includes lights, wipers, etc.). The entire unit is removed together. The turn signal switch on the B210 and 1200 models does not include any other functions (other than high beam).

Combination Switch—210 and Sentra

1. Disconnect the battery ground cable.
2. Remove the steering wheel as previously outlined. Observe the "caution" on the collapsible steering column.
3. Remove the steering column covers.
4. Disconnect the electrical plugs from the switch.
5. Remove the retaining screws and remove the switch.
6. Installation is the reverse of removal. Some turn signal switches have a tab which must fit into a hole in the steering shaft in order for the system to return the switch to the neutral position after the turn has been made. Be sure to align the tab and the hole when installing.

Turn Signal Switch—1200 and B210 Models

1. Disconnect battery ground cable.
2. Remove steering wheel.
3. Remove the four screws securing the

upper and lower shell covers to each other. Shell covers can then be taken out easily.
4. Disconnect the lead wires of the turn signal switch at the two connectors.
5. Loosen the two screws holding the switch assembly to the steering column jacket. The switch assembly can now be easily taken out.
6. Installation is the reverse of removal. Make sure that the location tab of the switch fits in the hole of the steering column jacket.

Steering Lock
REMOVAL AND INSTALLATION

The steering lock/ignition switch/warning buzzer assembly is attached to the steering column by special screws whose heads shear off when installed at the factory (so the lock cannot be removed easily). The screws must be drilled out to remove the assembly. The ignition switch or warning switch can be replaced without removing the assembly. The ignition switch is on the back of the assembly, and the warning switch on the side. The warning buzzer, which sounds when the driver's door is opened with the steering unlocked, is located behind the instrument panel.

Brakes

BRAKE SYSTEM

Adjustment

Front disc brakes are used on all models covered in this guide except some early 1200 models. All 1200, B210, and 210 Datsuns and Nissan Sentras are equipped with independent front and rear hydraulic systems with a warning light to indicate loss of pressure in either system. All models have rear hydraulic drum brakes.

The 1973 1200 is the only model covered here that does not have a power booster system to lessen the required brake pressure. The parking brake on all models operates the rear brakes through a cable system.

NOTE: *All front disc brakes covered in this guide are self-adjusting, needing no external adjustment. The drum brakes on the 1200 and B210 models require adjustment; 210 model drum brakes are automatically adjusted when the parking brake is applied (parking brake adjustment is also covered here).*

To adjust the brakes, jack up the car, remove the wheels, and safely support the rear with jackstands. Disconnect the parking brake linkage from the rear wheels, apply the brakes hard a few times to center the drums, and proceed as follows:

FRONT DRUM BRAKES

1. With the brake drum installed, insert the brake adjusting spoon through the backing plate. Tighten the cam adjusting stud clockwise until the brake shoes contact the brake drum (you will be unable to turn the drum freely).

2. Now turn the cam adjusting stud counterclockwise until the brake shoes separate slightly from the drums. The drums should turn freely.

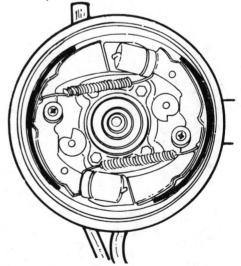

1200 front drum brake. All rear drums similar except utilize one wheel cylinder

3. Turn the brake drum, and if the brake shoe interferes (drags) on the drum, readjust the clearance. Depress the brake pedal and make sure the brake operates correctly.

Rear Brakes
1200

1. Remove the rubber grommets from the backing plate, and insert a brake adjusting spoon through the backing plate. Tighten the brake adjuster wedge clockwise, moving the brake shoes against the brake drum. You should now be unable to turn the brake drum.

2. Back off on the adjuster just enough that the brake drum will turn freely without dragging. Depress the brake pedal to make sure the brake operates effectively.

B210, 210 and Sentra

1. Make sure the hand brake lever assembly returns properly to its original position (down all the way).

2. Remove the rubber grommets from the adjuster holes in the backing plates.

3. Using a brake adjusting spoon or conventional screwdriver, turn the toothed adjusting nut to expand the brake shoes. Stop turning the adjusting nut when the shoes have made contact with the drum (drum won't turn).

4. Back off the adjusting nut several notches until the brake shoes are slightly away from the drum, with no drag. Test the brakes and make sure the operation is effective.

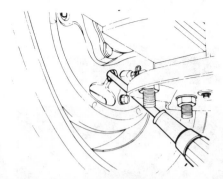

Rear brake adjustment. Brake adjusting spoon is recommended

PARKING BRAKE
All Models

1. Adjust rear brake shoe-to-drum clearance before adjusting hand brake.

2. Turn the adjusting nut on the front (short) end of the turnbuckle so that the operating stroke is 78.5 mm (3.091 in.), pulled by a force of 24 to 33 lbs. This corresponds to the sixth notch from the completely released lever position.

3. After the above adjustment is made, operate the lever twice at a force of 55 to 66 lbs. so as to seal it properly.

4. Adjust again as described above in number 2.

Parking brake adjustment turnbuckle

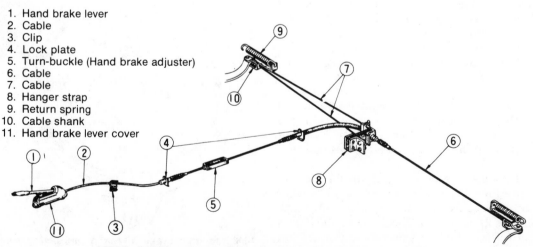

1. Hand brake lever
2. Cable
3. Clip
4. Lock plate
5. Turn-buckle (Hand brake adjuster)
6. Cable
7. Cable
8. Hanger strap
9. Return spring
10. Cable shank
11. Hand brake lever cover

1200 and B210 parking brake assembly. 210 and Sentra similar

5. Tighten the lock nut securely (see illustration).

6. If the adjustment is no longer effective on its threaded end, replace the front cable.

BRAKE PEDAL ADJUSTMENT

Before making this adjustment, make sure that the wheel brakes are properly adjusted. Adjust the pedal free play by means of the pedal pushrod locknut (on the floor side of the pedal). Adjust the pedal height by adjusting the brake lamp switch lock nut (and operating rod if equipped with a brake booster).

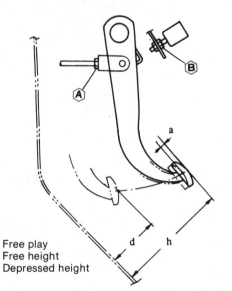

Free play
Free height
Depressed height

Brake pedal adjustment all models. "B" shows locknut

HYDRAULIC SYSTEM

Master Cylinder

REMOVAL AND INSTALLATION

Clean the outside of the cylinder thoroughly, particularly around the cap and fluid lines. Disconnect the fluid lines and cap them to exclude dirt. (Be careful not to allow *any* dirt into the system). Remove the clevis pin connecting the pushrod to the brake pedal arm inside the car. This pin need not be removed with the vacuum booster, if equipped. Unbolt the master cylinder from the firewall and remove. The adjustable pushrod is used to adjust brake pedal free-play (see Brake Pedal Adjustment above). After installation (which is the reverse of removal), bleed the system and check the pedal free-play.

NOTE: *Ordinary brake fluid will boil and cause brake failure under high temperatures developed in disc brake systems. Use only DOT 3 or 4 brake fluid developed for disc brake systems.*

OVERHAUL

CAUTION: *Master cylinders are supplied to Datsun by two manufacturers: Nabco and Tokico. Parts between these two manufacturers are not interchangeable. Be sure you obtain the correct rebuilding kit for your master cylinder.*

The master cylinder can be disassembled using the illustrations as a guide. Clean all parts in clean brake fluid. Replace the cylinder or piston as necessary if clearance between the two exceeds 0.006 in. Lubricate all parts in clean brake fluid on assembly. Master cylinder rebuilding kits, containing all the necessary parts, are available to simplify and cheapen the expense of overhaul.

BRAKE PROPORTIONING VALVE

All Datsuns covered in this guide are equipped with brake proportioning valves of several different types. The valves all do the same job, which is to separate the front and rear brake lines, allowing them to function independently, and preventing the rear brakes from locking before the front brakes. Damage, such as brake line leakage, in either the front or rear brake system will not affect

Brake Pedal Adjustments

	1200	B210	210	Sentra
Pedal free play (in.)	0.20−0.50	0.04−0.20	0.04−0.20	0.40−0.20
Pedal height (in.) ①	5.65−5.87	6.18	5.65−5.87	7.53−7.76 ② 7.60−7.83 ③
Depressed height (in.)	1.00	2.76	2.76	3.35

① Pedal height measured from floorboard to pedal pad
② Manual transaxle
③ Automatic transaxle

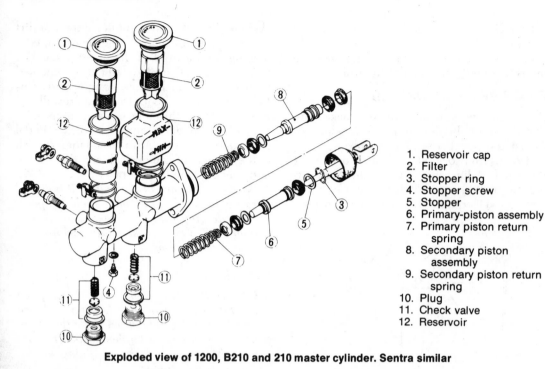

1. Reservoir cap
2. Filter
3. Stopper ring
4. Stopper screw
5. Stopper
6. Primary-piston assembly
7. Primary piston return spring
8. Secondary piston assembly
9. Secondary piston return spring
10. Plug
11. Check valve
12. Reservoir

Exploded view of 1200, B210 and 210 master cylinder. Sentra similar

the normal operation of the unaffected system. If, in the event of a panic stop, the rear brakes lock up before the front brakes, it could mean the proportioning valve is defective. In that case, replace the entire proportioning valve.

System Bleeding

Bleeding the brake system is required whenever air gets into the hydraulic fluid, causing a spongy feeling at the pedal and slow brake response. Air may find its way into the system through a worn master cylinder, worn wheel cylinders, a loose or broken brake line, or if any brake system component is removed from the system for repair.

NOTE: *The brake system must always be bled if a component is removed or the system disconnected in any way.*

1. Top up the master cylinder reservoir with the proper brake fluid. Make sure the fluid you use is approved for disc brakes (unless your car is a 1200 model with front drum brakes). All brake systems should use DOT 3 or 4 brake fluid.

2. Jack up the rear of the car and safely support it with jackstands.

3. Begin with the wheel farthest from the master cylinder. Clean all dirt off of the bleeder nipple. Fit a rubber hose over the bleeder nipple on the inside (facing under-

neath the car) of the brake backing plate. Submerge the other end of the hose in clean brake fluid in a clear glass jar.

NOTE: *Do not reuse any brake fluid that has been bled from the system.*

4. Have an assistant pump the brake pedal three or four times. On the bottom of the

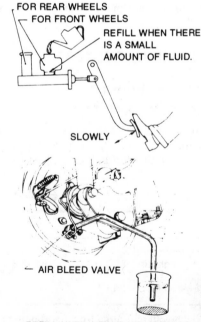

FOR REAR WHEELS
FOR FRONT WHEELS
REFILL WHEN THERE IS A SMALL AMOUNT OF FLUID.

SLOWLY

AIR BLEED VALVE

REFILL UNTIL NEW FLUID APPEARS

Bleeding the brakes

Brake System Troubleshooting

The Problem	Is Caused By	What to Do
The brake pedal goes to the floor	• Leak somewhere in the system • Brakes out of adjustment	• Check/correct fluid level; have system checked • Check brake adjusters
Spongy brake pedal	• Air in brake system • Brake fluid contaminated	• Have brake system bled • Have system drained, refilled and bled
The brake is hard	• Improperly adjusted brakes • Worn pads or linings • Kinked brake lines • Defective power brake booster • Low engine vacuum (power brakes)	• Have brakes adjusted • Check lining/pad wear • Have defective brake line replaced • Have booster checked • Check engine vacuum
The brake pedal "fades" under pressure (repeated hard stops will cause brake fade; brakes will return to normal when they cool down)	• Air in system • Incorrect brake fluid • Leaking master cylinder or wheel cylinders • Leaking hoses/lines	• Have brakes bled • Check fluid • Check master cylinder and wheel cylinders for leaks • Check lines for leaks
The car pulls to one side or brakes grab	• Incorrect tire pressure • Contaminated brake linings or pads • Worn brake linings • Loose or misaligned calipers • Defective proportioning valve • Front end out of alignment	• Check/correct tire pressure • Check linings for grease; if greasy, replace • Have linings replaced • Check caliper mountings • Have proportioning valve checked • Have wheel alignment checked
Brakes chatter or shudder	• Worn linings • Drums out-of-round • Wobbly rotor • Heat checked drums	• Check lining thickness • Have drums and linings ground • Have rotor checked for excessive wobble • Check drums for heat checking; if necessary, replace drums
Brakes produce noise (squealing, scraping, clicking)	• Worn linings • Loose calipers • Caliper anti-rattle springs missing • Scored or glazed drums or rotors	• Check pad and lining wear • Check caliper mountings • Check calipers for missing parts • Check for glazing (light glazing can be removed with sandpaper)
Brakes drag (will not release)	• Incorrect brake adjustment • Parking brake stuck or adjusted too tight • Caliper pistons seized • Defective metering valve or master cylinder • Broken brake return springs	• Have brakes checked • Check cable where it enters the brake plate. In winter, water frequently freezes here • Have calipers checked • Have system checked • Check brake return springs, replace if necessary
Brake system warning light stays lit	• One part of dual circuit inoperative, defective warning light switch, differential pressure valve not centered	• Have brake system checked

fourth stroke (pedal all the way down), loosen the bleeder screw behind the nipple (while your assistant keeps the pedal depressed) and allow the air bubbles to escape in the fluid. Quickly tighten the bleeder screw.

5. Repeat this procedure on the wheel until there are no more air bubbles in the brake fluid.

NOTE: *Continue to check the fluid level in the master cylinder during the bleeding procedure. Refill as necessary.*

6. Proceed to the other rear wheel and perform the same operation. When this wheel is bled, take the car down off of the jackstands, jack up the front end and support it with the stands. Bleed the front wheel farthest from the master cylinder then the wheel closest.

7. After bleeding all four wheels, check that the brake pedal is now firm. If not, repeat the bleeding operation.

FRONT DISC BRAKES

Disc Brake Pads

INSPECTION

You should be able to check the pad lining thickness without removing the pads. Check the Brake Specifications Chart at the end of this chapter to find the manufacturer's pad wear limit. However, this measurement may disagree with your state inspection laws. When replacing pads, always check the surface of the rotors for scoring or wear. The rotors should be removed for resurfacing if badly scored.

REMOVAL AND INSTALLATION

All four front brake pads must always be replaced as a set.

Annette Type

1. Raise and support the front of the car with jackstands. Remove the wheels.

2. Remove the clip, pull out the pins, and remove the pad springs.

3. Remove the pads by pulling them out with pliers.

4. To install, first lightly coat the yoke groove and end surface of the piston with grease. Do not allow grease to contact the pads or rotor.

5. Open the bleeder screw slightly and push the outer piston into the cylinder until its end aligns with the end of the boot retain-

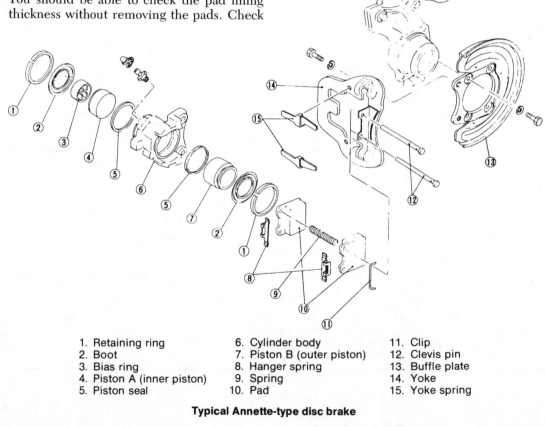

1. Retaining ring
2. Boot
3. Bias ring
4. Piston A (inner piston)
5. Piston seal
6. Cylinder body
7. Piston B (outer piston)
8. Hanger spring
9. Spring
10. Pad
11. Clip
12. Clevis pin
13. Buffle plate
14. Yoke
15. Yoke spring

Typical Annette-type disc brake

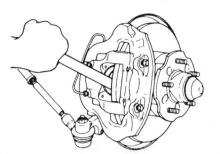

Pushing the inner piston in to install new brake pads, 1200, B210 and 210 calipers

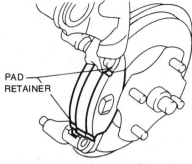

Sentra brake pad retainer location

ing ring. *Do not push too far;* if you do, the caliper will have to be disassembled. Install the inner pad.

6. Pull the yoke toward the outside of the car to push the inner piston into place. Install the outer pad.

7. Apply the brakes a few times to seat the pads. Check the master cylinder and add fluid if necessary. Bleed the brakes if necessary.

Sentra Pad

1. Jack up the front of the car and safely support it with jack stands.

2. Remove the caliper lock pin.

3. The caliper cylinder body swings upward for pad replacement. Remove the lower bolt and swing it up. Remove the pad retainers and pads.

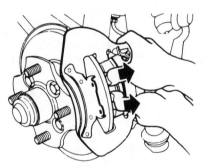

Make sure you don't push the piston in too far

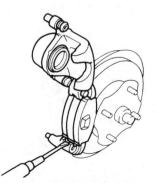

Swing the Sentra cylinder body up for pad access

CAUTION: *When the cylinder body is in the "up" position, DO NOT depress the brake pedal, or the piston will jump out.*

4. Before installation, clean the piston end and the pin bolts.

5. Apply a coat of PBC grease or equivalent to the pad-to-torque member clearance. NOTE: *DO NOT get any grease on the pads or brake rotor (disc).*

6. Install the inner pad. Swing the cylinder body down and to the other side.

7. Install the outer pad, then the pad retainers. Install the lock pin.

Calipers and Brake Discs

NOTE: *Use the Brake Identification Chart in this section to find the brake system your car uses. This information will be useful in buying replacement brake parts.*

OVERHAUL

Annette Type

1. Remove the pads.

2. Disconnect the brake tube.

3. Remove the two bottom strut assembly installation bolts to provide clearance.

4. Remove the caliper assembly mounting bolts.

5. Loosen the bleeder screw and press the pistons into their bores.

6. Clamp the yoke in a vise and tap the yoke head with a hammer to loosen the cylinder. Be careful that primary piston does not fall out.

7. Remove the bias ring from primary piston. Remove the retaining rings and boots from both pistons. Depress and remove the pistons from the cylinder. Remove the piston seal from the cylinder carefully with the fingers so as not to mar the cylinder wall.

8. Remove the yoke springs from the yoke.

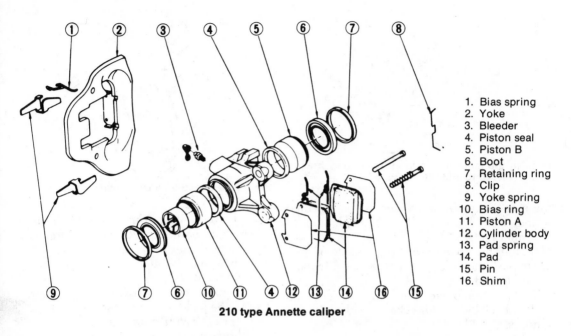

1. Bias spring
2. Yoke
3. Bleeder
4. Piston seal
5. Piston B
6. Boot
7. Retaining ring
8. Clip
9. Yoke spring
10. Bias ring
11. Piston A
12. Cylinder body
13. Pad spring
14. Pad
15. Pin
16. Shim

210 type Annette caliper

9. Wash all parts with clean brake fluid (do not use gasoline, kerosene, thinners or any other mineral solvent).

10. If the piston or cylinder is badly worn or scored, replace both. The piston surface is plated and must not be polished with emery paper. Replace all seals. The rotor can be removed and machined if scored, but final thickness must be at least 0.331 in. Runout must not exceed 0.001 in.

11. Lubricate the cylinder bore with clean brake fluid and install the piston seal.

12. Insert the bias ring into primary piston so that the rounded ring portion comes to the bottom of the piston. Primary piston has a small depression inside, while secondary does not.

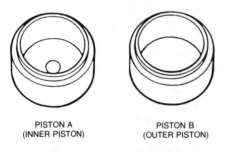

PISTON A
(INNER PISTON)

PISTON B
(OUTER PISTON)

Piston comparison (inner and outer)

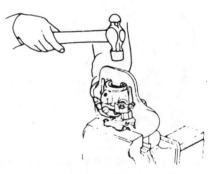

Tapping the yoke head with a hammer

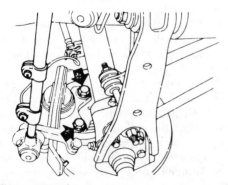

Caliper removal

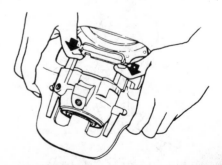

Assembling the yoke and cylinder (Annette type)

13. Lubricate the pistons with clean brake fluid and insert into the cylinder. Install the boot and retaining ring. The yoke groove of the bias ring of primary piston must align with the yoke groove of the cylinder.

14. Install the yoke springs to the yoke so the projecting portion faces to the disc (rotor).

15. Lubricate the sliding portion of the cylinder and yoke. Assemble the cylinder and yoke by tapping the yoke lightly.

16. Replace the caliper assembly and pads. Torque the mounting bolts to 33–41 ft. lbs. Rotor bolt torque is 20–27 ft. lbs. Strut bolt torque is 33–44 ft. lbs. Bleed the system of air.

Sentra Type

1. Separate cylinder body of caliper from the torque member by unbolting the two, swinging the cylinder body up (as in pad replacement) and sliding the pin out of the hole.

2. Remove the brake hose. Press out the piston with the dust seal and retainer ring.

3. Remove the piston seal.

4. Remove the guide pin, lock pin, guide pin boot and lock pin boot.

5. Clean and check all parts. Clean parts with clean brake fluid only (never use solvents). Check the inside surface of the cylinder for rust, wear, damage or foreign material. Minor rust damage may be removed with crocus cloth soaked in clean brake fluid. Check the torque member for wear, cracks or damage.

Check the piston for scoring, rust, wear or damage. Replace if any fault is detected.

CAUTION: *The piston sliding surface is plated. Do not attempt to polish the surface with even crocus cloth or fine emery cloth.*

6. Replace the piston seal and dust seal during assembly.

7. Check the guide pin for wear, cracks or damage.

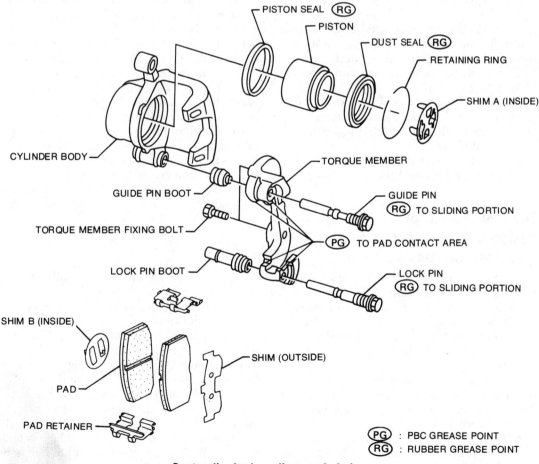

Sentra disc brake caliper exploded

Brake Identification Chart

Match the numbers on the chart with those below to identify your brake system

Model	1973	1974	1975	1976	1977	1978	1979	1980	1981	1982	1983
1200	①②⑤										
B210		①②	①②	①②	①③	①③					
210							①④	①④	①④	①④	
Sentra										⑥④	⑥④

① Annette Type front disc brakes
② Rear drum brakes with bolt-type adjuster
③ Rear drum brakes with internal, toothed adjusting nut
④ Rear drum brakes with automatic adjustment
⑤ Front drum brakes with top and bottom bolt-type adjusters
⑥ CL18B front disc brakes

8. Install the piston seal, applying rubber grease or brake fluid to the seal groove and seal.

9. Apply rubber grease or brake fluid to the sliding portions and the inside of the dust seal.

10. With the dust seal fitted to the piston, insert the dust seal into the groove on the cylinder body and install the piston.

11. Install the retainer ring and properly secure the dust seal.

12. Apply a coat of rubber grease to the guide pin and lock pin sliding surfaces. Install the lock pin boot, guide pin boot, lock pin and guide pin.

13. Attach the torque member to the cylinder body, and connect the brake hose.

Disc Brake Rotor

REMOVAL AND INSTALLATION

1200, B210 and 210

1. Block rear wheels with chocks, and firmly apply parking brake.

2. Jack up front of car and safely support it with jackstands.

3. Remove wheel and tire assembly.

4. Remove brake hose, brake caliper assembly.

5. Work off the small hub cap from the hub using thin screwdrivers or pry bars. If necessary, tap around it with a soft hammer while removing cap.

NOTE: *Use care while removing the cap, as there is an O-ring underneath that must not be damaged.*

6. Remove the cotter pin from the castellated nut and discard it (assemble the hub with a new cotter pin). Take out the adjusting cap and the wheel bearing lock nut.

7. Remove the wheel hub with the disc brake rotor from the spindle with the bearing installed. Be careful not to drop the outer bearing cone out of the hub when removing the knuckle from the knuckle spindle.

8. Remove the outer bearing cone.

9. Loosen the four bolts securing the brake disc; remove the brake disc rotor from the wheel hub assembly.

10. Install in the reverse order of removal, making sure wheel bearings are properly greased and that a new cotter pin is used. Install a new hub grease seal. Torque rotor bolts to 28–38 ft. lbs., and adjust wheel bearings by following the procedure outlined in this chapter.

Sentra

1. Remove the front hub and halfshaft as a unit, as described in Chapter 7 "Drive Train."

2. Remove the hub nut and then separate the halfshaft from the hub assembly.

3. Separate the wheel hub from the steering knuckle using a sliding hammer.

4. Remove the bolts securing the wheel hub to the disc rotor and remove the rotor.

5. Installation is the reverse of removal. Grease the end of the halfshaft before installing it into the front hub. Install a new hub grease seal. The rotor bolts should be torqued to 18–25 ft. lbs., and the halfshaft to hub bolt is torqued to 87–145 ft. lbs.

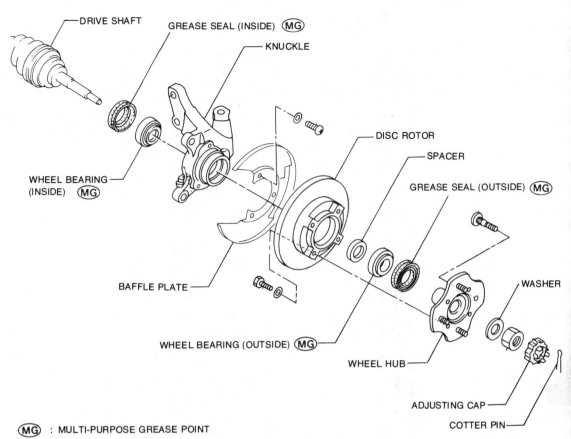

(MG) : MULTI-PURPOSE GREASE POINT

Sentra front disc and hub assembly

FRONT DRUM BRAKES

Some models of the 1200 are equipped with front drum brakes.

Brake Drums

REMOVAL AND INSTALLATION

1. Jack up the front of the vehicle so that the wheel which is to be serviced is off the ground. Be sure to loosen the lug nuts before the wheel comes off the ground.

2. Remove the wheel and tire assembly.

3. Pull the brake drum off the hub. If the drum cannot be easily removed, back off on the brake adjustment.

NOTE: *Never depress the brake pedal while the brake drum is removed.*

4. Install the brake drum in the reverse order of removal and adjust the brakes.

Brake Shoes

REMOVAL AND INSTALLATION

1. Jack up the vehicle until the wheel which is to be serviced is off the ground two or three inches. Remove the wheel and brake drum.

NOTE: *It is not absolutely essential to remove the hub assembly from the spindle, but it makes the job a great deal easier. If you can work with the hub in place, skip down to Step 7.*

2. Remove the hub dust cap.

3. Straighten the cotter pin and remove it from the spindle.

4. Unscrew the spindle nut and remove the adjusting cap, spindle nut, and spindle washer.

5. Wiggle the hub assembly until the outer bearing comes unseated and can be removed from the hub. Remove the outer bearing.

6. Pull the hub assembly off the spindle.

7. Unhook the return springs on the brake shoes and remove the shoes.

8. Apply brake grease to the adjuster assemblies and back the adjusters off the whole way using the bolts on the backing plate. Apply brake grease to the areas on the brake backing plate where the brake shoes make contact.

Brake Specifications

All measurements given are in inches unless noted

Model	Year	Lug Nut Torque (ft. lbs)	Master Cylinder Bore	Brake Disc		Drum		Minimum Lining Thickness	
				Minimum Thickness	Maximum Run-Out	Diameter	Max. Wear Limit	Front	Rear
1200	1973	58–65	0.6875	0.3307	0.0012	8.000	8.051	0.0630 (disc) 0.0591 (drum)	0.0591
B210	1974–78	58–65	0.750	0.331	0.0047	8.000	8.051	0.063	0.059
210	1979–82	58–72	0.8125	0.331	0.0047	8.000	8.050	0.063	0.059
Sentra	1982–83	58–72	0.750	0.433	0.0047	7.09	7.13	0.079	0.059

NOTE: Minimum lining thickness is as recommended by the manufacturer. Due to variation in state inspection regulations, the minimum allowable thickness may be different than recommended by the manufacturer.

9. Install the brake shoes in the reverse order of removal.

10. Install the hub, brake drum and wheel in the reverse order of removal. Adjust the wheel bearings.

Wheel Cylinders

REMOVAL AND INSTALLATION

1. Jack up the wheel to be serviced.

2. Remove the wheel, brake drum, hub assembly, and brake shoes.

3. Disconnect the brake hose from the wheel cylinder.

4. Unscrew the wheel cylinder securing nut and remove the wheel cylinder from the brake backing plate.

5. Install the wheel cylinder in the reverse order of removal, assemble the remaining components, and bleed the brake hydraulic system.

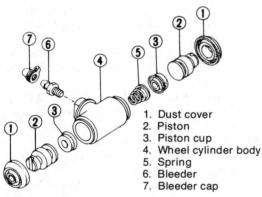

1. Dust cover
2. Piston
3. Piston cup
4. Wheel cylinder body
5. Spring
6. Bleeder
7. Bleeder cap

Typical wheel cylinder

OVERHAUL

NOTE: *Datsun obtains parts from two manufacturers: Nabco and Tokico. Parts are not interchangeable. The name of the manufacturer is usually on the wheel cylinder. Replacement wheel cylinder parts and complete rebuilt wheel cylinders are available from most auto parts stores under other names. Those parts must be replacements for the Tokico and Nabco originals, however.*

1. Remove the wheel cylinder from the backing plate.

2. Remove the dust boot and take out the piston. Discard the piston cup. The dust boot can be reused, if necessary, but it is better to replace it.

3. Wash all of the components in clean brake fluid.

4. Inspect the piston and piston bore. Re-

place any components which are severely corroded, scored, or worn. The piston and piston bore can be polished lightly with crocus cloth. Move the crocus cloth around the piston bore; *not* in and out of the piston bore.

5. Wash the wheel cylinder and piston thoroughly in clean brake fluid, allowing them to remain lubricated for assembly.

6. Coat all of the new components to be installed in the wheel cylinder with clean brake fluid prior to assembly.

7. Assemble the wheel cylinder and install it in the reverse order of removal. Assemble the remaining components and bleed the brake hydraulic system.

Front Wheel Bearings

ADJUSTMENT

1200, B210, 210

NOTE: *The Sentra, a front wheel drive vehicle, has pressed bearings which are not adjustable on the front wheels.*

The factory procedures for wheel bearing adjustment is of little use to the owner/mechanic, since it involves the use of a spring scale, an inch-pound torque wrench, and a foot-pound torque wrench. For the fol-

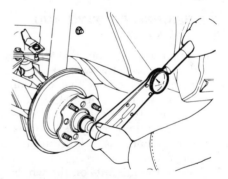

Tightening the hub nut with a torque wrench during wheel bearing adjustment

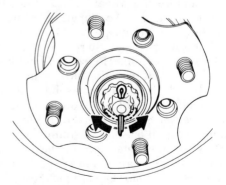

Split and spread the cotter pin

lowing procedure, you will only need a foot-pound torque wrench.

1. Jack up the car and safely support it with jackstands.

2. Remove the bearing dust cap and the cotter pin. Discard the cotter pin, as you will be replacing it with a new one.

3. Torque the spindle nut to 16–18 ft. lbs. on the 1200; 18–22 ft. lbs. on the B210, and 22–25 ft. lbs. on the 210 sedan and wagon.

4. Spin the wheel hub a few times to seat the bearing, then check the torque on the nut again.

5. Loosen the nut about 60° on all models except the 210. Loosen the 210 nut about 90°.

6. Install the adjusting cap and a new cotter pin. You may have to loosen the nut a bit to allow the cotter pin holes to align, but do not loosen the nut beyond 15°.

7. Reinstall the tire and wheel, and rotate the entire assembly. There should be no roughness or binding. Grasp the top of the tire and move it in and out. The play should be negligible. If there is excessive play, the wheel bearings must be retightened. If roughness persists, check the condition of the wheel bearings for nicks, pitting and damage.

8. Install the cap and lower the car from the stands.

WHEEL BEARING PACKING AND REPLACEMENT

It is important to remember that wheel bearings, although basically very durable, are subject to many elements that can quickly destroy them. Grit, misalignment, and improper preload are especially brutal to any roller bearing assembly. And like any bearing (ball, roller, needle, etc.), lubrication is extremely important.

1. Loosen the lug nuts on the wheel you intend to fix. Jack up the car and safely support it with jackstands.

2. Remove the wheel and tire. Remove the brake drum or brake caliper, following the procedure(s) in this chapter.

3. It is not necessary to remove the drum or disc from the hub. The outer wheel bearing will come off with the hub. Simply pull the hub and disc or drum assembly toward you and off the spindle. (Follow hub removal procedures for Sentra). Be sure to catch the bearing before it falls to the ground.

4. From the inner side of the hub, remove the inner grease seal, and lift the inner bearing from the hub. Discard the grease seal, as you will be replacing it with a new one.

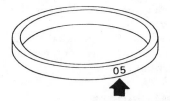

Sentra wheel bearing spacer size number

Packing wheel bearing with grease

5. Clean the bearings carefully in solvent, and allow them to air dry (or blow them out with compressed air, if available). You risk leaving bits of lint in the races if you dry them with a rag. Clean the grease caps, nuts, spindle, and the races in the hub thoroughly, and allow the parts to dry.

6. Inspect the bearings carefully. If they show any signs of wear (pitting, cracks, scoring, brinelling, burns, etc.), replace them along with the bearing cups in which they run in the hub. Do not mix old and new parts; you won't regret replacing everything if the parts look marginal.

7. If the cups are worn at all, remove them from the hub, using a brass rod as a drift. Use care not to damage the cup seats with the drift.

8. If the old cups were removed, install the new inner and outer cups into the hub, using either a tool made for the purpose, or a socket or piece of pipe of a large enough diameter to press on the outside rim of the cup only.

CAUTION: *Be careful not to cock the bearing cups in the hub. If they are not fully seated, the bearings will be impossible to adjust properly.*

9. Pack the inside area of the hub and cups with grease. Pack the inside of the grease cap while you're at it, but do not install the cap into the hub.

10. Pack the inner bearing with grease. Place a large glob of grease into the palm of one hand and push the inner bearing through it with a sliding motion. The grease must be forced through the side of the bearing and in

between each roller. Continue until the grease begins to ooze out the other side through the gaps between the rollers; the bearing must be completely packed with grease. Install the inner bearing into its cup in the hub, then press a new grease seal into place over it.

11. Install the hub and rotor or drum assembly onto the spindle. Pack the outer bearing with grease in the same manner as the inner bearing, then install the outer bearing into place in the hub.

12. Apply a thin coat of grease to the washer and the threaded portion of the spindle, then loosely install the washer and adjusting nut. Go on to the bearing preload adjustment.

Sentra

The Sentra front wheel bearings are fitted using spacers, which fit between the bearing race in the steering knuckle and the outer wheel bearing. The spacers are available from Nissan dealers and parts stores, and are numbered as to their size. New spacers must be installed whenever the knuckle is replaced, or when the bearings and/or their races are worn to an extent that end play is noticable at the front wheel. When new grease seals or bearings are installed, new spacers should be installed. Make sure they have the same mark as the spacers you have removed. If there is not much wear in your bearings, etc., and you are just repacking bearings, the old spacer can be reused.

1. With the front hub and halfshaft disassembled, install the outside grease seal and bearing into the wheel hub with a suitable drift.

2. Pack the seal lip with a quality multipurpose wheel bearing grease. Be sure that the grease seal is facing in the proper direction. Press the bearing into the inner race to install. Do not force the bearing.

3. Install the spacer. Spacer numbering ranges from number 05 to number 22, with each succeeding spacer being 0.0023 in. thicker.

4. Tighten the bolts securing the hub to the disc rotor.

5. Assemble the halfshaft into the knuckle and wheel hub. Install the rotor and hub assembly.

6. Tighten the hub nut to 87–145 ft. lbs.

7. Spin the wheel several times in both directions.

8. Measure wheel bearing preload. The rotation starting torque of the wheel bearings is ½ to 2 ft. lbs. Measured at the wheel hub bolt, you should obtain a reading of 3.1 to 10.8 lbs. on a pull scale.

9. If the bearing preload does not accord the specifications, reselect the spacer. When any axial end-play is present in the wheel bearing, replace the spacer with a smaller one. If bearing preload is greater and end-play is present, replace spacer with a larger one.

REAR DRUM BRAKES

Brake Drums
REMOVAL AND INSTALLATION

1. Raise the rear of the vehicle and support it on jack stands.

2. Remove the wheels.

3. Release the parking brake.

4. Pull off the brake drums. On some models there are two threaded service holes in each brake drum. If the drum will not come off, fit two correct size bolts in the service holes and screw them in: this will force the drum away from the axle.

5. If the drum cannot be easily removed, back off the brake adjustment.

NOTE: *Never depress the brake pedal while the brake drum is removed.*

6. Installation is the reverse of removal.

INSPECTION

After removing the brake drum, wipe out the accumulated dust with a damp cloth.

CAUTION: *Do not blow the brake dust out of the drums with compressed air or lung power. Brake linings contain asbestos, a known cancer causing substance. Dispose of the cloth after use.*

Inspect the drum for cracks, deep grooves, roughness, scoring, or out-of-roundness. Replace any brake drum which is cracked.

Smooth any slight scores by polishing the friction surface with the fine emery cloth. Heavy or extensive scoring will cause excessive brake lining wear and should be removed from the brake drum through resurfacing (most auto repair shops and machine shops provide this service).

Brake Shoes
REMOVAL AND INSTALLATION
All models

1. Jack up the rear of the car and safely support it with jackstands.

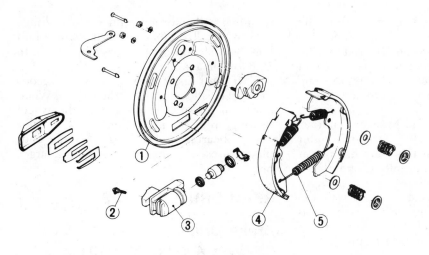

1. Brake disc
2. Bleeder
3. Wheel cylinder
4. Shoe assembly
5. Return spring

Exploded view of typical drum brake

2. Loosen the handbrake cable, remove the clevis pin from the wheel cylinder lever, disconnect the handbrake cable, and remove the return pull spring.

3. Remove the brake drum, shoe retainers, return springs, and brake shoes. Loosen the brake adjusters if the drums are difficult to remove. Place a heavy rubber band around the cylinder to prevent the piston from coming out.

4. Clean the backing plate and check the wheel cylinder for leaks. To remove the wheel cylinder, remove the brake line, dust cover, securing nuts or plates and adjusting shims. Clearance between cylinder and piston should not exceed 0.006 in.

5. The drums must be machined if scored or out-of-round more than 0.008 in. The drum inside diameter must not be machined beyond 8.04 in. Minimum safe lining thickness is 0.059 in. (0.039 in.-F10).

6. Follow Steps 6–9 for 510, 610, 710, and 810.

Wheel Cylinder

See correct section under "Brake Shoes Removal and Installation" for wheel cylinder removal and installation procedures. See the "Front Drum Brake Wheel Cylinder Overhaul" for overhaul procedures for the rear drum brake cylinders. Observe the "NOTE" about different manufacturers of wheel cylinder components.

Body

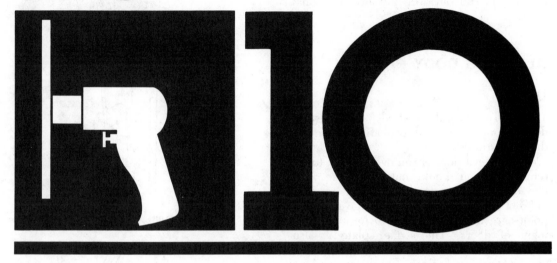

10

You can repair most minor auto body damage yourself. Minor damage usually falls into one of several categories: (1) small scratches and dings in the paint that can be repaired without the use of body filler, (2) deep scratches and dents that require body filler, but do not require pulling, or hammering metal back into shape and (3) rust-out repairs. The repair sequences illustrated in this chapter are typical of these types of repairs. If you want to get involved in more complicated repairs including pulling or hammering sheet metal back into shape, you will probably need more detailed instructions. Chilton's *Minor Auto Body Repair, 2nd Edition* is a comprehensive guide to repairing auto body damage yourself.

TOOLS AND SUPPLIES

The list of tools and equipment you may need to fix minor body damage ranges from very basic hand tools to a wide assortment of specialized body tools. Most minor scratches, dings and rust holes can be fixed using an electric drill, wire wheel or grinder attachment, half-round plastic file, sanding block, various grades of sandpaper (#36, which is coarse through #600, which is fine) in both wet and dry types, auto body plastic,

primer, touch-up paint, spreaders, newspaper and masking tape.

Most manufacturers of auto body repair products began supplying materials to professionals. Their knowledge of the best, most-used products has been translated into body repair kits for the do-it-yourselfer. Kits are available from a number of manufacturers and contain the necessary materials in the required amounts for the repair identified on the package.

Kits are available for a wide variety of uses, including:

- Rusted out metal
- All purpose kit for dents and holes
- Dents and deep scratches
- Fiberglass repair kit
- Epoxy kit for restyling.

Kits offer the advantage of buying what you need for the job. There is little waste and little chance of materials going bad from not being used. The same manufacturers also merchandise all of the individual products used—spreaders, dent pullers, fiberglass cloth, polyester resin, cream hardener, body filler, body files, sandpaper, sanding discs and holders, primer, spray paint, etc.

CAUTION: *Most of the products you will be using contain harmful chemicals, so be extremely careful. Always read the complete label before opening the containers. When* *you put them away for future use, be sure they are out of children's reach!*

Most auto body repair kits contain all the materials you need to do the job right in the kit. So, if you have a small rust spot or dent you want to fix, check the contents of the kit before you run out and buy any additional tools.

ALIGNING BODY PANELS

Doors

There are several methods of adjusting doors. Your vehicle will probably use one of those illustrated.

Whenever a door is removed and is to be reinstalled, you should matchmark the position of the hinges on the door pillars. The holes of the hinges and/or the hinge attaching points are usually oversize to permit alignment of doors. The striker plate is also moveable, through oversize holes, permitting up-and-down, in-and-out and fore-and-aft movement. Fore-and-aft movement is made by adding or subtracting shims from behind the striker and pillar post. The striker should be adjusted so that the door closes fully and remains closed, yet enters the lock freely.

DOOR HINGES

Don't try to cover up poor door adjustment with a striker plate adjustment. The gap on each side of the door should be equal and uniform and there should be no metal-to-metal contact as the door is opened or closed.

1. Determine which hinge bolts must be loosened to move the door in the desired direction.

2. Loosen the hinge bolt(s) just enough to allow the door to be moved with a padded pry bar.

3. Move the door a small amount and check the fit, after tightening the bolts. Be sure that there is no bind or interference with adjacent panels.

4. Repeat this until the door is properly positioned, and tighten all the bolts securely.

Hood, Trunk or Tailgate

As with doors, the outline of hinges should be scribed before removal. The hood and trunk can be aligned by loosening the hinge bolts in their slotted mounting holes and moving the hood or trunk lid as necessary.

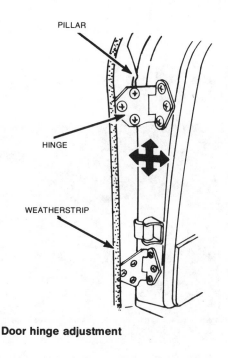

Door hinge adjustment

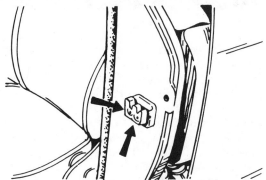

Move the door striker as indicated by arrows

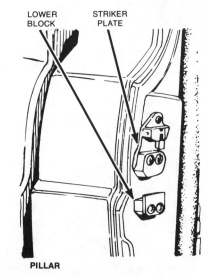

Striker plate and lower block

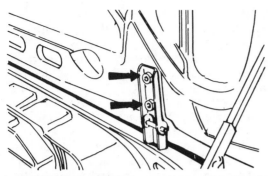

Loosen the hinge boots to permit fore-and-aft and horizontal adjustment

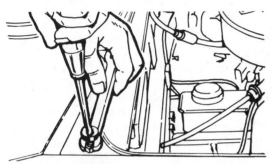

The hood is adjusted vertically by stop-screws at the front and/or rear

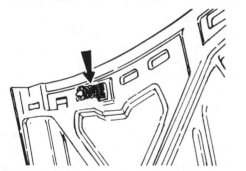

The hood pin can be adjusted for proper lock engagement

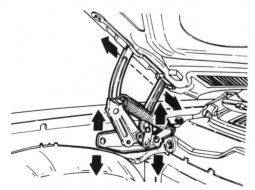

The height of the hood at the rear is adjusted by loosening the bolts that attach the hinge to the body and moving the hood up or down

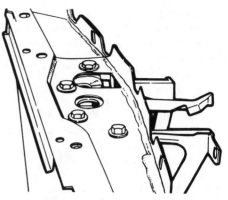

The base of the hood lock can also be repositioned slightly to give more positive lock engagement

The hood and trunk have adjustable catch locations to regulate lock engagement. Bumpers at the front and/or rear of the hood provide a vertical adjustment and the hood lockpin can be adjusted for proper engagement.

The tailgate on the station wagon can be adjusted by loosening the hinge bolts in their slotted mounting holes and moving the tailgate on its hinges. The latchplate and latch striker at the bottom of the tailgate opening can be adjusted to stop rattle. An adjustable bumper is located on each side.

RUST, UNDERCOATING, AND RUSTPROOFING

Rust

Rust is an electrochemical process. It works on ferrous metals (iron and steel) from the inside out due to exposure of unprotected surfaces to air and moisture. The possibility of rust exists practically nationwide—anywhere humidity, industrial pollution or chemical salts are present, rust can form. In coastal areas, the problem is high humidity and salt air; in snowy areas, the problem is chemical salt (de-icer) used to keep the roads clear, and in industrial areas, sulphur dioxide is present in the air from industrial pollution and is changed to sulphuric acid when it rains. The rusting process is accelerated by high temperatures, especially in snowy areas, when vehicles are driven over slushy roads and then left overnight in a heated garage.

Automotive styling also can be a contributor to rust formation. Spot welding of panels creates small pockets that trap moisture and form an environment for rust formation. Fortunately, auto manufacturers have been working hard to increase the corrosion protection of their products. Galvanized sheet metal enjoys much wider use, along with the increased use of plastic and various rust retardant coatings. Manufacturers are also designing out areas in the body where rust-forming moisture can collect.

To prevent rust, you must stop it before it gets started. On new vehicles, there are two ways to accomplish this.

First, the car or truck should be treated with a commercial rustproofing compound. There are many different brands of franchised rustproofers, but most processes involve spraying a waxy "self-healing" compound under the chassis, inside rocker panels, inside doors and fender liners and similar places where rust is likely to form. Prices for a quality rustproofing job range from $100–$250, depending on the area, the brand name and the size of the vehicle.

Ideally, the vehicle should be rustproofed as soon as possible following the purchase. The surfaces of the car or truck have begun to oxidize and deteriorate during shipping. In addition, the car may have sat on a dealer's lot or on a lot at the factory, and once the rust has progressed past the stage of light, powdery surface oxidation rustproofing is not likely to be worthwhile. Professional rustproofers feel that once rust has formed, rustproofing will simply seal in moisture already present. Most franchised rustproofing operations offer a 3–5 year warranty against rust-through, but will not support that warranty if the rustproofing is not applied within three months of the date of manufacture.

Undercoating should not be mistaken for rustproofing. Undercoating is a black, tarlike substance that is applied to the underside of a vehicle. Its basic function is to deaden noises that are transmitted from under the car. It simply cannot get into the crevices and seams where moisture tends to collect. In fact, it may clog up drainage holes and ventilation passages. Some undercoatings also tend to crack or peel with age and only create more moisture and corrosion attracting pockets.

The second thing you should do immediately after purchasing the car is apply a paint sealant. A sealant is a petroleum based product marketed under a wide variety of brand names. It has the same protective properties as a good wax, but bonds to the paint with a chemically inert layer that seals it from the air. If air can't get at the surface, oxidation cannot start.

The paint sealant kit consists of a base coat and a conditioning coat that should be applied every 6–8 months, depending on the manufacturer. The base coat must be applied before waxing, or the wax must first be removed.

Third, keep a garden hose handy for your car in winter. Use it a few times on nice days during the winter for underneath areas, and it will pay big dividends when spring arrives. Spraying under the fenders and other areas which even car washes don't reach will help remove road salt, dirt and other build-ups which help breed rust. Adjust the nozzle to a high-force spray. An old brush will help break up residue, permitting it to be washed away more easily.

It's a somewhat messy job, but worth it in the long run because rust often starts in those hidden areas.

At the same time, wash grime off the door sills and, more importantly, the under portions of the doors, plus the tailgate if you have a station wagon or truck. Applying a coat of wax to those areas at least once before and once during winter will help fend off rust.

When applying the wax to the under parts of the doors, you will note small drain holes. These holes often are plugged with undercoating or dirt. Make sure they are cleaned out to prevent water build-up inside the doors. A small punch or penknife will do the job.

Water from the high-pressure sprays in car washes sometimes can get into the housings for parking and taillights, so take a close look. If they contain water merely loosen the retaining screws and the water should run out.

Repairing Scratches and Small Dents

Step 1. This dent (arrow) is typical of a deep scratch or minor dent. If deep enough, the dent or scratch can be pulled out or hammered out from behind. In this case no straightening is necessary

Step 2. Using an 80-grit grinding disc on an electric drill grind the paint from the surrounding area down to bare metal. This will provide a rough surface for the body filler to grab

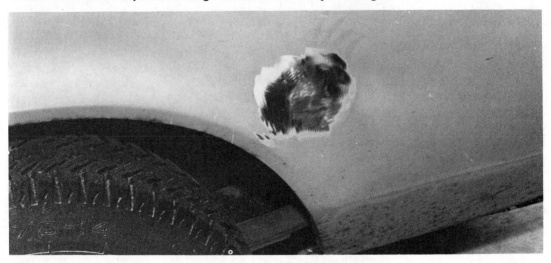

Step 3. The area should look like this when you're finished grinding

Step 4. Mix the body filler and cream hardener according to the directions

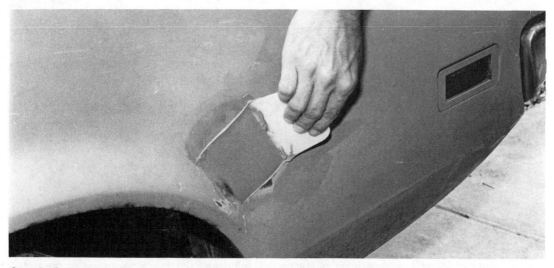

Step 5. Spread the body filler evenly over the entire area. Be sure to cover the area completely

Step 6. Let the body filler dry until the surface can just be scratched with your fingernail

Step 7. Knock the high spots from the body filler with a body file

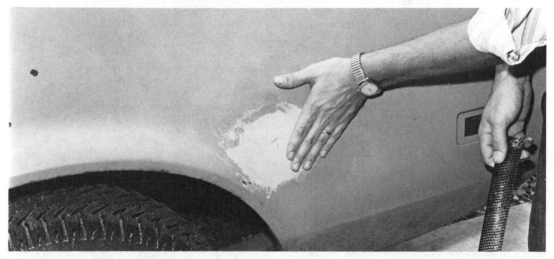

Step 8. Check frequently with the palm of your hand for high and low spots. If you wind up with low spots, you may have to apply another layer of filler

Step 9. Block sand the entire area with 320 grit paper

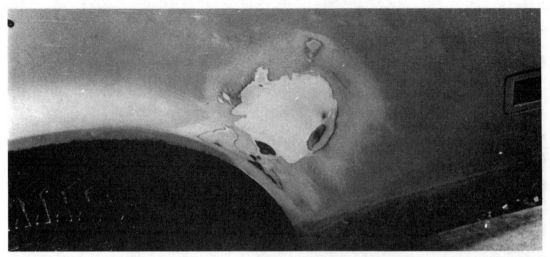

Step 10. When you're finished, the repair should look like this. Note the sand marks extending 2—3 inches out from the repaired area

Step 11. Prime the entire area with automotive primer

Step 12. The finished repair ready for the final paint coat. Note that the primer has covered the sanding marks (see Step 10). A repair of this size should be able to be spotpainted with good results

REPAIRING RUST HOLES

One thing you have to remember about rust: even if you grind away all the rusted metal in a panel, and repair the area with any of the kits available, *eventually* the rust will return. There are two reasons for this. One, rust is a chemical reaction that causes pressure under the repair from the inside out. That's how the blisters form. Two, the back side of the panel (and the repair) is wide open to moisture, and unpainted body filler acts like a sponge. That's why the best solution to rust problems is to remove the rusted panel and install a new one or have the rusted area cut out and a new piece of sheet metal welded in its place. The trouble with welding is the expense; sometimes it will cost more than the car or truck is worth.

One of the better solutions to do-it-yourself rust repair is the process using a fiberglass cloth repair kit (shown here). This will give a strong repair that resists cracking and moisture and is relatively easy to use. It can be used on large or small holes and also can be applied over contoured surfaces.

Step 1. Rust areas such as this are common and are easily fixed

Step 2. Grind away all traces of rust with a 24-grit grinding disc. Be sure to grind back 3—4 inches from the edge of the hole down to bare metal and be sure all traces of rust are removed

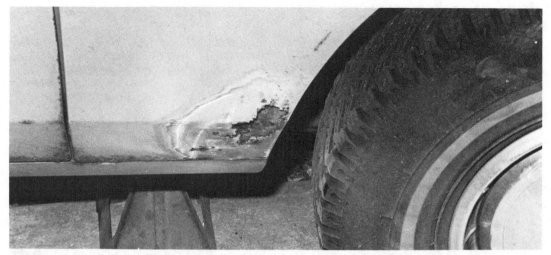

Step 3. Be sure all rust is removed from the edges of the metal. The edges must be ground back to un-rusted metal

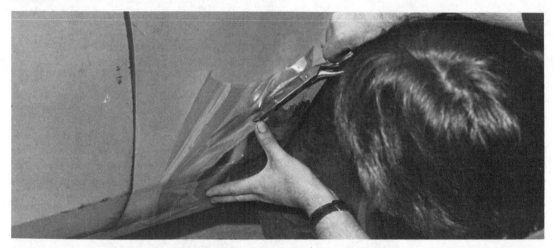

Step 4. If you are going to use release film, cut a piece about 2″ larger than the area you have sanded. Place the film over the repair and mark the sanded area on the film. Avoid any unnecessary wrinkling of the film

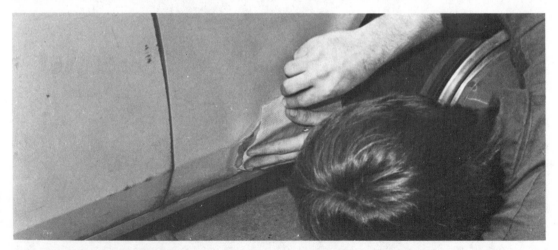

Step 5. Cut 2 pieces of fiberglass matte. One piece should be about 1″ smaller than the sanded area and the second piece should be 1″ smaller than the first. Use sharp scissors to avoid loose ends

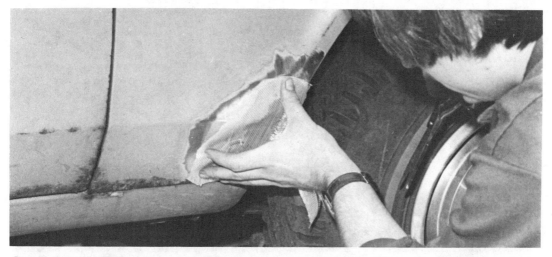

Step 6. Check the dimensions of the release film and cloth by holding them up to the repair area

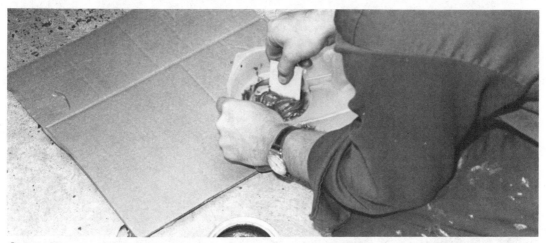

Step 7. Mix enough repair jelly and cream hardener in the mixing tray to saturate the fiberglass material or fill the repair area. Follow the directions on the container

Step 8. Lay the release sheet on a flat surface and spread an even layer of filler, large enough to cover the repair. Lay the smaller piece of fiberglass cloth in the center of the sheet and spread another layer of repair jelly over the fiberglass cloth. Repeat the operation for the larger piece of cloth. If the fiberglass cloth is not used, spread the repair jelly on the release film, concentrated in the middle of the repair

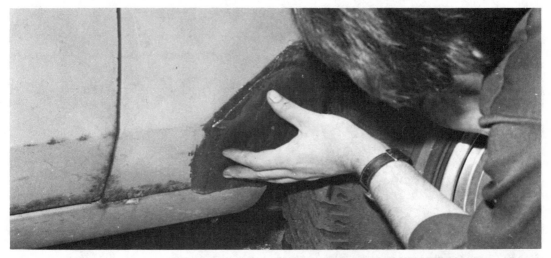

Step 9. Place the repair material over the repair area, with the release film facing outward

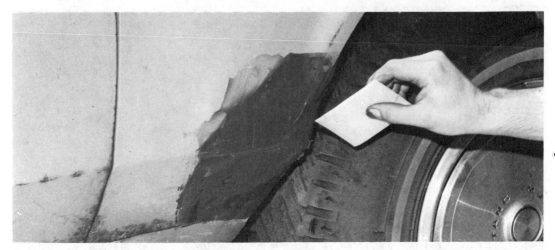

Step 10. Use a spreader and work from the center outward to smooth the material, following the body contours. Be sure to remove all air bubbles

Step 11. Wait until the repair has dried tack-free and peel off the release sheet. The ideal working temperature is 65—90° F. Cooler or warmer temperatures or high humidity may require additional curing time

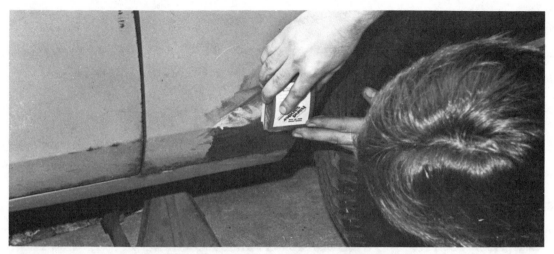

Step 12. Sand and feather-edge the entire area. The initial sanding can be done with a sanding disc on an electric drill if care is used. Finish the sanding with a block sander

Step 13. When the area is sanded smooth, mix some topcoat and hardener and apply it directly with a spreader. This will give a smooth finish and prevent the glass matte from showing through the paint

Step 14. Block sand the topcoat with finishing sandpaper

Step 15. To finish this repair, grind out the surface rust along the top edge of the rocker panel

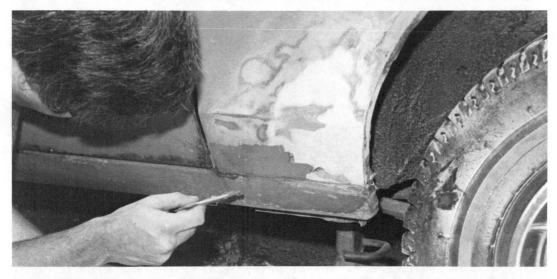

Step 16. Mix some more repair jelly and cream hardener and apply it directly over the surface

Step 17. When it dries tack-free, block sand the surface smooth

Step 18. If necessary, mask off adjacent panels and spray the entire repair with primer. You are now ready for a color coat

AUTO BODY CARE

There are hundreds—maybe thousands—of products on the market, all designed to protect or aid your car's finish in some manner. There are as many different products as there are ways to use them, but they all have one thing in common—the surface must be clean.

Washing

The primary ingredient for washing your car is water, preferably "soft" water. In many areas of the country, the local water supply is "hard" containing many minerals. The little rings or film that is left on your car's surface after it has dried is the result of "hard" water.

Since you usually can't change the local water supply, the next best thing is to dry the surface before it has a chance to dry itself.

Into the water you usually add soap. Don't use detergents or common, coarse soaps. Your car's paint never truly dries out, but is always evaporating residual oils into the air. Harsh detergents will remove these oils, causing the paint to dry faster than normal. Instead use warm water and a non-detergent soap made especially for waxed surfaces or a liquid soap made for waxed surfaces or a liquid soap made for washing dishes by hand.

Other products that can be used on painted surfaces include baking soda or plain soda water for stubborn dirt.

Wash the car completely, starting at the top, and rinse it completely clean. Abrasive grit should be loaded off under water pressure; scrubbing grit off will scratch the finish. The best washing tool is a sponge, cleaning mitt or soft towel. Whichever you choose, replace it often as each tends to absorb grease and dirt.

Other ways to get a better wash include:

• Don't wash your car in the sun or when the finish is hot.

• Use water pressure to remove caked-on dirt.

• Remove tree-sap and bird effluence immediately. Such substances will eat through wax, polish and paint.

One of the best implements to dry your car is a turkish towel or an old, soft bath towel. Anything with a deep nap will hold any dirt in suspension and not grind it into the paint.

Harder cloths will only grind the grit into the paint making more scratches. Always start drying at the top, followed by the hood and trunk and sides. You'll find there's always more dirt near the rocker panels and wheelwells which will wind up on the rest of the car if you dry these areas first.

Cleaners, Waxes and Polishes

Before going any farther you should know the function of various products.

Cleaners—remove the top layer of dead pigment or paint.

Rubbing or polishing compounds—used to remove stubborn dirt, get rid of minor scratches, smooth away imperfections and partially restore badly weathered paint.

Polishes—contain no abrasives or waxes; they shine the paint by adding oils to the paint.

Waxes—are a protective coating for the polish.

CLEANERS AND COMPOUNDS

Before you apply any wax, you'll have to remove oxidation, road film and other types of pollutants that washing alone will not remove.

The paint on your car never dries completely. There are always residual oils evaporating from the paint into the air. When enough oils are present in the paint, it has a healthy shine (gloss). When too many oils evaporate the paint takes on a whitish cast known as oxidation. The idea of polishing and waxing is to keep enough oil present in the painted surface to prevent oxidation; but when it occurs, the only recourse is to remove the top layer of "dead" paint, exposing the healthy paint underneath.

Products to remove oxidation and road film are sold under a variety of generic names—polishes, cleaner, rubbing compound, cleaner/polish, polish/cleaner, self-polishing wax, pre-wax cleaner, finish restorer and many more. Regardless of name there are two types of cleaners—abrasive cleaners (sometimes called polishing or rubbing compounds) that remove oxidation by grinding away the top layer of "dead" paint, or chemical cleaners that dissolve the "dead" pigment, allowing it to be wiped away.

Abrasive cleaners, by their nature, leave thousands of minute scratches in the finish, which must be polished out later. These should only be used in extreme cases, but are usually the only thing to use on badly oxidized paint finishes. Chemical cleaners are much milder but are not strong enough for severe cases of oxidation or weathered paint.

The most popular cleaners are liquid or paste abrasive polishing and rubbing compounds. Polishing compounds have a finer abrasive grit for medium duty work. Rubbing compounds are a coarser abrasive and for heavy duty work. Unless you are familiar with how to use compounds, be very careful. Excessive rubbing with any type of compound or cleaner can grind right through the paint to primer or bare metal. Follow the directions on the container—depending on type, the cleaner may or may not be OK for your paint. For example, some cleaners are not formulated for acrylic lacquer finishes.

When a small area needs compounding or heavy polishing, it's best to do the job by hand. Some people prefer a powered buffer for large areas. Avoid cutting through the paint along styling edges on the body. Small, hand operations where the compound is applied and rubbed using cloth folded into a thick ball allow you to work in straight lines along such edges.

To avoid cutting through on the edges when using a power buffer, try masking tape. Just cover the edge with tape while using power. Then finish the job by hand with the tape removed. Even then work carefully. The paint tends to be a lot thinner along the sharp ridges stamped into the panels.

Whether compounding by machine or by hand, only work on a small area and apply the compound sparingly. If the materials are spread too thin, or allowed to sit too long, they dry out. Once dry they lose the ability to deliver a smooth, clean finish. Also, dried out polish tends to cause the buffer to stick in one spot. This in turn can burn or cut through the finish.

WAXES AND POLISHES

Your car's finish can be protected in a number of ways. A cleaner/wax or polish/cleaner followed by wax or variations of each all provide good results. The two-step approach (polish followed by wax) is probably slightly better but consumes more time and effort. Properly fed with oils, your paint should never need cleaning, but despite the best polishing job, it won't last unless it's protected with wax. Without wax, polish must be renewed at least once a month to prevent oxidation. Years ago (some still swear by it today), the best wax was made from the Brazilian palm, the Carnuba, favored for its vegetable base and high melting point. However, modern synthetic waxes are harder, which means they protect against moisture better, and chemically inert silicone is used for a long lasting protection. The only problem with silicone wax is that it penetrates all layers of paint. To repaint or touch up a panel or car protected by silicone wax, you have to completely strip the finish to avoid "fish-eyes."

Under normal conditions, silicone waxes will last 4–6 months, but you have to be careful of wax build-up from too much waxing. Too thick a coat of wax is just as bad as no wax at all; it stops the paint from breathing.

Combination cleaners/waxes have become popular lately because they remove the old layer of wax plus light oxidation, while putting on a fresh coat of wax at the same time. Some cleaners/waxes contain abrasive cleaners which require caution, although many cleaner/waxes use a chemical cleaner.

Applying Wax or Polish

You may view polishing and waxing your car as a pleasant way to spend an afternoon, or as a boring chore, but it has to be done to keep the paint on your car. Caring for the paint doesn't require special tools, but you should follow a few rules.

1. Use a good quality wax.

2. Before applying any wax or polish, be sure the surface is completely clean. Just because the car looks clean, doesn't mean it's ready for polish or wax.

3. If the finish on your car is weathered, dull, or oxidized, it will probably have to be compounded to remove the old or oxidized paint. If the paint is simply dulled from lack of care, one of the non-abrasive cleaners known as polishing compounds will do the trick. If the paint is severely scratched or really dull, you'll probably have to use a rubbing compound to prepare the finish for waxing. If you're not sure which one to use, use the polishing compound, since you can easily ruin the finish by using too strong a compound.

4. Don't apply wax, polish or compound in direct sunlight, even if the directions on the can say you can. Most waxes will not cure properly in bright sunlight and you'll probably end up with a blotchy looking finish.

5. Don't rub the wax off too soon. The result will be a wet, dull looking finish. Let the wax dry thoroughly before buffing it off.

6. A constant debate among car enthusiasts is how wax should be applied. Some maintain pastes or liquids should be applied in a circular motion, but body shop experts have long thought that this approach results in barely detectable circular abrasions, especially on cars that are waxed frequently. They advise rubbing in straight lines, especially if any kind of cleaner is involved.

7. If an applicator is not supplied with the wax, use a piece of soft cheesecloth or very soft lint-free material. The same applies to buffing the surface.

SPECIAL SURFACES

One-step combination cleaner and wax formulas shouldn't be used on many of the special surfaces which abound on cars. The one-step materials contain abrasives to achieve a clean surface under the wax top coat. The abrasives are so mild that you could clean a car every week for a couple of years without fear of rubbing through the paint. But this same level of abrasiveness might, through repeated use, damage decals used for special trim effects. This includes wide stripes, wood-grain trim and other appliques.

Painted plastics must be cleaned with care. If a cleaner is too aggressive it will cut through the paint and expose the primer. If bright trim such as polished aluminum or chrome is painted, cleaning must be performed with even greater care. If rubbing compound is being used, it will cut faster than polish.

Abrasive cleaners will dull an acrylic finish. The best way to clean these newer finishes is with a non-abrasive liquid polish. Only dirt and oxidation, not paint, will be removed.

Taking a few minutes to read the instructions on the can of polish or wax will help prevent making serious mistakes. Not all preparations will work on all surfaces. And some are intended for power application while others will only work when applied by hand.

Don't get the idea that just pouring on some polish and then hitting it with a buffer will suffice. Power equipment speeds the operation. But it also adds a measure of risk. It's very easy to damage the finish if you use the wrong methods or materials.

Caring for Chrome

Read the label on the container. Many products are formulated specifically for chrome, but others contain abrasives that will scratch the chrome finish. If it isn't recommended for chrome, don't use it.

Never use steel wool or kitchen soap pads to clean chrome. Be careful not to get chrome cleaner on paint or interior vinyl surfaces. If you do, get it off immediately.

Troubleshooting

This section is designed to aid in the quick, accurate diagnosis of automotive problems. While automotive repairs can be made by many people, accurate troubleshooting is a rare skill for the amateur and professional alike.

In its simplest state, troubleshooting is an exercise in logic. It is essential to realize that an automobile is really composed of a series of systems. Some of these systems are interrelated; others are not. Automobiles operate within a framework of logical rules and physical laws, and the key to troubleshooting is a good understanding of all the automotive systems.

This section breaks the car or truck down into its component systems, allowing the problem to be isolated. The charts and diagnostic road maps list the most common problems and the most probable causes of trouble. Obviously it would be impossible to list every possible problem that could happen along with every possible cause, but it will locate MOST problems and eliminate a lot of unnecessary guesswork. The systematic format will locate problems within a given system, but, because many automotive systems are interrelated, the solution to your particular problem may be found in a number of systems on the car or truck.

USING THE TROUBLESHOOTING CHARTS

This book contains all of the specific information that the average do-it-yourself mechanic needs to repair and maintain his or her car or truck. The troubleshooting charts are designed to be used in conjunction with the specific procedures and information in the text. For instance, troubleshooting a point-type ignition system is fairly standard for all models, but you may be directed to the text to find procedures for troubleshooting an individual type of electronic ignition. You will also have to refer to the specification charts throughout the book for specifications applicable to your car or truck.

TOOLS AND EQUIPMENT

The tools illustrated in Chapter 1 (plus two more diagnostic pieces) will be adequate to troubleshoot most problems. The two other tools needed are a voltmeter and an ohmmeter. These can be purchased separately or in combination, known as a VOM meter.

In the event that other tools are required, they will be noted in the procedures.

Troubleshooting Engine Problems

See Chapters 2, 3, 4 for more information and service procedures.

Index to Systems

System	To Test	Group
Battery	Engine need not be running	1
Starting system	Engine need not be running	2
Primary electrical system	Engine need not be running	3
Secondary electrical system	Engine need not be running	4
Fuel system	Engine need not be running	5
Engine compression	Engine need not be running	6
Engine vacuum	Engine must be running	7
Secondary electrical system	Engine must be running	8
Valve train	Engine must be running	9
Exhaust system	Engine must be running	10
Cooling system	Engine must be running	11
Engine lubrication	Engine must be running	12

Index to Problems

Problem: Symptom	Begin at Specific Diagnosis, Number ____
Engine Won't Start:	
Starter doesn't turn	1.1, 2.1
Starter turns, engine doesn't	2.1
Starter turns engine very slowly	1.1, 2.4
Starter turns engine normally	3.1, 4.1
Starter turns engine very quickly	6.1
Engine fires intermittently	4.1
Engine fires consistently	5.1, 6.1
Engine Runs Poorly:	
Hard starting	3.1, 4.1, 5.1, 8.1
Rough idle	4.1, 5.1, 8.1
Stalling	3.1, 4.1, 5.1, 8.1
Engine dies at high speeds	4.1, 5.1
Hesitation (on acceleration from standing stop)	5.1, 8.1
Poor pickup	4.1, 5.1, 8.1
Lack of power	3.1, 4.1, 5.1, 8.1
Backfire through the carburetor	4.1, 8.1, 9.1
Backfire through the exhaust	4.1, 8.1, 9.1
Blue exhaust gases	6.1, 7.1
Black exhaust gases	5.1
Running on (after the ignition is shut off)	3.1, 8.1
Susceptible to moisture	4.1
Engine misfires under load	4.1, 7.1, 8.4, 9.1
Engine misfires at speed	4.1, 8.4
Engine misfires at idle	3.1, 4.1, 5.1, 7.1, 8.4

Sample Section

Test and Procedure	Results and Indications	Proceed to
4.1—Check for spark: Hold each spark plug wire approximately ¼″ from ground with gloves or a heavy, dry rag. Crank the engine and observe the spark.	If no spark is evident:	→ **4.2**
	If spark is good in some cases:	→ **4.3**
	If spark is good in all cases:	→ **4.6**

Specific Diagnosis

This section is arranged so that following each test, instructions are given to proceed to another, until a problem is diagnosed.

Section 1—Battery

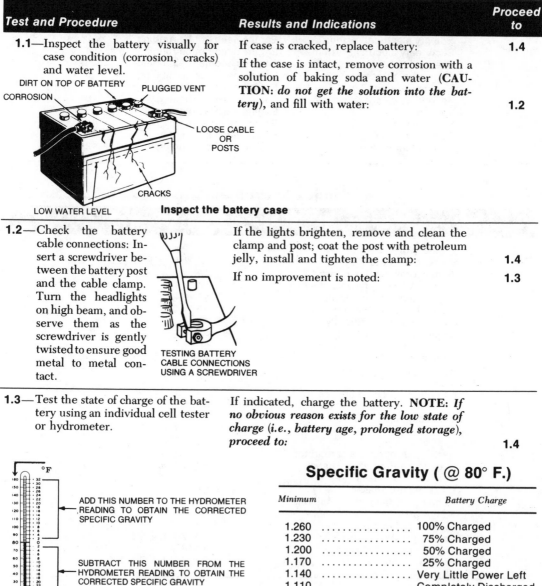

Test and Procedure	Results and Indications	Proceed to
1.1—Inspect the battery visually for case condition (corrosion, cracks) and water level.	If case is cracked, replace battery:	**1.4**
	If the case is intact, remove corrosion with a solution of baking soda and water (**CAUTION**: *do not get the solution into the battery*), and fill with water:	**1.2**

DIRT ON TOP OF BATTERY

CORROSION

PLUGGED VENT

LOOSE CABLE OR POSTS

CRACKS

LOW WATER LEVEL   **Inspect the battery case**

1.2—Check the battery cable connections: Insert a screwdriver between the battery post and the cable clamp. Turn the headlights on high beam, and observe them as the screwdriver is gently twisted to ensure good metal to metal contact.	If the lights brighten, remove and clean the clamp and post; coat the post with petroleum jelly, install and tighten the clamp:	**1.4**
	If no improvement is noted:	**1.3**

TESTING BATTERY CABLE CONNECTIONS USING A SCREWDRIVER

1.3—Test the state of charge of the battery using an individual cell tester or hydrometer.	If indicated, charge the battery. **NOTE:** *If no obvious reason exists for the low state of charge (i.e., battery age, prolonged storage), proceed to:*	**1.4**

°F

ADD THIS NUMBER TO THE HYDROMETER READING TO OBTAIN THE CORRECTED SPECIFIC GRAVITY

SUBTRACT THIS NUMBER FROM THE HYDROMETER READING TO OBTAIN THE CORRECTED SPECIFIC GRAVITY

Specific Gravity (@ 80° F.)

Minimum	Battery Charge
1.260	100% Charged
1.230	75% Charged
1.200	50% Charged
1.170	25% Charged
1.140	Very Little Power Left
1.110	Completely Discharged

The effects of temperature on battery specific gravity (left) and amount of battery charge in relation to specific gravity (right)

1.4—Visually inspect battery cables for cracking, bad connection to ground, or bad connection to starter.	If necessary, tighten connections or replace the cables:	**2.1**

Section 2—Starting System
See Chapter 3 for service procedures

Test and Procedure	Results and Indications	Proceed to

Note: Tests in Group 2 are performed with coil high tension lead disconnected to prevent accidental starting.

Test and Procedure	Results and Indications	Proceed to
2.1—Test the starter motor and solenoid: Connect a jumper from the battery post of the solenoid (or relay) to the starter post of the solenoid (or relay).	If starter turns the engine normally:	2.2
	If the starter buzzes, or turns the engine very slowly:	2.4
	If no response, replace the solenoid (or relay).	3.1
	If the starter turns, but the engine doesn't, ensure that the flywheel ring gear is intact. If the gear is undamaged, replace the starter drive.	3.1
2.2—Determine whether ignition override switches are functioning properly (clutch start switch, neutral safety switch), by connecting a jumper across the switch(es), and turning the ignition switch to "start".	If starter operates, adjust or replace switch:	3.1
	If the starter doesn't operate:	2.3
2.3—Check the ignition switch "start" position: Connect a 12V test lamp or voltmeter between the starter post of the solenoid (or relay) and ground. Turn the ignition switch to the "start" position, and jiggle the key.	If the lamp doesn't light or the meter needle doesn't move when the switch is turned, check the ignition switch for loose connections, cracked insulation, or broken wires. Repair or replace as necessary:	3.1
	If the lamp flickers or needle moves when the key is jiggled, replace the ignition switch.	3.3

Checking the ignition switch "start" position

STARTER RELAY
(IF EQUIPPED)

Test and Procedure	Results and Indications	Proceed to
2.4—Remove and bench test the starter, according to specifications in the engine electrical section.	If the starter does not meet specifications, repair or replace as needed:	3.1
	If the starter is operating properly:	2.5
2.5—Determine whether the engine can turn freely: Remove the spark plugs, and check for water in the cylinders. Check for water on the dipstick, or oil in the radiator. Attempt to turn the engine using an 18″ flex drive and socket on the crankshaft pulley nut or bolt.	If the engine will turn freely only with the spark plugs out, and hydrostatic lock (water in the cylinders) is ruled out, check valve timing:	9.2
	If engine will not turn freely, and it is known that the clutch and transmission are free, the engine must be disassembled for further evaluation:	Chapter 3

Section 3—Primary Electrical System

Test and Procedure	Results and Indications	Proceed to
3.1—Check the ignition switch "on" position: Connect a jumper wire between the distributor side of the coil and ground, and a 12V test lamp between the switch side of the coil and ground. Remove the high tension lead from the coil. Turn the ignition switch on and jiggle the key.	If the lamp lights:	**3.2**
	If the lamp flickers when the key is jiggled, replace the ignition switch:	**3.3**
	If the lamp doesn't light, check for loose or open connections. If none are found, remove the ignition switch and check for continuity. If the switch is faulty, replace it:	**3.3**

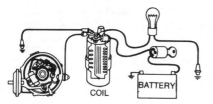

Checking the ignition switch "on" position

3.2—Check the ballast resistor or resistance wire for an open circuit, using an ohmmeter. See Chapter 3 for specific tests.	Replace the resistor or resistance wire if the resistance is zero. **NOTE:** *Some ignition systems have no ballast resistor.*	**3.3**

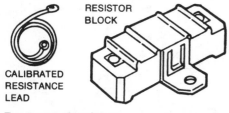

Two types of resistors

3.3—On point-type ignition systems, visually inspect the breaker points for burning, pitting or excessive wear. Gray coloring of the point contact surfaces is normal. Rotate the crankshaft until the contact heel rests on a high point of the distributor cam and adjust the point gap to specifications. On electronic ignition models, remove the distributor cap and visually inspect the armature. Ensure that the armature pin is in place, and that the armature is on tight and rotates when the engine is cranked. Make sure there are no cracks, chips or rounded edges on the armature.	If the breaker points are intact, clean the contact surfaces with fine emery cloth, and adjust the point gap to specifications. If the points are worn, replace them. On electronic systems, replace any parts which appear defective. If condition persists:	**3.4**

Test and Procedure	Results and Indications	Proceed to
3.4—On point-type ignition systems, connect a dwell-meter between the distributor primary lead and ground. Crank the engine and observe the point dwell angle. On electronic ignition systems, conduct a stator (magnetic pickup assembly) test. See Chapter 3.	On point-type systems, adjust the dwell angle if necessary. **NOTE:** *Increasing the point gap decreases the dwell angle and vice-versa.*	**3.6**
	If the dwell meter shows little or no reading;	**3.5**
	On electronic ignition systems, if the stator is bad, replace the stator. If the stator is good, proceed to the other tests in Chapter 3.	

CLOSE   OPEN

NORMAL DWELL

WIDE GAP

SMALL DWELL

INSUFFICIENT DWELL

NARROW GAP

LARGE DWELL

EXCESSIVE DWELL

Dwell is a function of point gap

3.5—On the point-type ignition systems, check the condenser for short: connect an ohmeter across the condenser body and the pigtail lead.	If any reading other than infinite is noted, replace the condenser	**3.6**

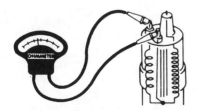

OHMMETER

Checking the condenser for short

3.6—Test the coil primary resistance: On point-type ignition systems, connect an ohmmeter across the coil primary terminals, and read the resistance on the low scale. Note whether an external ballast resistor or resistance wire is used. On electronic ignition systems, test the coil primary resistance as in Chapter 3.	Point-type ignition coils utilizing ballast resistors or resistance wires should have approximately 1.0 ohms resistance. Coils with internal resistors should have approximately 4.0 ohms resistance. If values far from the above are noted, replace the coil.	**4.1**

OHMMETER

Check the coil primary resistance

Section 4—Secondary Electrical System
See Chapters 2–3 for service procedures

Test and Procedure	Results and Indications	Proceed to
4.1—Check for spark: Hold each spark plug wire approximately ¼″ from ground with gloves or a heavy, dry rag. Crank the engine, and observe the spark.	If no spark is evident:	**4.2**
	If spark is good in some cylinders:	**4.3**
	If spark is good in all cylinders:	**4.6**

Check for spark at the plugs

4.2—Check for spark at the coil high tension lead: Remove the coil high tension lead from the distributor and position it approximately ¼″ from ground. Crank the engine and observe spark. **CAUTION: *This test should not be performed on engines equipped with electronic ignition.***	If the spark is good and consistent:	**4.3**
	If the spark is good but intermittent, test the primary electrical system starting at 3.3:	**3.3**
	If the spark is weak or non-existent, replace the coil high tension lead, clean and tighten all connections and retest. If no improvement is noted:	**4.4**
4.3—Visually inspect the distributor cap and rotor for burned or corroded contacts, cracks, carbon tracks, or moisture. Also check the fit of the rotor on the distributor shaft (where applicable).	If moisture is present, dry thoroughly, and retest per 4.1:	**4.1**
	If burned or excessively corroded contacts, cracks, or carbon tracks are noted, replace the defective part(s) and retest per 4.1:	**4.1**
	If the rotor and cap appear intact, or are only slightly corroded, clean the contacts thoroughly (including the cap towers and spark plug wire ends) and retest per 4.1:	
	If the spark is good in all cases:	**4.6**
	If the spark is poor in all cases:	**4.5**

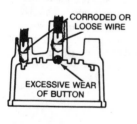

CORRODED OR LOOSE WIRE

EXCESSIVE WEAR OF BUTTON

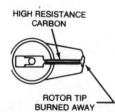

HIGH RESISTANCE CARBON

ROTOR TIP BURNED AWAY

Inspect the distributor cap and rotor

Test and Procedure	Results and Indications	Proceed to

4.4—Check the coil secondary resistance: On point-type systems connect an ohmmeter across the distributor side of the coil and the coil tower. Read the resistance on the high scale of the ohmmeter. On electronic ignition systems, see Chapter 3 for specific tests.

The resistance of a satisfactory coil should be between 4,000 and 10,000 ohms. If resistance is considerably higher (i.e., 40,000 ohms) replace the coil and retest per 4.1. **NOTE:** *This does not apply to high performance coils.*

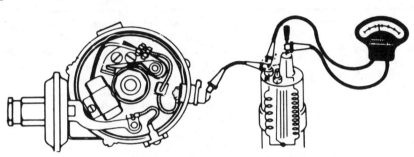

Testing the coil secondary resistance

4.5—Visually inspect the spark plug wires for cracking or brittleness. Ensure that no two wires are positioned so as to cause induction firing (adjacent and parallel). Remove each wire, one by one, and check resistance with an ohmmeter.

Replace any cracked or brittle wires. If any of the wires are defective, replace the entire set. Replace any wires with excessive resistance (over $8000\,\Omega$ per foot for suppression wire), and separate any wires that might cause induction firing.

4.6

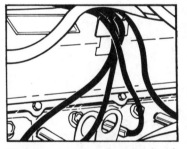

Misfiring can be the result of spark plug leads to adjacent, consecutively firing cylinders running parallel and too close together

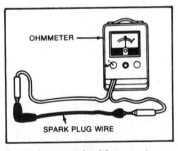

On point-type ignition systems, check the spark plug wires as shown. On electronic ignitions, do not remove the wire from the distributor cap terminal; instead, test through the cap

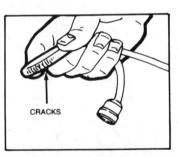

Spark plug wires can be checked visually by bending them in a loop over your finger. This will reveal any cracks, burned or broken insulation. Any wire with cracked insulation should be replaced

4.6—Remove the spark plugs, noting the cylinders from which they were removed, and evaluate according to the color photos in the middle of this book.

See following.

See following.

Test and Procedure	Results and Indications	Proceed to
4.7—Examine the location of all the plugs.	The following diagrams illustrate some of the conditions that the location of plugs will reveal.	4.8

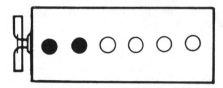

Two adjacent plugs are fouled in a 6-cylinder engine, 4-cylinder engine or either bank of a V-8. This is probably due to a blown head gasket between the two cylinders

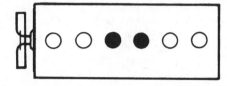

The two center plugs in a 6-cylinder engine are fouled. Raw fuel may be "boiled" out of the carburetor into the intake manifold after the engine is shut-off. Stop-start driving can also foul the center plugs, due to overly rich mixture. Proper float level, a new float needle and seat or use of an insulating spacer may help this problem

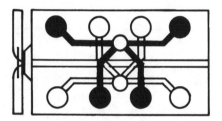

An unbalanced carburetor is indicated. Following the fuel flow on this particular design shows that the cylinders fed by the right-hand barrel are fouled from overly rich mixture, while the cylinders fed by the left-hand barrel are normal

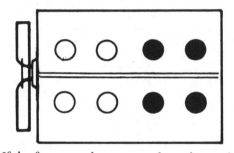

If the four rear plugs are overheated, a cooling system problem is suggested. A thorough cleaning of the cooling system may restore coolant circulation and cure the problem

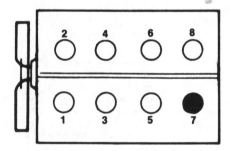

Finding one plug overheated may indicate an intake manifold leak near the affected cylinder. If the overheated plug is the second of two adjacent, consecutively firing plugs, it could be the result of ignition cross-firing. Separating the leads to these two plugs will eliminate cross-fire

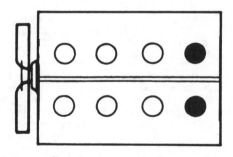

Occasionally, the two rear plugs in large, lightly used V-8's will become oil fouled. High oil consumption and smoky exhaust may also be noticed. It is probably due to plugged oil drain holes in the rear of the cylinder head, causing oil to be sucked in around the valve stems. This usually occurs in the rear cylinders first, because the engine slants that way

Test and Procedure	Results and Indications	Proceed to
4.8—Determine the static ignition timing. Using the crankshaft pulley timing marks as a guide, locate top dead center on the compression stroke of the number one cylinder.	The rotor should be pointing toward the No. 1 tower in the distributor cap, and, on electronic ignitions, the armature spoke for that cylinder should be lined up with the stator.	**4.8**
4.9—Check coil polarity: Connect a voltmeter negative lead to the coil high tension lead, and the positive lead to ground (**NOTE:** *Reverse the hook-up for positive ground systems*). Crank the engine momentarily. **Checking coil polarity**	If the voltmeter reads up-scale, the polarity is correct: If the voltmeter reads down-scale, reverse the coil polarity (switch the primary leads):	**5.1** **5.1**

Section 5—Fuel System
See Chapter 4 for service procedures

Test and Procedure	Results and Indications	Proceed to
5.1—Determine that the air filter is functioning efficiently: Hold paper elements up to a strong light, and attempt to see light through the filter.	Clean permanent air filters in solvent (or manufacturer's recommendation), and allow to dry. Replace paper elements through which light cannot be seen:	**5.2**
5.2—Determine whether a flooding condition exists: Flooding is identified by a strong gasoline odor, and excessive gasoline present in the throttle bore(s) of the carburetor. 	If flooding is not evident: If flooding is evident, permit the gasoline to dry for a few moments and restart. If flooding doesn't recur: If flooding is persistent:	**5.3** **5.7** **5.5**
	If the engine floods repeatedly, check the choke butterfly flap	
5.3—Check that fuel is reaching the carburetor: Detach the fuel line at the carburetor inlet. Hold the end of the line in a cup (not styrofoam), and crank the engine. 	If fuel flows smoothly: If fuel doesn't flow (**NOTE:** *Make sure that there is fuel in the tank*), or flows erratically:	**5.7** **5.4**
	Check the fuel pump by disconnecting the output line (fuel pump-to-carburetor) at the carburetor and operating the starter briefly	

Test and Procedure	Results and Indications	Proceed to
5.4—Test the fuel pump: Disconnect all fuel lines from the fuel pump. Hold a finger over the input fitting, crank the engine (with electric pump, turn the ignition or pump on); and feel for suction.	If suction is evident, blow out the fuel line to the tank with low pressure compressed air until bubbling is heard from the fuel filler neck. Also blow out the carburetor fuel line (both ends disconnected):	5.7
	If no suction is evident, replace or repair the fuel pump: **NOTE:** *Repeated oil fouling of the spark plugs, or a no-start condition, could be the result of a ruptured vacuum booster pump diaphragm, through which oil or gasoline is being drawn into the intake manifold (where applicable).*	5.7
5.5—Occasionally, small specks of dirt will clog the small jets and orifices in the carburetor. With the engine cold, hold a flat piece of wood or similar material over the carburetor, where possible, and crank the engine.	If the engine starts, but runs roughly the engine is probably not run enough. If the engine won't start:	5.9
5.6—Check the needle and seat: Tap the carburetor in the area of the needle and seat.	If flooding stops, a gasoline additive (e.g., Gumout) will often cure the problem:	5.7
	If flooding continues, check the fuel pump for excessive pressure at the carburetor (according to specifications). If the pressure is normal, the needle and seat must be removed and checked, and/or the float level adjusted:	5.7
5.7—Test the accelerator pump by looking into the throttle bores while operating the throttle.	If the accelerator pump appears to be operating normally:	5.8
	If the accelerator pump is not operating, the pump must be reconditioned. Where possible, service the pump with the carburetor(s) installed on the engine. If necessary, remove the carburetor. Prior to removal:	5.8

Check for gas at the carburetor by looking down the carburetor throat while someone moves the accelerator

Test and Procedure	Results and Indications	Proceed to
5.8—Determine whether the carburetor main fuel system is functioning: Spray a commercial starting fluid into the carburetor while attempting to start the engine.	If the engine starts, runs for a few seconds, and dies:	5.9
	If the engine doesn't start:	6.1

Test and Procedure	Results and Indications	Proceed to
5.9—Uncommon fuel system malfunctions: See below:	If the problem is solved: If the problem remains, remove and recondition the carburetor.	**6.1**

Condition	Indication	Test	Prevailing Weather Conditions	Remedy
Vapor lock	Engine will not restart shortly after running.	Cool the components of the fuel system until the engine starts. Vapor lock can be cured faster by draping a wet cloth over a mechanical fuel pump.	Hot to very hot	Ensure that the exhaust manifold heat control valve is operating. Check with the vehicle manufacturer for the recommended solution to vapor lock on the model in question.
Carburetor icing	Engine will not idle, stalls at low speeds.	Visually inspect the throttle plate area of the throttle bores for frost.	High humidity, 32–40° F.	Ensure that the exhaust manifold heat control valve is operating, and that the intake manifold heat riser is not blocked.
Water in the fuel	Engine sputters and stalls; may not start.	Pump a small amount of fuel into a glass jar. Allow to stand, and inspect for droplets or a layer of water.	High humidity, extreme temperature changes.	For droplets, use one or two cans of commercial gas line anti-freeze. For a layer of water, the tank must be drained, and the fuel lines blown out with compressed air.

Section 6—Engine Compression
See Chapter 3 for service procedures

6.1—Test engine compression: Remove all spark plugs. Block the throttle wide open. Insert a compression gauge into a spark plug port, crank the engine to obtain the maximum reading, and record.	If compression is within limits on all cylinders:	**7.1**
	If gauge reading is extremely low on all cylinders:	**6.2**
	If gauge reading is low on one or two cylinders: (If gauge readings are identical and low on two or more adjacent cylinders, the head gasket must be replaced.)	**6.2**

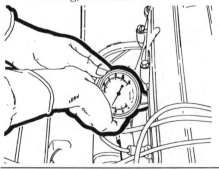

Checking compression

6.2—Test engine compression (wet): Squirt approximately 30 cc. of engine oil into each cylinder, and retest per 6.1.	If the readings improve, worn or cracked rings or broken pistons are indicated:	**See Chapter 3**
	If the readings do not improve, burned or excessively carboned valves or a jumped timing chain are indicated: NOTE: *A jumped timing chain is often indicated by difficult cranking.*	**7.1**

Section 7—Engine Vacuum
See Chapter 3 for service procedures

Test and Procedure	Results and Indications	Proceed to
7.1—Attach a vacuum gauge to the intake manifold beyond the throttle plate. Start the engine, and observe the action of the needle over the range of engine speeds.	See below.	**See below**

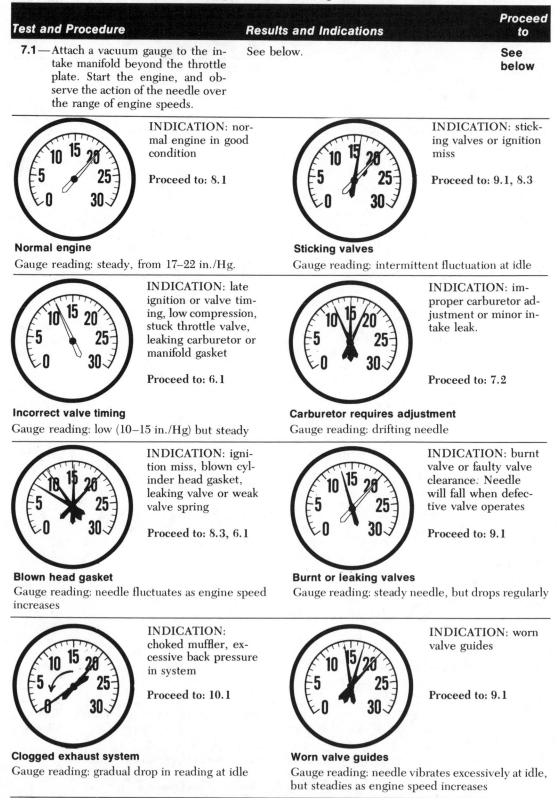

INDICATION: normal engine in good condition

Proceed to: 8.1

Normal engine
Gauge reading: steady, from 17–22 in./Hg.

INDICATION: sticking valves or ignition miss

Proceed to: 9.1, 8.3

Sticking valves
Gauge reading: intermittent fluctuation at idle

INDICATION: late ignition or valve timing, low compression, stuck throttle valve, leaking carburetor or manifold gasket

Proceed to: 6.1

Incorrect valve timing
Gauge reading: low (10–15 in./Hg) but steady

INDICATION: improper carburetor adjustment or minor intake leak.

Proceed to: 7.2

Carburetor requires adjustment
Gauge reading: drifting needle

INDICATION: ignition miss, blown cylinder head gasket, leaking valve or weak valve spring

Proceed to: 8.3, 6.1

Blown head gasket
Gauge reading: needle fluctuates as engine speed increases

INDICATION: burnt valve or faulty valve clearance. Needle will fall when defective valve operates

Proceed to: 9.1

Burnt or leaking valves
Gauge reading: steady needle, but drops regularly

INDICATION: choked muffler, excessive back pressure in system

Proceed to: 10.1

Clogged exhaust system
Gauge reading: gradual drop in reading at idle

INDICATION: worn valve guides

Proceed to: 9.1

Worn valve guides
Gauge reading: needle vibrates excessively at idle, but steadies as engine speed increases

White pointer = steady gauge hand   Black pointer = fluctuating gauge hand

Test and Procedure	Results and Indications	Proceed to
7.2—Attach a vacuum gauge per 7.1, and test for an intake manifold leak. Squirt a small amount of oil around the intake manifold gaskets, carburetor gaskets, plugs and fittings. Observe the action of the vacuum gauge.	If the reading improves, replace the indicated gasket, or seal the indicated fitting or plug:	**8.1**
	If the reading remains low:	**7.3**
7.3—Test all vacuum hoses and accessories for leaks as described in 7.2. Also check the carburetor body (dashpots, automatic choke mechanism, throttle shafts) for leaks in the same manner.	If the reading improves, service or replace the offending part(s):	**8.1**
	If the reading remains low:	**6.1**

Section 8—Secondary Electrical System
See Chapter 2 for service procedures

Test and Procedure	Results and Indications	Proceed to
8.1—Remove the distributor cap and check to make sure that the rotor turns when the engine is cranked. Visually inspect the distributor components.	Clean, tighten or replace any components which appear defective.	**8.2**
8.2—Connect a timing light (per manufacturer's recommendation) and check the dynamic ignition timing. Disconnect and plug the vacuum hose(s) to the distributor if specified, start the engine, and observe the timing marks at the specified engine speed.	If the timing is not correct, adjust to specifications by rotating the distributor in the engine: (Advance timing by rotating distributor opposite normal direction of rotor rotation, retard timing by rotating distributor in same direction as rotor rotation.)	**8.3**
8.3—Check the operation of the distributor advance mechanism(s): To test the mechanical advance, disconnect the vacuum lines from the distributor advance unit and observe the timing marks with a timing light as the engine speed is increased from idle. If the mark moves smoothly, without hesitation, it may be assumed that the mechanical advance is functioning properly. To test vacuum advance and/or retard systems, alternately crimp and release the vacuum line, and observe the timing mark for movement. If movement is noted, the system is operating.	If the systems are functioning:	**8.4**
	If the systems are not functioning, remove the distributor, and test on a distributor tester:	**8.4**
8.4—Locate an ignition miss: With the engine running, remove each spark plug wire, one at a time, until one is found that doesn't cause the engine to roughen and slow down.	When the missing cylinder is identified:	**4.1**

Section 9—Valve Train
See Chapter 3 for service procedures

Test and Procedure	Results and Indications	Proceed to
9.1—Evaluate the valve train: Remove the valve cover, and ensure that the valves are adjusted to specifications. A mechanic's stethoscope may be used to aid in the diagnosis of the valve train. By pushing the probe on or near push rods or rockers, valve noise often can be isolated. A timing light also may be used to diagnose valve problems. Connect the light according to manufacturer's recommendations, and start the engine. Vary the firing moment of the light by increasing the engine speed (and therefore the ignition advance), and moving the trigger from cylinder to cylinder. Observe the movement of each valve.	Sticking valves or erratic valve train motion can be observed with the timing light. The cylinder head must be disassembled for repairs.	**See Chapter 3**
9.2—Check the valve timing: Locate top dead center of the No. 1 piston, and install a degree wheel or tape on the crankshaft pulley or damper with zero corresponding to an index mark on the engine. Rotate the crankshaft in its direction of rotation, and observe the opening of the No. 1 cylinder intake valve. The opening should correspond with the correct mark on the degree wheel according to specifications.	If the timing is not correct, the timing cover must be removed for further investigation.	**See Chapter 3**

Section 10—Exhaust System

Test and Procedure	Results and Indications	Proceed to
10.1—Determine whether the exhaust manifold heat control valve is operating: Operate the valve by hand to determine whether it is free to move. If the valve is free, run the engine to operating temperature and observe the action of the valve, to ensure that it is opening.	If the valve sticks, spray it with a suitable solvent, open and close the valve to free it, and retest. If the valve functions properly: If the valve does not free, or does not operate, replace the valve:	**10.2** **10.2**
10.2—Ensure that there are no exhaust restrictions: Visually inspect the exhaust system for kinks, dents, or crushing. Also note that gases are flowing freely from the tailpipe at all engine speeds, indicating no restriction in the muffler or resonator.	Replace any damaged portion of the system:	**11.1**

Section 11—Cooling System
See Chapter 3 for service procedures

Test and Procedure	Results and Indications	Proceed to
11.1—Visually inspect the fan belt for glazing, cracks, and fraying, and replace if necessary. Tighten the belt so that the longest span has approximately ½" play at its mid-point under thumb pressure (see Chapter 1).	Replace or tighten the fan belt as necessary:	**11.2**

Checking belt tension

Test and Procedure	Results and Indications	Proceed to
11.2—Check the fluid level of the cooling system.	If full or slightly low, fill as necessary:	**11.5**
	If extremely low:	**11.3**
11.3—Visually inspect the external portions of the cooling system (radiator, radiator hoses, thermostat elbow, water pump seals, heater hoses, etc.) for leaks. If none are found, pressurize the cooling system to 14–15 psi.	If cooling system holds the pressure:	**11.5**
	If cooling system loses pressure rapidly, reinspect external parts of the system for leaks under pressure. If none are found, check dipstick for coolant in crankcase. If no coolant is present, but pressure loss continues:	**11.4**
	If coolant is evident in crankcase, remove cylinder head(s), and check gasket(s). If gaskets are intact, block and cylinder head(s) should be checked for cracks or holes.	
	If the gasket(s) is blown, replace, and purge the crankcase of coolant:	**12.6**
	NOTE: *Occasionally, due to atmospheric and driving conditions, condensation of water can occur in the crankcase. This causes the oil to appear milky white. To remedy, run the engine until hot, and change the oil and oil filter.*	
11.4—Check for combustion leaks into the cooling system: Pressurize the cooling system as above. Start the engine, and observe the pressure gauge. If the needle fluctuates, remove each spark plug wire, one at a time, noting which cylinder(s) reduce or eliminate the fluctuation.	Cylinders which reduce or eliminate the fluctuation, when the spark plug wire is removed, are leaking into the cooling system. Replace the head gasket on the affected cylinder bank(s).	

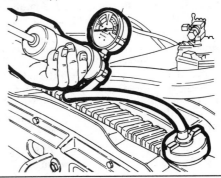

Pressurizing the cooling system

Test and Procedure	Results and Indications	Proceed to
11.5—Check the radiator pressure cap: Attach a radiator pressure tester to the radiator cap (wet the seal prior to installation). Quickly pump up the pressure, noting the point at which the cap releases.	If the cap releases within ± 1 psi of the specified rating, it is operating properly:	**11.6**
	If the cap releases at more than ± 1 psi of the specified rating, it should be replaced:	**11.6**

Checking radiator pressure cap

Test and Procedure	Results and Indications	Proceed to
11.6—Test the thermostat: Start the engine cold, remove the radiator cap, and insert a thermometer into the radiator. Allow the engine to idle. After a short while, there will be a sudden, rapid increase in coolant temperature. The temperature at which this sharp rise stops is the thermostat opening temperature.	If the thermostat opens at or about the specified temperature:	**11.7**
	If the temperature doesn't increase: (If the temperature increases slowly and gradually, replace the thermostat.)	**11.7**
11.7—Check the water pump: Remove the thermostat elbow and the thermostat, disconnect the coil high tension lead (to prevent starting), and crank the engine momentarily.	If coolant flows, replace the thermostat and retest per 11.6:	**11.6**
	If coolant doesn't flow, reverse flush the cooling system to alleviate any blockage that might exist. If system is not blocked, and coolant will not flow, replace the water pump.	

Section 12—Lubrication
See Chapter 3 for service procedures

Test and Procedure	Results and Indications	Proceed to
12.1—Check the oil pressure gauge or warning light: If the gauge shows low pressure, or the light is on for no obvious reason, remove the oil pressure sender. Install an accurate oil pressure gauge and run the engine momentarily.	If oil pressure builds normally, run engine for a few moments to determine that it is functioning normally, and replace the sender.	—
	If the pressure remains low:	**12.2**
	If the pressure surges:	**12.3**
	If the oil pressure is zero:	**12.3**
12.2—Visually inspect the oil: If the oil is watery or very thin, milky, or foamy, replace the oil and oil filter.	If the oil is normal:	**12.3**
	If after replacing oil the pressure remains low:	**12.3**
	If after replacing oil the pressure becomes normal:	—

Test and Procedure	Results and Indications	Proceed to
12.3—Inspect the oil pressure relief valve and spring, to ensure that it is not sticking or stuck. Remove and thoroughly clean the valve, spring, and the valve body.	If the oil pressure improves: If no improvement is noted:	— **12.4**
12.4—Check to ensure that the oil pump is not cavitating (sucking air instead of oil): See that the crankcase is neither over nor underfull, and that the pickup in the sump is in the proper position and free from sludge.	Fill or drain the crankcase to the proper capacity, and clean the pickup screen in solvent if necessary. If no improvement is noted:	**12.5**
12.5—Inspect the oil pump drive and the oil pump:	If the pump drive or the oil pump appear to be defective, service as necessary and retest per 12.1:	**12.1**
	If the pump drive and pump appear to be operating normally, the engine should be disassembled to determine where blockage exists:	**See Chapter 3**
12.6—Purge the engine of ethylene glycol coolant: Completely drain the crankcase and the oil filter. Obtain a commercial butyl cellosolve base solvent, designated for this purpose, and follow the instructions precisely. Following this, install a new oil filter and refill the crankcase with the proper weight oil. The next oil and filter change should follow shortly thereafter (1000 miles).		

TROUBLESHOOTING EMISSION CONTROL SYSTEMS

See Chapter 4 for procedures applicable to individual emission control systems used on specific combinations of engine/transmission/model.

TROUBLESHOOTING THE CARBURETOR

See Chapter 4 for service procedures

Carburetor problems cannot be effectively isolated unless all other engine systems (particularly ignition and emission) are functioning properly and the engine is properly tuned.

Condition	Possible Cause
Engine cranks, but does not start	1. Improper starting procedure 2. No fuel in tank 3. Clogged fuel line or filter 4. Defective fuel pump 5. Choke valve not closing properly 6. Engine flooded 7. Choke valve not unloading 8. Throttle linkage not making full travel 9. Stuck needle or float 10. Leaking float needle or seat 11. Improper float adjustment
Engine stalls	1. Improperly adjusted idle speed or mixture **Engine hot** 2. Improperly adjusted dashpot 3. Defective or improperly adjusted solenoid 4. Incorrect fuel level in fuel bowl 5. Fuel pump pressure too high 6. Leaking float needle seat 7. Secondary throttle valve stuck open 8. Air or fuel leaks 9. Idle air bleeds plugged or missing 10. Idle passages plugged **Engine Cold** 11. Incorrectly adjusted choke 12. Improperly adjusted fast idle speed 13. Air leaks 14. Plugged idle or idle air passages 15. Stuck choke valve or binding linkage 16. Stuck secondary throttle valves 17. Engine flooding—high fuel level 18. Leaking or misaligned float
Engine hesitates on acceleration	1. Clogged fuel filter 2. Leaking fuel pump diaphragm 3. Low fuel pump pressure 4. Secondary throttle valves stuck, bent or misadjusted 5. Sticking or binding air valve 6. Defective accelerator pump 7. Vacuum leaks 8. Clogged air filter 9. Incorrect choke adjustment (engine cold)
Engine feels sluggish or flat on acceleration	1. Improperly adjusted idle speed or mixture 2. Clogged fuel filter 3. Defective accelerator pump 4. Dirty, plugged or incorrect main metering jets 5. Bent or sticking main metering rods 6. Sticking throttle valves 7. Stuck heat riser 8. Binding or stuck air valve 9. Dirty, plugged or incorrect secondary jets 10. Bent or sticking secondary metering rods. 11. Throttle body or manifold heat passages plugged 12. Improperly adjusted choke or choke vacuum break.
Carburetor floods	1. Defective fuel pump. Pressure too high. 2. Stuck choke valve 3. Dirty, worn or damaged float or needle valve/seat 4. Incorrect float/fuel level 5. Leaking float bowl

Condition	Possible Cause
Engine idles roughly and stalls	1. Incorrect idle speed 2. Clogged fuel filter 3. Dirt in fuel system or carburetor 4. Loose carburetor screws or attaching bolts 5. Broken carburetor gaskets 6. Air leaks 7. Dirty carburetor 8. Worn idle mixture needles 9. Throttle valves stuck open 10. Incorrectly adjusted float or fuel level 11. Clogged air filter
Engine runs unevenly or surges	1. Defective fuel pump 2. Dirty or clogged fuel filter 3. Plugged, loose or incorrect main metering jets or rods 4. Air leaks 5. Bent or sticking main metering rods 6. Stuck power piston 7. Incorrect float adjustment 8. Incorrect idle speed or mixture 9. Dirty or plugged idle system passages 10. Hard, brittle or broken gaskets 11. Loose attaching or mounting screws 12. Stuck or misaligned secondary throttle valves
Poor fuel economy	1. Poor driving habits 2. Stuck choke valve 3. Binding choke linkage 4. Stuck heat riser 5. Incorrect idle mixture 6. Defective accelerator pump 7. Air leaks 8. Plugged, loose or incorrect main metering jets 9. Improperly adjusted float or fuel level 10. Bent, misaligned or fuel-clogged float 11. Leaking float needle seat 12. Fuel leak 13. Accelerator pump discharge ball not seating properly 14. Incorrect main jets
Engine lacks high speed performance or power	1. Incorrect throttle linkage adjustment 2. Stuck or binding power piston 3. Defective accelerator pump 4. Air leaks 5. Incorrect float setting or fuel level 6. Dirty, plugged, worn or incorrect main metering jets or rods 7. Binding or sticking air valve 8. Brittle or cracked gaskets 9. Bent, incorrect or improperly adjusted secondary metering rods 10. Clogged fuel filter 11. Clogged air filter 12. Defective fuel pump

TROUBLESHOOTING FUEL INJECTION PROBLEMS

Each fuel injection system has its own unique components and test procedures, for which it is impossible to generalize. Refer to Chapter 4 of this Repair & Tune-Up Guide for specific test and repair procedures, if the vehicle is equipped with fuel injection.

TROUBLESHOOTING ELECTRICAL PROBLEMS

See Chapter 5 for service procedures

For any electrical system to operate, it must make a complete circuit. This simply means that the power flow from the battery must make a complete circle. When an electrical component is operating, power flows from the battery to the component, passes through the component causing it to perform its function (lighting a light bulb), and then returns to the battery through the ground of the circuit. This ground is usually (but not always) the metal part of the car or truck on which the electrical component is mounted.

Perhaps the easiest way to visualize this is to think of connecting a light bulb with two wires attached to it to the battery. If one of the two wires attached to the light bulb were attached to the negative post of the battery and the other were attached to the positive post of the battery, you would have a complete circuit. Current from the battery would flow to the light bulb, causing it to light, and return to the negative post of the battery.

The normal automotive circuit differs from this simple example in two ways. First, instead of having a return wire from the bulb to the battery, the light bulb returns the current to the battery through the chassis of the vehicle. Since the negative battery cable is attached to the chassis and the chassis is made of electrically conductive metal, the chassis of the vehicle can serve as a ground wire to complete the circuit. Secondly, most automotive circuits contain switches to turn components on and off as required.

Every complete circuit from a power source must include a component which is using the power from the power source. If you were to disconnect the light bulb from the wires and touch the two wires together (don't do this) the power supply wire to the component would be grounded before the normal ground connection for the circuit.

Because grounding a wire from a power source makes a complete circuit—less the required component to use the power—this phenomenon is called a short circuit. Common causes are: broken insulation (exposing the metal wire to a metal part of the car or truck), or a shorted switch.

Some electrical components which require a large amount of current to operate also have a relay in their circuit. Since these circuits carry a large amount of current, the thickness of the wire in the circuit (gauge size) is also greater. If this large wire were connected from the component to the control switch on the instrument panel, and then back to the component, a voltage drop would occur in the circuit. To prevent this potential drop in voltage, an electromagnetic switch (relay) is used. The large wires in the circuit are connected from the battery to one side of the relay, and from the opposite side of the relay to the component. The relay is normally open, preventing current from passing through the circuit. An additional, smaller, wire is connected from the relay to the control switch for the circuit. When the control switch is turned on, it grounds the smaller wire from the relay and completes the circuit. This closes the relay and allows current to flow from the battery to the component. The horn, headlight, and starter circuits are three which use relays.

It is possible for larger surges of current to pass through the electrical system of your car or truck. If this surge of current were to reach an electrical component, it could burn it out. To prevent this, fuses, circuit breakers or fusible links are connected into the current supply wires of most of the major electrical systems. When an electrical current of excessive power passes through the component's fuse, the fuse blows out and breaks the circuit, saving the component from destruction.

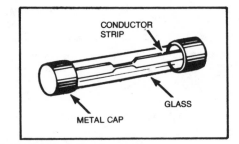

Typical automotive fuse

A circuit breaker is basically a self-repairing fuse. The circuit breaker opens the circuit the same way a fuse does. However, when either the short is removed from the circuit or the surge subsides, the circuit breaker resets itself and does not have to be replaced as a fuse does.

A fuse link is a wire that acts as a fuse. It is normally connected between the starter relay and the main wiring harness. This connection is usually under the hood. The fuse link (if installed) protects all the

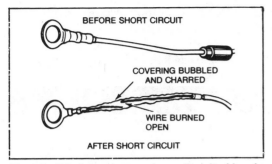

Most fusible links show a charred, melted insulation when they burn out

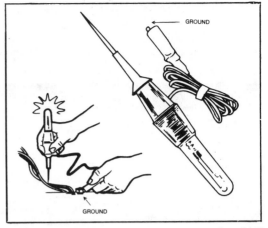

The test light will show the presence of current when touched to a hot wire and grounded at the other end

chassis electrical components, and is the probable cause of trouble when none of the electrical components function, unless the battery is disconnected or dead.

Electrical problems generally fall into one of three areas:

1. The component that is not functioning is not receiving current.

2. The component itself is not functioning.

3. The component is not properly grounded.

The electrical system can be checked with a test light and a jumper wire. A test light is a device that looks like a pointed screwdriver with a wire attached to it and has a light bulb in its handle. A jumper wire is a piece of insulated wire with an alligator clip attached to each end.

If a component is not working, you must follow a systematic plan to determine which of the three causes is the villain.

1. Turn on the switch that controls the inoperable component.

2. Disconnect the power supply wire from the component.

3. Attach the ground wire on the test light to a good metal ground.

4. Touch the probe end of the test light to the end of the power supply wire that was disconnected from the component. If the component is receiving current, the test light will go on.

NOTE: *Some components work only when the ignition switch is turned on.*

If the test light does not go on, then the problem is in the circuit between the battery and the component. This includes all the switches, fuses, and relays in the system. Follow the wire that runs back to the battery. The problem is an open circuit between the battery and the component. If the fuse is blown and, when replaced, immediately blows again, there is a short circuit in the system which must be located and repaired. If there is a switch in the system, bypass it with a jumper wire. This is done by connecting one end of the jumper wire to the power supply wire into the switch and the other end of the jumper wire to the wire coming out of the switch. If the test light lights with the jumper wire installed, the switch or whatever was bypassed is defective.

NOTE: *Never substitute the jumper wire for the component, since it is required to use the power from the power source.*

5. If the bulb in the test light goes on, then the current is getting to the component that is not working. This eliminates the first of the three possible causes. Connect the power supply wire and connect a jumper wire from the component to a good metal ground. Do this with the switch which controls the component turned on, and also the ignition switch turned on if it is required for the component to work. If the component works with the jumper wire installed, then it has a bad ground. This is usually caused by the metal area on which the component mounts to the chassis being coated with some type of foreign matter.

6. If neither test located the source of the trouble, then the component itself is defective. Remember that for any electrical system to work, all connections must be clean and tight.

Troubleshooting Basic Turn Signal and Flasher Problems
See Chapter 5 for service procedures

Most problems in the turn signals or flasher system can be reduced to defective flashers or bulbs, which are easily replaced. Occasionally, the turn signal switch will prove defective.
F = Front   R = Rear   ● = Lights off   ○ = Lights on

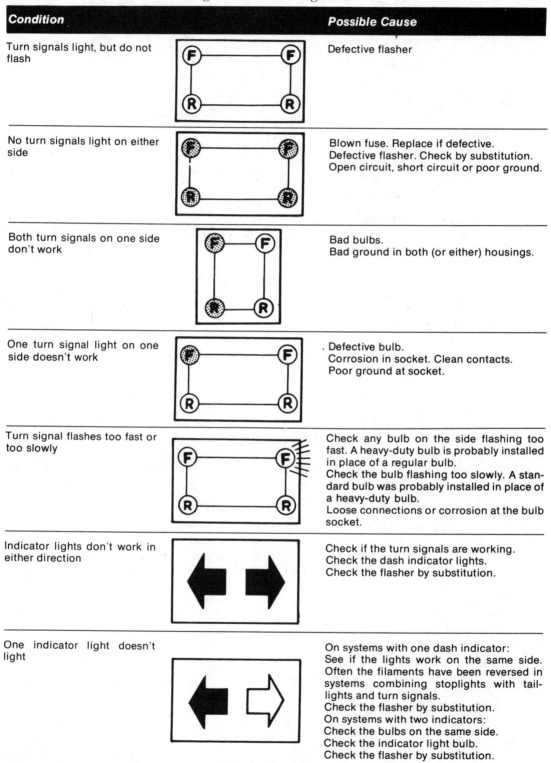

Condition	Possible Cause
Turn signals light, but do not flash	Defective flasher
No turn signals light on either side	Blown fuse. Replace if defective. Defective flasher. Check by substitution. Open circuit, short circuit or poor ground.
Both turn signals on one side don't work	Bad bulbs. Bad ground in both (or either) housings.
One turn signal light on one side doesn't work	. Defective bulb. Corrosion in socket. Clean contacts. Poor ground at socket.
Turn signal flashes too fast or too slowly	Check any bulb on the side flashing too fast. A heavy-duty bulb is probably installed in place of a regular bulb. Check the bulb flashing too slowly. A standard bulb was probably installed in place of a heavy-duty bulb. Loose connections or corrosion at the bulb socket.
Indicator lights don't work in either direction	Check if the turn signals are working. Check the dash indicator lights. Check the flasher by substitution.
One indicator light doesn't light	On systems with one dash indicator: See if the lights work on the same side. Often the filaments have been reversed in systems combining stoplights with taillights and turn signals. Check the flasher by substitution. On systems with two indicators: Check the bulbs on the same side. Check the indicator light bulb. Check the flasher by substitution.

Troubleshooting Lighting Problems
See Chapter 5 for service procedures

Condition	Possible Cause
One or more lights don't work, but others do	1. Defective bulb(s) 2. Blown fuse(s) 3. Dirty fuse clips or light sockets 4. Poor ground circuit
Lights burn out quickly	1. Incorrect voltage regulator setting or defective regulator 2. Poor battery/alternator connections
Lights go dim	1. Low/discharged battery 2. Alternator not charging 3. Corroded sockets or connections 4. Low voltage output
Lights flicker	1. Loose connection 2. Poor ground. (Run ground wire from light housing to frame) 3. Circuit breaker operating (short circuit)
Lights "flare"—Some flare is normal on acceleration—If excessive, see "Lights Burn Out Quickly"	High voltage setting
Lights glare—approaching drivers are blinded	1. Lights adjusted too high 2. Rear springs or shocks sagging 3. Rear tires soft

Troubleshooting Dash Gauge Problems
Most problems can be traced to a defective sending unit or faulty wiring. Occasionally, the gauge itself is at fault. See Chapter 5 for service procedures.

Condition	Possible Cause
COOLANT TEMPERATURE GAUGE	
Gauge reads erratically or not at all	1. Loose or dirty connections 2. Defective sending unit. 3. Defective gauge. To test a bi-metal gauge, remove the wire from the sending unit. Ground the wire for an instant. If the gauge registers, replace the sending unit. To test a magnetic gauge, disconnect the wire at the sending unit. With ignition ON gauge should register COLD. Ground the wire; gauge should register HOT.
AMMETER GAUGE—TURN HEADLIGHTS ON (DO NOT START ENGINE). NOTE REACTION	
Ammeter shows charge Ammeter shows discharge Ammeter does not move	1. Connections reversed on gauge 2. Ammeter is OK 3. Loose connections or faulty wiring 4. Defective gauge

Condition	*Possible Cause*

OIL PRESSURE GAUGE

Gauge does not register or is inaccurate	1. On mechanical gauge, Bourdon tube may be bent or kinked. 2. Low oil pressure. Remove sending unit. Idle the engine briefly. If no oil flows from sending unit hole, problem is in engine. 3. Defective gauge. Remove the wire from the sending unit and ground it for an instant with the ignition ON. A good gauge will go to the top of the scale. 4. Defective wiring. Check the wiring to the gauge. If it's OK and the gauge doesn't register when grounded, replace the gauge. 5. Defective sending unit.

ALL GAUGES

All gauges do not operate All gauges read low or erratically All gauges pegged	1. Blown fuse 2. Defective instrument regulator 3. Defective or dirty instrument voltage regulator 4. Loss of ground between instrument voltage regulator and frame 5. Defective instrument regulator

WARNING LIGHTS

Light(s) do not come on when ignition is ON, but engine is not started Light comes on with engine running	1. Defective bulb 2. Defective wire 3. Defective sending unit. Disconnect the wire from the sending unit and ground it. Replace the sending unit if the light comes on with the ignition ON. 4. Problem in individual system 5. Defective sending unit

Troubleshooting Clutch Problems

It is false economy to replace individual clutch components. The pressure plate, clutch plate and throwout bearing should be replaced as a set, and the flywheel face inspected, whenever the clutch is overhauled. See Chapter 6 for service procedures.

Condition	*Possible Cause*
Clutch chatter	1. Grease on driven plate (disc) facing 2. Binding clutch linkage or cable 3. Loose, damaged facings on driven plate (disc) 4. Engine mounts loose 5. Incorrect height adjustment of pressure plate release levers 6. Clutch housing or housing to transmission adapter misalignment 7. Loose driven plate hub
Clutch grabbing	1. Oil, grease on driven plate (disc) facing 2. Broken pressure plate 3. Warped or binding driven plate. Driven plate binding on clutch shaft
Clutch slips	1. Lack of lubrication in clutch linkage or cable (linkage or cable binds, causes incomplete engagement) 2. Incorrect pedal, or linkage adjustment 3. Broken pressure plate springs 4. Weak pressure plate springs 5. Grease on driven plate facings (disc)

Troubleshooting Clutch Problems (cont.)

Condition	Possible Cause
Incomplete clutch release	1. Incorrect pedal or linkage adjustment or linkage or cable binding 2. Incorrect height adjustment on pressure plate release levers 3. Loose, broken facings on driven plate (disc) 4. Bent, dished, warped driven plate caused by overheating
Grinding, whirring grating noise when pedal is depressed	1. Worn or defective throwout bearing 2. Starter drive teeth contacting flywheel ring gear teeth. Look for milled or polished teeth on ring gear.
Squeal, howl, trumpeting noise when pedal is being released (occurs during first inch to inch and one-half of pedal travel)	Pilot bushing worn or lack of lubricant. If bushing appears OK, polish bushing with emery cloth, soak lube wick in oil, lube bushing with oil, apply film of chassis grease to clutch shaft pilot hub, reassemble. NOTE: Bushing wear may be due to misalignment of clutch housing or housing to transmission adapter
Vibration or clutch pedal pulsation with clutch disengaged (pedal fully depressed)	1. Worn or defective engine transmission mounts 2. Flywheel run out. (Flywheel run out at face not to exceed 0.005") 3. Damaged or defective clutch components

Troubleshooting Manual Transmission Problems
See Chapter 6 for service procedures

Condition	Possible Cause
Transmission jumps out of gear	1. Misalignment of transmission case or clutch housing. 2. Worn pilot bearing in crankshaft. 3. Bent transmission shaft. 4. Worn high speed sliding gear. 5. Worn teeth or end-play in clutch shaft. 6. Insufficient spring tension on shifter rail plunger. 7. Bent or loose shifter fork. 8. Gears not engaging completely. 9. Loose or worn bearings on clutch shaft or mainshaft. 10. Worn gear teeth. 11. Worn or damaged detent balls.
Transmission sticks in gear	1. Clutch not releasing fully. 2. Burred or battered teeth on clutch shaft, or sliding sleeve. 3. Burred or battered transmission mainshaft. 4. Frozen synchronizing clutch. 5. Stuck shifter rail plunger. 6. Gearshift lever twisting and binding shifter rail. 7. Battered teeth on high speed sliding gear or on sleeve. 8. Improper lubrication, or lack of lubrication. 9. Corroded transmission parts. 10. Defective mainshaft pilot bearing. 11. Locked gear bearings will give same effect as stuck in gear.
Transmission gears will not synchronize	1. Binding pilot bearing on mainshaft, will synchronize in high gear only. 2. Clutch not releasing fully. 3. Detent spring weak or broken. 4. Weak or broken springs under balls in sliding gear sleeve. 5. Binding bearing on clutch shaft, or binding countershaft. 6. Binding pilot bearing in crankshaft. 7. Badly worn gear teeth. 8. Improper lubrication. 9. Constant mesh gear not turning freely on transmission mainshaft. Will synchronize in that gear only.

Condition	Possible Cause
Gears spinning when shifting into gear from neutral	1. Clutch not releasing fully. 2. In some cases an extremely light lubricant in transmission will cause gears to continue to spin for a short time after clutch is released. 3. Binding pilot bearing in crankshaft.
Transmission noisy in all gears	1. Insufficient lubricant, or improper lubricant. 2. Worn countergear bearings. 3. Worn or damaged main drive gear or countergear. 4. Damaged main drive gear or mainshaft bearings. 5. Worn or damaged countergear anti-lash plate.
Transmission noisy in neutral only	1. Damaged main drive gear bearing. 2. Damaged or loose mainshaft pilot bearing. 3. Worn or damaged countergear anti-lash plate. 4. Worn countergear bearings.
Transmission noisy in one gear only	1. Damaged or worn constant mesh gears. 2. Worn or damaged countergear bearings. 3. Damaged or worn synchronizer.
Transmission noisy in reverse only	1. Worn or damaged reverse idler gear or idler bushing. 2. Worn or damaged mainshaft reverse gear. 3. Worn or damaged reverse countergear. 4. Damaged shift mechanism.

TROUBLESHOOTING AUTOMATIC TRANSMISSION PROBLEMS

Keeping alert to changes in the operating characteristics of the transmission (changing shift points, noises, etc.) can prevent small problems from becoming large ones. If the problem cannot be traced to loose bolts, fluid level, misadjusted linkage, clogged filters or similar problems, you should probably seek professional service.

Transmission Fluid Indications

The appearance and odor of the transmission fluid can give valuable clues to the overall condition of the transmission. Always note the appearance of the fluid when you check the fluid level or change the fluid. Rub a small amount of fluid between your fingers to feel for grit and smell the fluid on the dipstick.

If the fluid appears:	It indicates:
Clear and red colored	Normal operation
Discolored (extremely dark red or brownish) or smells burned	Band or clutch pack failure, usually caused by an overheated transmission. Hauling very heavy loads with insufficient power or failure to change the fluid often result in overheating. Do not confuse this appearance with newer fluids that have a darker red color and a strong odor (though not a burned odor).
Foamy or aerated (light in color and full of bubbles)	1. The level is too high (gear train is churning oil) 2. An internal air leak (air is mixing with the fluid). Have the transmission checked professionally.
Solid residue in the fluid	Defective bands, clutch pack or bearings. Bits of band material or metal abrasives are clinging to the dipstick. Have the transmission checked professionally.
Varnish coating on the dipstick	The transmission fluid is overheating

TROUBLESHOOTING DRIVE AXLE PROBLEMS

First, determine when the noise is most noticeable.

Drive Noise: Produced under vehicle acceleration.

Coast Noise: Produced while coasting with a closed throttle.

Float Noise: Occurs while maintaining constant speed (just enough to keep speed constant) on a level road.

External Noise Elimination

It is advisable to make a thorough road test to determine whether the noise originates in the rear axle or whether it originates from the tires, engine, transmission, wheel bearings or road surface. Noise originating from other places cannot be corrected by servicing the rear axle.

ROAD NOISE

Brick or rough surfaced concrete roads produce noises that seem to come from the rear axle. Road noise is usually identical in Drive or Coast and driving on a different type of road will tell whether the road is the problem.

TIRE NOISE

Tire noise can be mistaken as rear axle noise, even though the tires on the front are at fault. Snow tread and mud tread tires or tires worn unevenly will frequently cause vibrations which seem to originate elsewhere; *temporarily, and for test purposes only,* inflate the tires to 40–50 lbs. This will significantly alter the noise produced by the tires, but will not alter noise from the rear axle. Noises from the rear axle will normally cease at speeds below 30 mph on coast, while tire noise will continue at lower tone as speed is decreased. The rear axle noise will usually change from drive conditions to coast conditions, while tire noise will not. Do not forget to lower the tire pressure to normal after the test is complete.

ENGINE/TRANSMISSION NOISE

Determine at what speed the noise is most pronounced, then stop in a quiet place. With the transmission in Neutral, run the engine through speeds corresponding to road speeds where the noise was noticed. Noises produced with the vehicle standing still are coming from the engine or transmission.

FRONT WHEEL BEARINGS

Front wheel bearing noises, sometimes confused with rear axle noises, will not change when comparing drive and coast conditions. While holding the speed steady, lightly apply the footbrake. This will often cause wheel bearing noise to lessen, as some of the weight is taken off the bearing. Front wheel bearings are easily checked by jacking up the wheels and spinning the wheels. Shaking the wheels will also determine if the wheel bearings are excessively loose.

REAR AXLE NOISES

Eliminating other possible sources can narrow the cause to the rear axle, which normally produces noise from worn gears or bearings. Gear noises tend to peak in a narrow speed range, while bearing noises will usually vary in pitch with engine speeds.

Noise Diagnosis

The Noise Is:	Most Probably Produced By:
1. Identical under Drive or Coast	Road surface, tires or front wheel bearings
2. Different depending on road surface	Road surface or tires
3. Lower as speed is lowered	Tires
4. Similar when standing or moving	Engine or transmission
5. A vibration	Unbalanced tires, rear wheel bearing, unbalanced driveshaft or worn U-joint
6. A knock or click about every two tire revolutions	Rear wheel bearing
7. Most pronounced on turns	Damaged differential gears
8. A steady low-pitched whirring or scraping, starting at low speeds	Damaged or worn pinion bearing
9. A chattering vibration on turns	Wrong differential lubricant or worn clutch plates (limited slip rear axle)
10. Noticed only in Drive, Coast or Float conditions	Worn ring gear and/or pinion gear

Troubleshooting Steering & Suspension Problems

Condition	Possible Cause
Hard steering (wheel is hard to turn)	1. Improper tire pressure 2. Loose or glazed pump drive belt 3. Low or incorrect fluid 4. Loose, bent or poorly lubricated front end parts 5. Improper front end alignment (excessive caster) 6. Bind in steering column or linkage 7. Kinked hydraulic hose 8. Air in hydraulic system 9. Low pump output or leaks in system 10. Obstruction in lines 11. Pump valves sticking or out of adjustment 12. Incorrect wheel alignment
Loose steering (too much play in steering wheel)	1. Loose wheel bearings 2. Faulty shocks 3. Worn linkage or suspension components 4. Loose steering gear mounting or linkage points 5. Steering mechanism worn or improperly adjusted 6. Valve spool improperly adjusted 7. Worn ball joints, tie-rod ends, etc.
Veers or wanders (pulls to one side with hands off steering wheel)	1. Improper tire pressure 2. Improper front end alignment 3. Dragging or improperly adjusted brakes 4. Bent frame 5. Improper rear end alignment 6. Faulty shocks or springs 7. Loose or bent front end components 8. Play in Pitman arm 9. Steering gear mountings loose 10. Loose wheel bearings 11. Binding Pitman arm 12. Spool valve sticking or improperly adjusted 13. Worn ball joints
Wheel oscillation or vibration transmitted through steering wheel	1. Low or uneven tire pressure 2. Loose wheel bearings 3. Improper front end alignment 4. Bent spindle 5. Worn, bent or broken front end components 6. Tires out of round or out of balance 7. Excessive lateral runout in disc brake rotor 8. Loose or bent shock absorber or strut
Noises (see also "Troubleshooting Drive Axle Problems")	1. Loose belts 2. Low fluid, air in system 3. Foreign matter in system 4. Improper lubrication 5. Interference or chafing in linkage 6. Steering gear mountings loose 7. Incorrect adjustment or wear in gear box 8. Faulty valves or wear in pump 9. Kinked hydraulic lines 10. Worn wheel bearings
Poor return of steering	1. Over-inflated tires 2. Improperly aligned front end (excessive caster) 3. Binding in steering column 4. No lubrication in front end 5. Steering gear adjusted too tight
Uneven tire wear (see "How To Read Tire Wear")	1. Incorrect tire pressure 2. Improperly aligned front end 3. Tires out-of-balance 4. Bent or worn suspension parts

HOW TO READ TIRE WEAR

The way your tires wear is a good indicator of other parts of the suspension. Abnormal wear patterns are often caused by the need for simple tire maintenance, or for front end alignment.

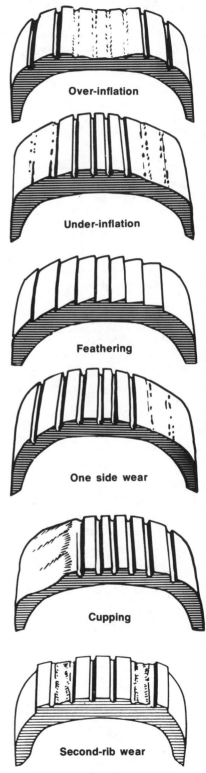

Excessive wear at the center of the tread indicates that the air pressure in the tire is consistently too high. The tire is riding on the center of the tread and wearing it prematurely. Occasionally, this wear pattern can result from outrageously wide tires on narrow rims. The cure for this is to replace either the tires or the wheels.

Over-inflation

This type of wear usually results from consistent under-inflation. When a tire is under-inflated, there is too much contact with the road by the outer treads, which wear prematurely. When this type of wear occurs, and the tire pressure is known to be consistently correct, a bent or worn steering component or the need for wheel alignment could be indicated.

Under-inflation

Feathering is a condition when the edge of each tread rib develops a slightly rounded edge on one side and a sharp edge on the other. By running your hand over the tire, you can usually feel the sharper edges before you'll be able to see them. The most common causes of feathering are incorrect toe-in setting or deteriorated bushings in the front suspension.

Feathering

When an inner or outer rib wears faster than the rest of the tire, the need for wheel alignment is indicated. There is excessive camber in the front suspension, causing the wheel to lean too much putting excessive load on one side of the tire. Misalignment could also be due to sagging springs, worn ball joints, or worn control arm bushings. Be sure the vehicle is loaded the way it's normally driven when you have the wheels aligned.

One side wear

Cups or scalloped dips appearing around the edge of the tread almost always indicate worn (sometimes bent) suspension parts. Adjustment of wheel alignment alone will seldom cure the problem. Any worn component that connects the wheel to the suspension can cause this type of wear. Occasionally, wheels that are out of balance will wear like this, but wheel imbalance usually shows up as bald spots between the outside edges and center of the tread.

Cupping

Second-rib wear is usually found only in radial tires, and appears where the steel belts end in relation to the tread. It can be kept to a minimum by paying careful attention to tire pressure and frequently rotating the tires. This is often considered normal wear but excessive amounts indicate that the tires are too wide for the wheels.

Second-rib wear

Troubleshooting Disc Brake Problems

Condition	Possible Cause
Noise—groan—brake noise emanating when slowly releasing brakes (creep-groan)	Not detrimental to function of disc brakes—no corrective action required. (This noise may be eliminated by slightly increasing or decreasing brake pedal efforts.)
Rattle—brake noise or rattle emanating at low speeds on rough roads, (front wheels only).	1. Shoe anti-rattle spring missing or not properly positioned. 2. Excessive clearance between shoe and caliper. 3. Soft or broken caliper seals. 4. Deformed or misaligned disc. 5. Loose caliper.
Scraping	1. Mounting bolts too long. 2. Loose wheel bearings. 3. Bent, loose, or misaligned splash shield.
Front brakes heat up during driving and fail to release	1. Operator riding brake pedal. 2. Stop light switch improperly adjusted. 3. Sticking pedal linkage. 4. Frozen or seized piston. 5. Residual pressure valve in master cylinder. 6. Power brake malfunction. 7. Proportioning valve malfunction.
Leaky brake caliper	1. Damaged or worn caliper piston seal. 2. Scores or corrosion on surface of cylinder bore.
Grabbing or uneven brake action—Brakes pull to one side	1. Causes listed under "Brakes Pull". 2. Power brake malfunction. 3. Low fluid level in master cylinder. 4. Air in hydraulic system. 5. Brake fluid, oil or grease on linings. 6. Unmatched linings. 7. Distorted brake pads. 8. Frozen or seized pistons. 9. Incorrect tire pressure. 10. Front end out of alignment. 11. Broken rear spring. 12. Brake caliper pistons sticking. 13. Restricted hose or line. 14. Caliper not in proper alignment to braking disc. 15. Stuck or malfunctioning metering valve. 16. Soft or broken caliper seals. 17. Loose caliper.
Brake pedal can be depressed without braking effect	1. Air in hydraulic system or improper bleeding procedure. 2. Leak past primary cup in master cylinder. 3. Leak in system. 4. Rear brakes out of adjustment. 5. Bleeder screw open.
Excessive pedal travel	1. Air, leak, or insufficient fluid in system or caliper. 2. Warped or excessively tapered shoe and lining assembly. 3. Excessive disc runout. 4. Rear brake adjustment required. 5. Loose wheel bearing adjustment. 6. Damaged caliper piston seal. 7. Improper brake fluid (boil). 8. Power brake malfunction. 9. Weak or soft hoses.

Troubleshooting Disc Brake Problems (cont.)

Condition	Possible Cause
Brake roughness or chatter (pedal pumping)	1. Excessive thickness variation of braking disc. 2. Excessive lateral runout of braking disc. 3. Rear brake drums out-of-round. 4. Excessive front bearing clearance.
Excessive pedal effort	1. Brake fluid, oil or grease on linings. 2. Incorrect lining. 3. Frozen or seized pistons. 4. Power brake malfunction. 5. Kinked or collapsed hose or line. 6. Stuck metering valve. 7. Scored caliper or master cylinder bore. 8. Seized caliper pistons.
Brake pedal fades (pedal travel increases with foot on brake)	1. Rough master cylinder or caliper bore. 2. Loose or broken hydraulic lines/connections. 3. Air in hydraulic system. 4. Fluid level low. 5. Weak or soft hoses. 6. Inferior quality brake shoes or fluid. 7. Worn master cylinder piston cups or seals.

Troubleshooting Drum Brakes

Condition	Possible Cause
Pedal goes to floor	1. Fluid low in reservoir. 2. Air in hydraulic system. 3. Improperly adjusted brake. 4. Leaking wheel cylinders. 5. Loose or broken brake lines. 6. Leaking or worn master cylinder. 7. Excessively worn brake lining.
Spongy brake pedal	1. Air in hydraulic system. 2. Improper brake fluid (low boiling point). 3. Excessively worn or cracked brake drums. 4. Broken pedal pivot bushing.
Brakes pulling	1. Contaminated lining. 2. Front end out of alignment. 3. Incorrect brake adjustment. 4. Unmatched brake lining. 5. Brake drums out of round. 6. Brake shoes distorted. 7. Restricted brake hose or line. 8. Broken rear spring. 9. Worn brake linings. 10. Uneven lining wear. 11. Glazed brake lining. 12. Excessive brake lining dust. 13. Heat spotted brake drums. 14. Weak brake return springs. 15. Faulty automatic adjusters. 16. Low or incorrect tire pressure.

Condition	Possible Cause
Squealing brakes	1. Glazed brake lining. 2. Saturated brake lining. 3. Weak or broken brake shoe retaining spring. 4. Broken or weak brake shoe return spring. 5. Incorrect brake lining. 6. Distorted brake shoes. 7. Bent support plate. 8. Dust in brakes or scored brake drums. 9. Linings worn below limit. 10. Uneven brake lining wear. 11. Heat spotted brake drums.
Chirping brakes	1. Out of round drum or eccentric axle flange pilot.
Dragging brakes	1. Incorrect wheel or parking brake adjustment. 2. Parking brakes engaged or improperly adjusted. 3. Weak or broken brake shoe return spring. 4. Brake pedal binding. 5. Master cylinder cup sticking. 6. Obstructed master cylinder relief port. 7. Saturated brake lining. 8. Bent or out of round brake drum. 9. Contaminated or improper brake fluid. 10. Sticking wheel cylinder pistons. 11. Driver riding brake pedal. 12. Defective proportioning valve. 13. Insufficient brake shoe lubricant.
Hard pedal	1. Brake booster inoperative. 2. Incorrect brake lining. 3. Restricted brake line or hose. 4. Frozen brake pedal linkage. 5. Stuck wheel cylinder. 6. Binding pedal linkage. 7. Faulty proportioning valve.
Wheel locks	1. Contaminated brake lining. 2. Loose or torn brake lining. 3. Wheel cylinder cups sticking. 4. Incorrect wheel bearing adjustment. 5. Faulty proportioning valve.
Brakes fade (high speed)	1. Incorrect lining. 2. Overheated brake drums. 3. Incorrect brake fluid (low boiling temperature). 4. Saturated brake lining. 5. Leak in hydraulic system. 6. Faulty automatic adjusters.
Pedal pulsates	1. Bent or out of round brake drum.
Brake chatter and shoe knock	1. Out of round brake drum. 2. Loose support plate. 3. Bent support plate. 4. Distorted brake shoes. 5. Machine grooves in contact face of brake drum (Shoe Knock). 6. Contaminated brake lining. 7. Missing or loose components. 8. Incorrect lining material. 9. Out-of-round brake drums. 10. Heat spotted or scored brake drums. 11. Out-of-balance wheels.

Troubleshooting Drum Brakes (cont.)

Condition	Possible Cause
Brakes do not self adjust	1. Adjuster screw frozen in thread. 2. Adjuster screw corroded at thrust washer. 3. Adjuster lever does not engage star wheel. 4. Adjuster installed on wrong wheel.
Brake light glows	1. Leak in the hydraulic system. 2. Air in the system. 3. Improperly adjusted master cylinder pushrod. 4. Uneven lining wear. 5. Failure to center combination valve or proportioning valve.

Appendix

General Conversion Table

Multiply by	To convert		To	
2.54	Inches		Centimeters	.3937
30.48	Feet		Centimeters	.0328
.914	Yards		Meters	1.094
1.609	Miles		Kilometers	.621
6.45	Square inches		Square cm.	.155
.836	Square yards		Square meters	1.196
16.39	Cubic inches		Cubic cm.	.061
28.3	Cubic feet		Liters	.0353
.4536	Pounds		Kilograms	2.2045
3.785	Gallons		Liters	.264
.068	Lbs./sq. in. (psi)		Atmospheres	14.7
.138	Foot pounds		Kg. m.	7.23
1.014	H.P. (DIN)		H.P. (SAE)	.9861
—	To obtain		From	Multiply by

Note: 1 cm. equals 10 mm.; 1 mm. equals .0394".

Conversion—Common Fractions to Decimals and Millimeters

Common Fractions	Decimal Fractions	Millimeters (approx.)	Common Fractions	Decimal Fractions	Millimeters (approx.)	Common Fractions	Decimal Fractions	Millimeters (approx.)
1/128	.008	0.20	11/32	.344	8.73	43/64	.672	17.07
1/64	.016	0.40	23/64	.359	9.13	11/16	.688	17.46
1/32	.031	0.79	3/8	.375	9.53	45/64	.703	17.86
3/64	.047	1.19	25/64	.391	9.92	23/32	.719	18.26
1/16	.063	1.59	13/32	.406	10.32	47/64	.734	18.65
5/64	.078	1.98	27/64	.422	10.72	3/4	.750	19.05
3/32	.094	2.38	7/16	.438	11.11	49/64	.766	19.45
7/64	.109	2.78	29/64	.453	11.51	25/32	.781	19.84
1/8	.125	3.18	15/32	.469	11.91	51/64	.797	20.24
9/64	.141	3.57	31/64	.484	12.30	13/16	.813	20.64
5/32	.156	3.97	1/2	.500	12.70	53/64	.828	21.03
11/64	.172	4.37	33/64	.516	13.10	27/32	.844	21.43
3/16	.188	4.76	17/32	.531	13.49	55/64	.859	21.83
13/64	.203	5.16	35/64	.547	13.89	7/8	.875	22.23
7/32	.219	5.56	9/16	.563	14.29	57/64	.891	22.62
15/64	.234	5.95	37/64	.578	14.68	29/32	.906	23.02
1/4	.250	6.35	19/32	.594	15.08	59/64	.922	23.42
17/64	.266	6.75	39/64	.609	15.48	15/16	.938	23.81
9/32	.281	7.14	5/8	.625	15.88	61/64	.953	24.21
19/64	.297	7.54	41/64	.641	16.27	31/32	.969	24.61
5/16	.313	7.94	21/32	.656	16.67	63/64	.984	25.00
21/64	.328	8.33						

Conversion—Millimeters to Decimal Inches

mm	inches	mm	inches	mm	inches	mm	inches	mm	inches
1	.039 370	31	1.220 470	61	2.401 570	91	3.582 670	210	8.267 700
2	.078 740	32	1.259 840	62	2.440 940	92	3.622 040	220	8.661 400
3	.118 110	33	1.299 210	63	2.480 310	93	3.661 410	230	9.055 100
4	.157 480	34	1.338 580	64	2.519 680	94	3.700 780	240	9.448 800
5	.196 850	35	1.377 949	65	2.559 050	95	3.740 150	250	9.842 500
6	.236 220	36	1.417 319	66	2.598 420	96	3.779 520	260	10.236 200
7	.275 590	37	1.456 689	67	2.637 790	97	3.818 890	270	10.629 900
8	.314 960	38	1.496 050	68	2.677 160	98	3.858 260	280	11.032 600
9	.354 330	39	1.535 430	69	2.716 530	99	3.897 630	290	11.417 300
10	.393 700	40	1.574 800	70	2.755 900	100	3.937 000	300	11.811 000
11	.433 070	41	1.614 170	71	2.795 270	105	4.133 848	310	12.204 700
12	.472 440	42	1.653 540	72	2.834 640	110	4.330 700	320	12.598 400
13	.511 810	43	1.692 910	73	2.874 010	115	4.527 550	330	12.992 100
14	.551 180	44	1.732 280	74	2.913 380	120	4.724 400	340	13.385 800
15	.590 550	45	1.771 650	75	2.952 750	125	4.921 250	350	13.779 500
16	.629 920	46	1.811 020	76	2.992 120	130	5.118 100	360	14.173 200
17	.669 290	47	1.850 390	77	3.031 490	135	5.314 950	370	14.566 900
18	.708 660	48	1.889 760	78	3.070 860	140	5.511 800	380	14.960 600
19	.748 030	49	1.929 130	79	3.110 230	145	5.708 650	390	15.354 300
20	.787 400	50	1.968 500	80	3.149 600	150	5.905 500	400	15.748 000
21	.826 770	51	2.007 870	81	3.188 970	155	6.102 350	500	19.685 000
22	.866 140	52	2.047 240	82	3.228 340	160	6.299 200	600	23.622 000
23	.905 510	53	2.086 610	83	3.267 710	165	6.496 050	700	27.559 000
24	.944 880	54	2.125 980	84	3.307 080	170	6.692 900	800	31.496 000
25	.984 250	55	2.165 350	85	3.346 450	175	6.889 750	900	35.433 000
26	1.023 620	56	2.204 720	86	3.385 820	180	7.086 600	1000	39.370 000
27	1.062 990	57	2.244 090	87	3.425 190	185	7.283 450	2000	78.740 000
28	1.102 360	58	2.283 460	88	3.464 560	190	7.480 300	3000	118.110 000
29	1.141 730	59	2.322 830	89	3.503 903	195	7.677 150	4000	157.480 000
30	1.181 100	60	2.362 200	90	3.543 300	200	7.874 000	5000	196.850 000

To change decimal millimeters to decimal inches, position the decimal point where desired on either side of the millimeter measurement shown and reset the inches decimal by the same number of digits in the same direction. For example, to convert 0.001 mm to decimal inches, reset the decimal behind the 1 mm (shown on the chart) to 0.001; change the decimal inch equivalent (0.039″ shown) to 0.000039″.

Tap Drill Sizes

Screw & Tap Size	National Fine or S.A.E. Threads Per Inch	Use Drill Number
No. 5	44	37
No. 6	40	33
No. 8	36	29
No. 10	32	21
No. 12	28	15
1/4	28	3
5/16	24	1
3/8	24	Q
7/16	20	W
1/2	20	29/64
9/16	18	33/64
5/8	18	37/64
3/4	16	11/16
7/8	14	13/16
1 1/8	12	1 3/64
1 1/4	12	1 11/64
1 1/2	12	1 27/64

Tap Drill Sizes

Screw & Tap Size	National Coarse or U.S.S. Threads Per Inch	Use Drill Number
No. 5	40	39
No. 6	32	36
No. 8	32	29
No. 10	24	25
No. 12	24	17
1/4	20	8
5/16	18	F
3/8	16	5/16
7/16	14	U
1/2	13	27/64
9/16	12	31/64
5/8	11	17/32
3/4	10	21/32
7/8	9	49/64
1	8	7/8
1 1/8	7	63/64
1 1/4	7	1 7/64
1 1/2	6	1 11/32

Decimal Equivalent Size of the Number Drills

Drill No.	Decimal Equivalent	Drill No.	Decimal Equivalent	Drill No.	Decimal Equivalent
80	.0135	53	.0595	26	.1470
79	.0145	52	.0635	25	.1495
78	.0160	51	.0670	24	.1520
77	.0180	50	.0700	23	.1540
76	.0200	49	.0730	22	.1570
75	.0210	48	.0760	21	.1590
74	.0225	47	.0785	20	.1610
73	.0240	46	.0810	19	.1660
72	.0250	45	.0820	18	.1695
71	.0260	44	.0860	17	.1730
70	.0280	43	.0890	16	.1770
69	.0292	42	.0935	15	.1800
68	.0310	41	.0960	14	.1820
67	.0320	40	.0980	13	.1850
66	.0330	39	.0995	12	.1890
65	.0350	38	.1015	11	.1910
64	.0360	37	.1040	10	.1935
63	.0370	36	.1065	9	.1960
62	.0380	35	.1100	8	.1990
61	.0390	34	.1110	7	.2010
60	.0400	33	.1130	6	.2040
59	.0410	32	.1160	5	.2055
58	.0420	31	.1200	4	.2090
57	.0430	30	.1285	3	.2130
56	.0465	29	.1360	2	.2210
55	.0520	28	.1405	1	.2280
54	.0550	27	.1440		

Decimal Equivalent Size of the Letter Drills

Letter Drill	Decimal Equivalent	Letter Drill	Decimal Equivalent	Letter Drill	Decimal Equivalent
A	.234	J	.277	S	.348
B	.238	K	.281	T	.358
C	.242	L	.290	U	.368
D	.246	M	.295	V	.377
E	.250	N	.302	W	.386
F	.257	O	.316	X	.397
G	.261	P	.323	Y	.404
H	.266	Q	.332	Z	.413
I	.272	R	.339		

Anti-Freeze Chart

Temperatures Shown in Degrees Fahrenheit +32 is Freezing

Cooling System Capacity Quarts	Quarts of ETHYLENE GLYCOL Needed for Protection to Temperatures Shown Below														
	1	2	3	4	5	6	7	8	9	10	11	12	13	14
10	+24°	+16°	+ 4°	−12°	−34°	−62°								
11	+25	+18	+ 8	− 6	−23	−47								
12	+26	+19	+10	0	−15	−34	−57°							
13	+27	+21	+13	+ 3	− 9	−25	−45							
14			+15	+ 6	− 5	−18	−34							
15			+16	+ 8	0	−12	−26							
16			+17	+10	+ 2	− 8	−19	−34	−52°					
17			+18	+12	+ 5	− 4	−14	−27	−42					
18			+19	+14	+ 7	0	−10	−21	−34	−50°				
19			+20	+15	+ 9	+ 2	− 7	−16	−28	−42				
20				+16	+10	+ 4	− 3	−12	−22	−34	−48°			
21				+17	+12	+ 6	0	− 9	−17	−28	−41			
22				+18	+13	+ 8	+ 2	− 6	−14	−23	−34	−47°		
23				+19	+14	+ 9	+ 4	− 3	−10	−19	−29	−40		
24				+19	+15	+10	+ 5	0	− 8	−15	−23	−34	−46°	
25				+20	+16	+12	+ 7	+ 1	− 5	−12	−20	−29	−40	−50°
26					+17	+13	+ 8	+ 3	− 3	− 9	−16	−25	−34	−44
27					+18	+14	+ 9	+ 5	− 1	− 7	−13	−21	−29	−39
28					+18	+15	+10	+ 6	+ 1	− 5	−11	−18	−25	−34
29					+19	+16	+12	+ 7	+ 2	− 3	− 8	−15	−22	−29
30					+20	+17	+13	+ 8	+ 4	− 1	− 6	−12	−18	−25

For capacities over 30 quarts divide true capacity by 3. Find quarts Anti-Freeze for the ⅓ and multiply by 3 for quarts to add.

For capacities under 10 quarts multiply true capacity by 3. Find quarts Anti-Freeze for the tripled volume and divide by 3 for quarts to add.

To Increase the Freezing Protection of Anti-Freeze Solutions Already Installed

Cooling System Capacity Quarts	Number of Quarts of ETHYLENE GLYCOL Anti-Freeze Required to Increase Protection													
	From +20° F. to					From +10° F. to					From 0° F. to			
	0°	−10°	−20°	−30°	−40°	0°	−10°	−20°	−30°	−40°	−10°	−20°	−30°	−40°
10	1¾	2¼	3	3½	3¾	¾	1½	2¼	2¾	3¼	¾	1½	2	2½
12	2	2¾	3½	4	4½	1	1¾	2½	3¼	3¾	1	1¾	2½	3¼
14	2¼	3¼	4	4¾	5½	1¼	2	3	3¾	4½	1	2	3	3½
16	2½	3½	4½	5¼	6	1¼	2½	3½	4¼	5¼	1¼	2¼	3¼	4
18	3	4	5	6	7	1½	2¾	4	5	5¾	1½	2½	3¾	4¾
20	3¼	4½	5¾	6¾	7½	1¾	3	4¼	5½	6½	1½	2¾	4¼	5¼
22	3½	5	6¼	7¼	8¼	1¾	3¼	4¾	6	7¼	1¾	3¼	4½	5½
24	4	5½	7	8	9	2	3½	5	6½	7½	1¾	3½	5	6
26	4¼	6	7½	8¾	10	2	4	5½	7	8¼	2	3¾	5½	6¾
28	4½	6¼	8	9½	10½	2¼	4¼	6	7½	9	2	4	5¾	7¼
30	5	6¾	8½	10	11½	2½	4½	6½	8	9½	2¼	4¼	6¼	7¾

Test radiator solution with proper hydrometer. Determine from the table the number of quarts of solution to be drawn off from a full cooling system and replace with undiluted anti-freeze, to give the desired increased protection. For example, to increase protection of a 22-quart cooling system containing Ethylene Glycol (permanent type) anti-freeze, from +20° F. to −20° F. will require the replacement of 6¼ quarts of solution with undiluted anti-freeze.

Index

A

Air cleaner, 6, 96-97
Air conditioning, 14
Air induction valve filter, 7
Air injection system, 100-103
Alternator, 45-47
Automatic transmission, 135
    Adjustment, 136-137
    Identification, 6
    Pan removal, 135
    Removal, 137-138
Axle, 142
    Fluid recommendations, 24
    Lubricant level, 24
Axle ratio, 144
Axle shaft, 142

B

Back-up light switch, 137
Ball joints, 149
Battery, 18, 50-51
    Jump starting, 25
    Maintenance, 18-20
Belt tension adjustment, 10-12
Body, 175
    Washing, cleaning, 189-191
Bolt and fastener specifications, 72-73
Brakes
    Adjustment, 159, 161
    Bleeding, 162-164
    Caliper, 165
    Fluid level, 15-16
    Fluid recommendations, 16
    Front brakes, 159, 164-165
    Identification, 168
    Master cylinder, 161
    Parking brake, 160
    Pedal adjustments, 161
    Rear brakes, 160
    Rotor, 168
    Shoes, 169, 173
    Specifications, 170
Breaker points, 32-34

C

Camber, 151
Camshaft and bearings, 62-64, 86, 88
Capacities, 19
Carbon canister, 8, 94
Carburetor
    Adjustment, 42-43
    Overhaul, 111-112
    Replacement, 104-108
    Specifications, 105
Caster, 151
Catalytic converter, 103
Charging system, 45-47

Chassis lubrication, 24
Choke, 103, 110-111
Clutch
    Adjustment, 132-133
    Master cylinder, 133-134
    Replacement, 133
    Slave cylinder, 135
    Specifications, 128
Coil (ignition), 197-199
Condenser, 32-34
Connecting rod and bearings, 56, 81-82, 90
Control arm, 149
Conversion tables, 226
Cooling system, 12-13
Crankcase ventilation (PCV), 7, 93
Crankshaft, 56, 82, 88
    Specifications, 56
Cylinder head, 58
    Reconditioning, 73-80
    Removal and installation, 58-60
    Torque sequence, 59

D

Dashpot, 109
Dents and scratches, 179
Differential, 143
    Fluid change, 24
    Ratios, 144
Disc brakes, 164
Distributor
    Removal and installation, 44-45
    Breaker points, 32-34
Door panels, 176
Drive axle, 142
Driveshaft, 139
Drum brakes, 169, 173
Dwell angle, 34
Dwell meter, 2-3

E

Electrical
    Chassis, 115-117
    Engine, 44
Electronic ignition, 35-38
    Troubleshooting, 37-38
Emission controls, 92
Engine, 44, 51
    Camshaft, 62-64
    Cooling, 67-69
    Cylinder head torque sequence, 59
    Design, 51
    Exhaust manifold, 61
    Front cover, 61-62
    Identification, 5, 52
    Intake manifold, 61
    Oil recommendations, 21-22
    Pistons and rings, 64-65
    Rebuilding, 70
        Precautions, 70

Removal and installation, 52-58
Rocker arm (or shaft), 60-61
Specifications, 54
Timing belt, 63
Timing chain (or gears), 62-63
Torque specifications, 58
Tune-up, 27
Evaporative canister, 8
Evaporative system, 93
Exhaust gas recirculation, 97-100
Exhaust manifold, 61

F

Fan belt adjustment, 10-12
Fast idle adjustment, 110
Firing order, 45
Float level adjustment, 109-110
Fluid level checks, 15
    Battery, 18
    Coolant, 16
    Engine oil, 15
    Brake master cylinder, 15-16
    Clutch master cylinder, 15-16
    Power steering pump, 18
    Rear axle, 16
    Steering gear, 16
    Transmission, 15
Fluid recommendations, 16, 18, 21-22
Front suspension, 145
    Ball joints, 149
    lower control arm, 149
    Wheel alignment, 150-152
        Specifications, 153
Front wheel bearing, 171-172
Fuel filter, 21
Fuel pump, 103-104
Fuel system, 103
Fuel tank, 112-114
Fuses and flashers, 127
Fusible links, 126

G

Gear ratio, 144
Gearshift linkage adjustment, 136
    Automatic, 136-137
Generator (see Alternator), 45-47

H

Halfshafts, 141
Hand brake, 160
Headlights, 125-126
Heater, 117-120
Heat control valve, 9
History, 5
Hydraulic clutch, 134
    Bleeding, 135

I

Identification, 5
    Vehicle, 5

Engine, 5, 52
Transmission, 6
Idle speed and mixture, 42-43
Ignition switch, 123
Ignition timing, 38-40
Instrument cluster, 121-124
Intake manifold, 61

J

Jacking points, 24
    Cautions, 26
Jump starting, 25

L

Lighting, 125
Lower control arm, 149
Lubrication, 21
    Chassis, 24
    Differential, 24
    Engine, 22-23
    Transmission, 23-24

M

Main seal, 65-66
Maintenance intervals, 1
Manifolds, 61
    Intake, 61
    Exhaust, 61
Manual transmission, 128
    Identification, 6
Master cylinder, 161
Metric bolts, 73
Metric conversion tables, 226
Model identification, 5

N

Neutral safety switch, 137

O

Oil and fuel recommendations, 21-22
Oil change, 22-23
Oil filter (engine), 23
Oil pan, 65
Oil pump, 66-67
Oil level (engine), 15
Oil viscosity chart, 22

P

Parking brake, 160
Pistons and rings, 57, 84-85, 87, 90
    Installation, 64-65
    Positioning, 64-65
PCV valve, 7
    Filter, 93
Points, 32-34
Power steering pump, 18
Pushrods, 80

R

Radiator, 67
Radio, 120-121
Rear axle, 142
    Fluid change, 24
Rear suspension, 152
Rear main oil seal, 65-66
Regulator, 47-48
Rings, 57, 84-85, 87, 90
Rocker arm (or shaft), 60-61, 79
Routine maintenance, 1
Rust spots, 177, 183

S

Safety notice, 3-4
Scratches and dents, 179
Seat belts, 123-125
Serial number location, 5
Shock absorbers, 146, 156-157
    Front, 146
    Rear, 156
Solenoid, 48, 50
Spark plugs, 30-32
    Cables, 31-32
Spark timing control system, 94-95
Specifications
    Alternator and regulator, 47
    Battery and starter, 51
    Brakes, 170
    Capacities, 19
    Carburetor, 105-107
    Crankshaft and connecting rod, 56
    Fuses, 126
    General engine, 54
    Piston and ring, 57
    Torque, 58
    Tune-up, 28
    Valve, 58
    Wheel alignment, 153
Speedometer cable, 122-123
Springs, 145, 155-156
    Front, 146
    Rear, 155
Starter, 48-50
Steering, 145, 152, 157
    Gear, 16, 151
    Lock, 158
    Wheel, 157
Stripped threads, 71
Struts, 145, 147-148
Suspension, 145
Synthetic oils, 21-22

T

Thermostat, 68-69
Thread repair, 71
Throttle linkage adjustment, 108-109
Throttle opener control system, 95-96
Tie-rod, 150
Timing (ignition), 38-40
Timing chain, 62-63, 90-91
Timing chain cover, 61
Tires, 20-21
Toe, 151
Tools, 2-3, 70, 175, 192
Torque specifications, 58
Towing, 24, 26
Transmission, 128
    Automatic, 135
    Manual, 128
        Removal, 128-131
    Fluid change, 23-24
Troubleshooting, 192
Tune-up, 27
    Procedures, 27
    Specifications, 28-29
Turn signal switch, 157-158

U

U-joints, 141

V

Vacuum hoses, 103
Valves, 40
    Adjustment, 40-41
    Service, 75-78
    Specifications, 58
    Springs, 78
Vehicle identification, 5

W

Water pump, 67-68
Wheel alignment, 150-152
    Specifications, 153
Wheel bearings, 171, 172
Wheel cylinders, 171, 174
Windshield wipers, 17-18
    Arm, 17, 18
    Blade, 17, 18
    Linkage, 121
    Motor, 121